Amazonian *Caboclo* Society

First published in 1993 by
Berg Publishers
221 Waterman Street, Providence, RI 02906, USA
150 Cowley Road, Oxford, OX4 1JJ, UK

Library of Congress Cataloguing-in-Publication Data
A CIP catalogue record for this book is available from the Library of Congress

British Library Cataloguing in Publication Data
A CIP catalogue record for this book is available from the British Library

ISBN 0 85496 756 7

Printed in the United States by Edwards Brothers, Ann Arbor, M.I.

Contents

List of Figures

List of Tables

List of Maps

Roraima
Amapá
R Amazon
SANTARÉM
R.Tapajós
Amazonas
Pará
Maranhão
Ceará
LEGAL AMAZONIA
Piauí
Acre
NORTHEAST
Rondônia
Goiás
Bahia
Mato
Grosso
Federal District
CENTRE-SOUTH
Minas Gerais
São Paulo
Paraná
Rio Grande do Sul
1 Rio Grande do Norte
2 Paraíba
3 Pernambuco
4 Alagoas
5 Sergipe
6 Espírito Santo
7 Rio de Janeiro
8 Guanabara
9 Santa Catarina
0 kilometres 500

Map 1 Brazil

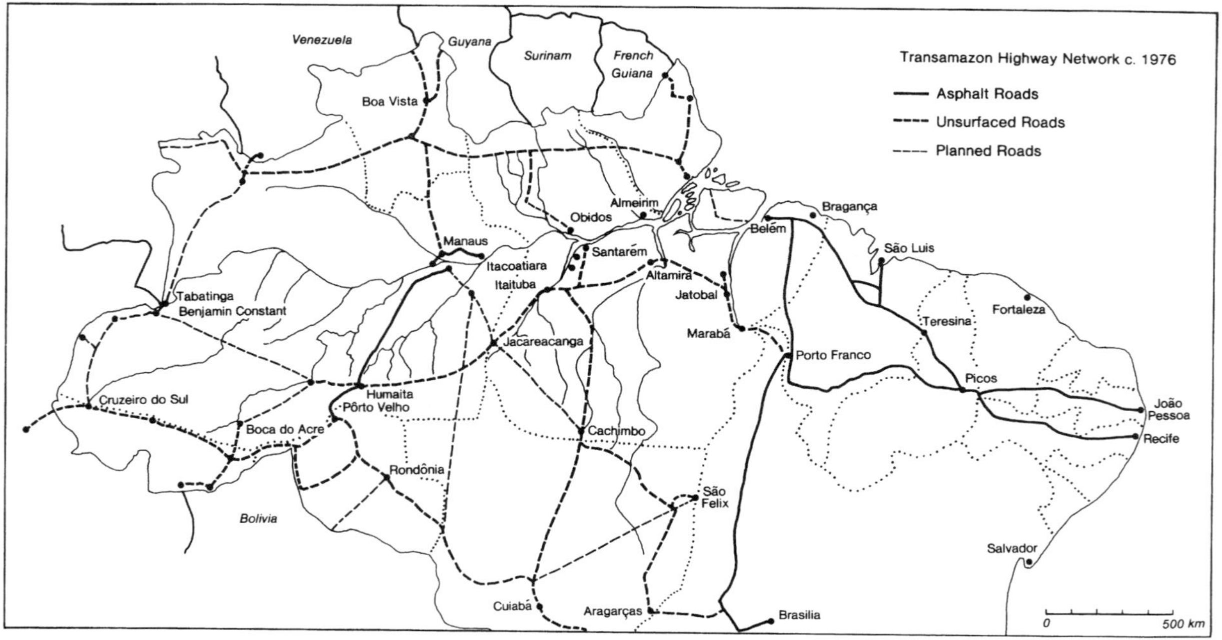

Map 2 Amazonia

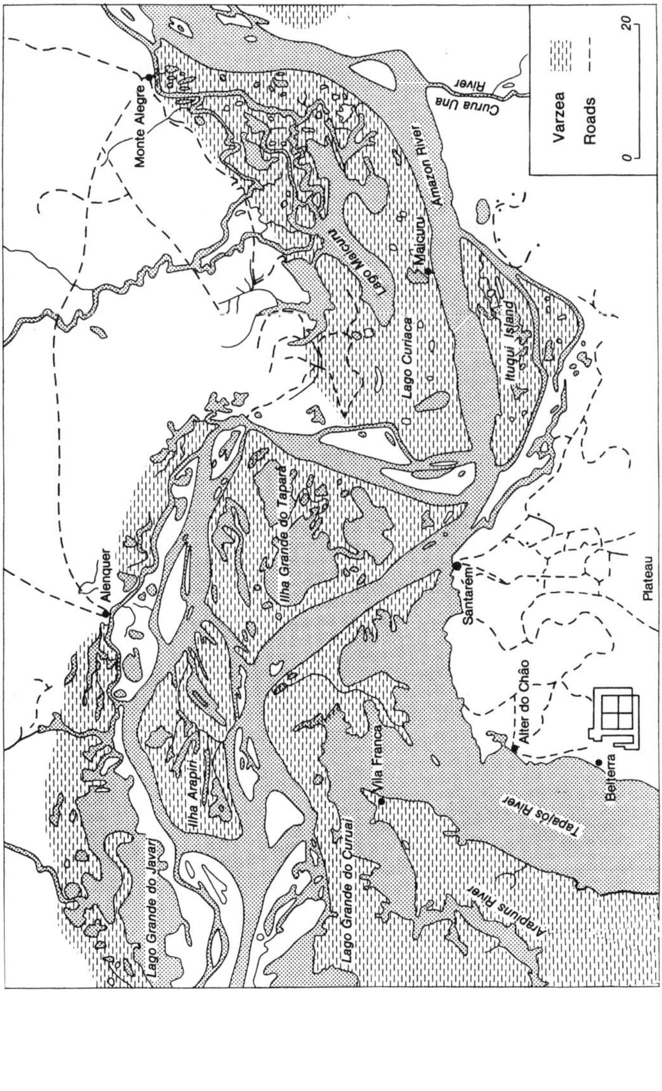

Map 3 Santrém

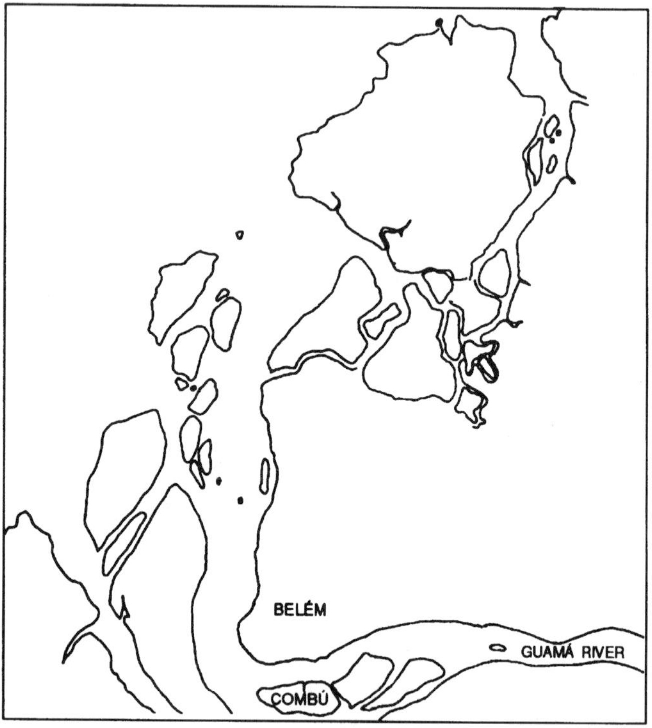

Map 4 Combú

Glossary

açaí: (Euterpe oleracea Mart.) palm fruit, important food source.
aldeia: village; Indian section of colonial settlements.
ambulante: itinerant rural trader.
arigó: pejorative term used to describe immigrants from the North-east.
aviamento: pyramid trading system established during the 'rubber period'.
bairro: neighbourhood.
banco: market stall.
boias-frias: day-wage agricultural workers recruited from urban sites.
borracha: collected rubber.
brazil nut: (Bertholletia excelsa Humb.); in the vernacular, *castanha* (*do Para*).
bugre manso: tame wild man (Indian).
caboclo: a term which refers to deculturated Indians, people of mixed ethnic ancestry, 'traditional' (i.e. pre-*Transamazônica*) Amazonian peasants.
cacau: (Theobroma cacao L.); cocoa.
capoeira: secondary growth forest. pre-*Transamazônica* synonymous with 'fallow'.
crente: Protestant
desenvolvimento: literally, 'development'; in Amazonian discourse, refers generally to increased integration of region and state, and not infrequently, ironically.
enchente: the annual (Jan.–July) flood of the Amazon River which submerges the *várzeas*, varying in onset, height and duration.
farinha: meal; in Amazonia, in absence of a qualifier (e.g. 'maize' meal) refers to fried manioc.
favelado: urban squatter; despite the popular representation of favelados (and favelas – the squatter neighbourhoods) as marginal, they are a central feature of Brazilian urbanization.
filho de criação: adopted/fostered child.
fregues: customer, client.
FUNAI: National Indian Foundation (federal agency).
futuro: literally, 'the future'; in Amazonian discourse connotes optimistic assessment of effects of national integration.
garimpeiro: gold-miner.
GETAT: federal agency instituted to resolve land conflicts in Southern Para.

hyleia: Amazonian humid tropical forest.
INCRA: Institute for Colonization and Agrarian Reform (federal agency).
mandioca: (Manihot esculenta Rodr.); manioc; the 'sweet' version is macaxeira. The tubers provide farinha, tapioca, tucupí; the leaves may also be eaten (*manisoba*) and the stalks are used as cuttings.
neo-Amazonian: either non-Indian Amazonian or post-*Transamazônica* colonist (i.e. contrasted with *caboclo*).
nordestino: person from the Northeast region of Brazil.
parentes: kin, family.
patrão: boss.
planalto: plateau.
posseiro: squatter.
quintal: yard in which perennials cultivated and ducks and chickens raised.
ribeirinho: Amazonians whose livelihoods are largely riverine.
roça: small piece of cultivable land.
RTU: Rubber Tappers' Union (Conselho Nacional do Seringueiros)
seringa: rubber (hevea brasiliensis).
seringueiro: rubber-tapper
sítio: smallholding, farm; overlaps with second-home, weekend retreat.
SUDAM: Superintendency for the Development of Amazonia (federal agency).
taberna: small trading establishment.
taipa: wattle and daub.
terra firme: upland forest
Transamazônica: main trunk of highway system begun in 1970 which bisects Brazilian Amazonia.
umbanda: syncretic, spirit-possession belief system, part of range of Brazilian systems including *candomble, macumba, batuque,* Kardecism.
várzea: floodplain of the Amazon River; refers to both floodland subject to both tidal and annual invasion.
UDR: (União Democratica Ruralista) reactionary ranchers' organization which has been in the forefront of fight against Amazonian smallholders.
vipi: V(ery) I(mportant) P(erson).

Preface

The title of this book requires some explanation. It identifies a broad area – Amazonia – and a topic within it – *caboclo* society – but the actual scope of the book is more modest. While the research on which the book is based did take place in Amazonia – and among *caboclos* – the discussion is based on work in only a few communities and is informed by an experience of wider Amazonia largely confined to selected secondary sources and discussions with more widely travelled Amazonianists. During the time spent in Brazilian Amazonia – 1975–6 and the summers of 1988, 1989 and 1990 – I hardly ventured far afield: the environs of Santarém and the Guamá estuary. When I speak of 'Amazonia', then, the reader should take this to mean 'Brazilian Amazonia' in the first instance, 'lower Amazonia' (that part of the river which passes through the state of Pará) in the second, and a very small number of communities in the third.

Similarly, I use the term *caboclo* in a way which reflects experience in a narrow domain. When preparing to go to the field, I consulted a senior Amazonianist (who would no doubt prefer to be thought of as an Indianist), who was amazed that anyone wanted to spend time among 'Indian-killers'. Although I was taken aback at his characterization (and at the implications it bore for me as a naive fellow-traveller) and would dispute it, that reaction has underscored a certain hesitancy about even using the term *caboclo*. Among its many connotations, *caboclo* has unquestionably unpleasant usages and it is impossible to use the term without bearing the weight of possible misunderstanding. A suitable alternative term, however, does not come to mind. 'Amazonian peasant' is anodyne by comparison, but 'peasant' itself is hardly unencumbered with unflattering connotations. Furthermore, most of the *caboclos*/peasants I know have ill fit the stereotypes: they may at times be 'rural cultivators', but they also drive taxis, work as boatmakers or domestics, follow international football, and in some cases are fluent in the bureaucratic discourse of 'sustainable development'.

The pejorative readings of *caboclo* have in recent years been challenged by a new orthodoxy. Indeed, the received view according to which *caboclos* were inauthentic and pathological Amazonians has been superseded in some publications by an enthusiastic rendering according to which the *caboclo* is the long-unrecognized Amazonian New Man (and less often, Woman), the wise manager of the threatened forest.

These sorts of clarification – and the need for them – constitute one of the main preoccupations of this book: the ethnohistory of a people without an official 'ethno'. There are many 'Amazonias' and many versions of '*caboclo*', and the focal meanings of these terms are matters of dispute, but what is less contentious is the fact that *caboclo* society historically has tended to be treated as an afterthought, an unignorable presence, but a matter of no great import. The 'invisibility' of the title registers the averted gaze as much as it does the reality of *caboclo* society.

This book is concerned with an enigma, an invisible society which has, recently, become almost visible. Amazonian peasant societies – *caboclos* in the vernacular – are not literally invisible; rather they have been treated as marginal in relation to an overdetermined naturalism represented by a forest of mythic proportions and marginal in relation to 'proper' Amazonian social formations, Indian societies (and, on the distant horizon, the promise of modernity). As a result they are functionally invisible, portrayed as contingent, structureless, *ad hoc*, pathological and perhaps, like Buffon's sloth, only one maladaptation away from extinction.

A difficulty facing contemporary Amazonianist researchers is to account for the fact that so many have kept so silent for so long about lumpen-Amazonia. Over the past twenty years, Amazonia has been rediscovered, and Amazonia-as-nature and Amazonia-as-Indian-society are joined by a new set of representations. Some of these other 'Amazonias' are now well-known. They include 'Amazonia-as-eco-disaster', 'Amazonia-as-social-conflict' as well as 'Amazonia-as-unlikely-place-to-have-opera-house'. The Amazonia occupied by historical peasant societies, however, is still largely inchoate, and I suspect that one of the reasons for this is that to draw too much attention to *caboclo* societies is to highlight the obvious omissions of the past.

If farce follows tragedy, perhaps – it seems – the third time around it is better to draw a veil.

There are tensions between the general and the specific which are impossible to overcome. For one thing, the book is hardly exhaustive (indeed it is highly preliminary) with regard to a pan-Amazonian concept of *caboclo*, and the ethnographic examples themselves hardly represent complete accounts. Second, while there is a unity called 'Amazonia', it is internally differentiated and embraces a variety of social forms (including a diversity of 'peasant societies'), and what binds it together representationally is the imagery of naturalism. Thus, ethnographic case studies – of which, in any case, there are few concerning *caboclos* – must be heavily qualified with regard to their representativeness. Under these circumstances, an ethnographic case study runs the risk of being sequestered, while at the same time the generalizations run the risk of being vapid. What I attempt to do in the middle ground is to draw attention to a kind of Amazonian society which has been under-represented in the anthropological literature, the long-established Amazonian peasantry, and in doing so try to explain why it is that such societies have remained relatively invisible by examining the sorts of construction placed on the notion of 'Amazonian society'. While there is an ethnographic purpose in this, and material from two quite different Amazonian peasantries is presented, the arguments are in the main concerned with issues of contextualization and revision. This oblique approach, I would argue, is a necessary – though tentative – step in trying to re-situate in history peasant societies traditionally depicted as structureless and malign footnotes to the romanticized 'conquest of the tropics'.

There are, of course, many competing conceptions of Amazonia – the Brazilian frontier, the tropical ecosystem, the threatened home of the noble savage, a site of unregulated modernization experiments, to name but a few – and there are struggles on the ground as well as struggles beyond Amazonia focused on these different conceptions. As Amazonia becomes more familiar, however, it becomes more fragmented, and the comfortable generalizations of a few years ago are abandoned in the face of research which has exposed the degree of ignorance which has prevailed in the past at the same time it reveals how much of Amazonia has been lost before being understood at all.

Recognition that Amazonia – as both a natural and social landscape – is disappearing or being in unpredictable and largely undesirable ways radically altered at the same time that basic research is still being carried out (or in the worst circumstances, merely contemplated) has provided a subtext to basic research, and one of the consequences has been that virtually all research has policy implications. The contrast between pure and applied research, always a contested heuristic, is impossible to maintain.

For the anthropological researcher one of the great difficulties in approaching Amazonian peasant society concerns the degree to which the study of a local society has any bearing beyond strict limits. There is, for example, a diversity of 'peasant societies' in Amazonia all adequately described by the term, but differing so markedly and in so many respects that the fact that they are all 'Amazonian' seems beside the point. The relationship between fishing communities in Eastern Pará and coffee-growers in Acre may be both real and trivial. In this book I try to evade the problem of representativeness by presenting the ethnographic examples in the context of a problematic pan-Amazonian conception, that of the *caboclo*.

Caboclo, as noted above, is not a concept without definitional problems, but it is no less useful for that. The concept *caboclo* provides a platform for discussing what seems to me a vital if neglected theme in Amazonian studies, the relationship between Amazonian colonial history and the structure of the widely disparaged contemporary *caboclo* societies and cultures. One of the major effects of the increase in scientific and development activity in Amazonia has been, frequently, the reduction of 'the dilemmas of Amazonian development' to a series of management exercises: how to extract wealth without destroying the forest, how to accommodate 'land hungry' peasants, how to conserve genetic resources, how to insulate Amerindians. While this distribution of effort certainly includes positive features, it is also symptomatic of a tendency to regard Amazonia primarily not as a social space, but as a natural one in which society is to varying degrees tolerated. Against this view I would propose that there is a largely overlooked social dimension, that of *caboclo* society, examples of which have assumed different forms in different parts of the region, but which share a crucial defining feature, namely that they bear the marks of external structures – that of merchant capital for example – for which Amazonia has from the sixteenth century until the present represented a vast resource potential. When the region has intermittently 'fulfilled its potential' – most notably during the period of the rubber boom – the issue of 'Amazonian society' has faded in the face of incipient 'development'. When the region has had less direct links with the world economy, its constitutent non-Amerindian societies have been characterized as 'stagnant', if not simply invisible. Throughout its colonial and modern history the peasant societies which have endured regardless of Amazonia's relative position within the world economy have generally been regarded as transitory and, commonly, definitively pathological. Generally speaking, such societies as have emerged in the interstices of colonial apparatus have never been granted full status as integral social forms. They are treated as contingent, incomplete, haphazard meldings of the detritus of aboriginal social formations and the remnants of European commercial experiments. They are defined in terms of what they are not (aboriginal, national) rather than in positive terms.

While both historical and contemporary characterizations of the cyclical process of 'development/stagnation' in Amazonia have shared many of the same terms of reference – the forbidding forest, marginal societies, the delivery of civilization by invaders, the relatively unquestioned desirability of 'integrating' Amazonia – in the contemporary period the possibilities for conquest seem to be more confidently within grasp. As a result, those representative features of traditional 'stagnant' Amazonia are viewed – whether realistically or not – as effaceable, untidy reminders of pre-modern Amazonia.

The structure of the book is as follows: the first part (*Caboclos out of History*) introduces the notion of historical Amazonian peasantries (chapter 1: Introduction) and looks at the ways *caboclos* have been represented in the literature (Chapter 2: Invisible *Caboclos*, Visible Nature). In Chapter 3, I look at the way in which ecological and modernizationist perspectives have informed (or not) understanding of *caboclo* societies. Throughout, the emphasis is on the marginal position which *caboclos* have maintained in relation to Amazonian research.

In the second part (*Caboclcs* in History), Chapter 4 introduces material on the Lower Amazon city/municipality of Santarém, a major conurbation long overshadowed by Belém and Manaus, the capitals, respectively, of the states of Pará and Amazonas. Although Santarém did not feature directly in the execution of *Transamazônica* (it is the northern terminus of the highway which bisects *Transamazônica*), it was affected directly by the failure of *Transamazônica* settler recolonization projects (large increase in immigrant colonization of upland forest) and the subsequent shift to pastoral development. Chapter 5 (Exploring Santareno Identity: Kinship, Domestic Groups and Social Organization) looks at the structure of kindreds in Santarém. Kinship is a highly flexible idiom which permits Santarenos to accommodate the contradictory demands of regional and national pressures.

In Chapter 6 (Petty Commodity Production and Formal Subsumption) I look at three versions of 'Santareno peasantry' (*caboclo, nordestino*, and Japanese). A provisional model of peasant differentiation is presented and it is argued that the characterization 'peasant stagnation' disguises the dynamism of quite distinct versions of social reproduction. In Chapter 7 (Merchant Capital, Social Reproduction and Blockage) the dynamic (and static) qualities evident in the development of a traditional peasantry are discussed in relation to the formative influences of merchant capital in Amazonia. It is argued that in the aftermath of the rubber boom, the apparatus of merchant capital permitted the fluorescence of diverse forms of petty commodity production, a tendency blocked by subsequent efforts (following *Transamazônica*) to effect the complete integration of Amazonia into the national economy.

Finally, in Chapter 8 (Maintaining the Image of Sustainability) I examine the way in which the role of Amazonian peasantries has been recast in light of proposals for 'sustainable development'. Using material from the island of Combú, in the Guamá/Amazon estuary, I argue that without an understanding of the historical development of such peasantries their elevation from 'mere *caboclos*' to 'traditional forest managers' renders them no less invisible.

I have used the term 'invisibility' to draw attention to what seems one of the most durable – and mystifying – features in representations of Amazonia: the natural domain is held to be pre-eminent. Society is represented as a contingency. In the face of a venal programme of national integration, in the face of a rising First World environmental consciousness, and in the face of a global investment programme in which 'natural resources' take precedence over 'human resources', 'invisibility' also underlines the fact that the various responses to the so-called dilemmas of Amazonian development have rarely seen fit to consider the people of Amazonia as a significant constituency. They are acknowledged, but by and large they are hidden by more pressing 'global' concerns.

Unlike many other peasantries scrutinized by anthropologists, Amazonian ones are missing a crucial feature: they have no obvious pre-capitalist antecendents. They do not represent updatings of aboriginal societies, nor do they represent examples of white settler colonies *à la* North America. Instead, they are like the societies described by Mintz (1974) in the Caribbean, reconstituted, bound together by externalities, forced into existence as effects of expansionary European empires, then abandoned and left to make their way as the curtain falls on a stage designed for Imperial audiences. That they are ersatz is a point repeatedly made, stagnant, half-caste, neither one thing nor another, as though this is somehow a failing of the child and not the parents who, having cultivated it for a while, slope off to pursue bigger and better things unburdened by the offspring of early forays into primitive accumulation.

I gratefully acknowledge the support of the Leverhulme Trust and the University of London Central Research Fund.

Thanks to June Wyer, Zoë, and Zachary, Charles and Margaret Nugent for many things. In Santarém, Dutra and Zuila kept an eye out. On Combú, John Rombold and Anthony Anderson were generous hosts. In London, Oxford and Melbourne, Joel Kahn, Maila Stivens, Josep Llobera, John Gledhill, Gareth Stanton, Allen Abramson, Mike Rowlands, Humphrey Ocean, Mike Gilsenan, Olivia Harris and my colleagues at Goldsmiths' have been sources of much support. I am most grateful to Anna Howells for help with the diagrams and maps.

Part I

Caboclos Out of History

Chapter 1

Introduction

Portrayals of Amazonia have been dominated by two sets of images. On the one hand, there is the tropical forest whose description is unavoidably, and romantically, hyperbolic; and on the other, there are the representations of the archetypal primitive Other captured staring straight into the lens. Increasingly, however, another set of images has come to be included, that in which Amazonia appears as a new frontier in which social injustice and ecological mayhem compete for space in the frame.

The shift from the romantically exotic to the horrifically exotic is closely associated with the building of the *Transamazônica* (Transamazon Highway), the major piece of a road system which has made the interior of Brazilian Amazonia accessible in a way denied throughout the 450 years during which 'the Amazon River' was synonymous with 'Amazonia'.

The rediscovery of Amazonia has been realized in a number of ways. In terms of the state, Amazonia has been presented as a suitable terrain for absorbing many of Brazil's disenfranchised. For foreign capital, in alliance with the state via the now widely discredited 'Brazilian model' of development (cf. Roxborough 1979; Branford and Kucinski 1988), the opening up of Amazonia has created an investment climate uncluttered by regulation. For many scientific researchers, however, increased accessibility has presented less an opportunity for basic research than salvage operations, for an overwhelming feature of neo-Amazonian development is the fact that the large-scale forms of intervention have guaranteed the setting into motion of processes which are inimical to Amazonian life-forms and Amazonian societies and – if prognostications about the effects of massive release of carbon into the atmosphere and depletion of genetic stock prove correct – will have consequences which reach far beyond Amazonia.

For anthropological research, this salvage aspect is not novel because the Amerindian societies which have been the main focus of modern research represent a small fraction of the aboriginal social formations which existed at the time of conquest whose only unity is provided by the expression 'lowland societies'. For those interested in Amazonian peasantries, the situation is somewhat different in that the *Transamazônica* has created new kinds of peasantries, and it is these new types which have been the focus of most peasant research in the region since 1970 when the building of the road was initiated.

This book, however, is concerned with a peasantry which stands somewhat outside the two main areas of interest in Amazonian anthropology, namely a peasantry constructed in the course of an unsuccessful incorporation of Amazonia within the colony and, later, nation. It is a peasantry which was, until recently, a 'modern' product, but 'pre-modernized'.

Within the terms of reference of both anthropology and neo-Amazonian development, historical peasantries are problematic. In relation to the former, historical peasantries have been presented as the direct antagonists of Amerindian societies, *ad hoc* vanguardists of periodically encroaching national colonists and, later, the modern state. In relation to neo-Amazonian developers, historical peasantries represent what is to be overcome through modernization. They are regarded by this lobby as decadent, stagnant, structureless, in many ways typifying the 'backward' peasant society whose failure to 'develop' justifies large-scale technocratic intervention in Amazonia.

While this study is mainly focused on one historical peasantry of Amazonia, the people of Santarém do Pará, the issues raised concern a wider field, one bound, respectively, by representations of Amazonia as primarily a 'natural environment' and modernizationist claims for the possibilities of 'development'.

The naturalistic representations, evident in both scholarly and journalistic writing, implicitly (and often explicitly) subscribe to a view in which *social system* is subsumed under *ecosystem* (Nugent 1981, 1990; this issue is taken up in detail in chapters 2 and 3). What is systematic in Amazonia, following these prescriptions, is nature; society is intrusive, and to the degree that it is structured, this is a reflection of the rigidities of ecosystemic constraints (cf. the vast literature on 'protein capture'). Amerindian social formations, for example, are widely regarded as representing a limiting case *vis-à-vis* the pre-modern possibilities for adaptation in such an untoward environment in spite of the strong evidence that pre-colonial social formations were more complex than is commonly acknowledged and displayed a number of features which refute the stereotypical forest-dwelling noble savage notion (cf. Roosevelt 1980, 1987).

Between these two edges of the field – with the pristine, naturalized Amerindian at one end and the modern frontier entrepreneur at the other – lie historical peasantries in Amazonia, and in relation to the Amazonians at either edge, such peasantries are anomalies: they are neither 'natural' in the way Amerindians are represented, nor are they a visibly desirable part of the modernization apparatus, and unsurprisingly – in terms of the way Amazonia receives increasing international attention as modernization is inflicted on it – peasants are regarded at best as bystanders and at worst as the main promulgators of Amazonian destruction.

What is happening in Amazonia is both more mysterious than stories of its imminent demise would suggest and less so. The mysterious aspect centres on the fact that while the underlying causes of social conflict and environmental destruction are well documented (fiscal incentives for unproductive land-clearing, unregulated goldmining, non-enforcement of statutes protecting Indians lands, and so on), what is occurring in Amazonia is regularly presented as a tragedy taking place on a remote frontier, beyond supervision and indeed out of sight. When Amazonian 'nationalists' declare the need to *integrar para não entregar* (integrate rather than deliver the region to foreign hands), one need not look far – Carajás, for example – to see a high level of complicity between those who are 'defending' Amazonia and those allegedly being defended against (see, in particular, Treece 1987; Hall 1989).

The less than mysterious aspect concerns the fact that Amazonia is a cheap source of raw materials (bauxite, iron ore, gold, timber, manganese); that by holding it out as a 'frontier' opportunity for the Brazilian landless, Amazonia serves as a cheap political sop; and that, crucially, the representation of Amazonia as an ideal site for the application of the techniques of 'progress' depends on projecting Amazonia as bereft of anything which might qualify for the appelation 'society'. (Amerindians do not, in the vernacular, qualify as 'society'. They are 'natural' in the perverse discourse of modernization, a management problem in the same way that 'nutrient poor soils' are a problem.)[1]

That this rediscovery of Amazonia has not to any significant degree included the rediscovery of its peasants is not to say that those interested in Amazonia have not been aware of their existence. It is to say, however, that the idea of peasant society in Amazonia has not been – and continues not to be – taken very seriously. This reveals itself in a number of ways. For example, in a recent book critical of the trajectory of Amazonian development, Stone (1986) begins the chapter on the rubber boom, Amazonia's 'golden age', with the observation that:

> Socially, the end of the boom had major consequences. Weeds grew on the broad boulevards, and the opera houses in Manaus and in Belém shut down with the collapse of commercial enterprise of all sorts. The big ships stopped coming from Europe and from the south. (1986: 76)

Charitably, in 'social' terms, the appearance of weeds and the disappearance of opera houses might be undesirable, and the closing down of commerical enterprise and absence of big ships were probably not causes of celebration, but what conception of Amazonian society would merit such a brief commentary that the facts above can be described, 'socially', as 'major consequences'?

What is alluded to as 'social' in the quote above is a set of disappointments which reflect primarily non-Amazonian interests: how it has failed be integrated – profitably exploited – and it is the story most frequently told today as Amazonia is again presented as a viable candidate for integration into the modern world.

For this story to be credible, however, much has to be ignored, including the fact that Amazonia is already integrated

1. The 'naturalness' of Amazonian societies has been a recurrent theme since conquest. One of the best-known formulations, attributed to Gilberto Freyre, places Indians as the naturally fecund complement to European brains and African brawn.

into the modern world economy. Something else which must be overlooked is the fact that there are societies in Amazonia. These aberrant suppositions – the need for modernization, the absence of 'viable' societies – make it possible to inflict on Amazonia an unregulated expropriation of resources: the mass felling of commercially valueless timber in order to extract a few valuable trees; the creation of hydroelectric dams whose local utility is marginal at best; the 'creation' of cattle pasture whose major product is tax relief, not beef. They also make it possible to displace an established peasantry by land speculators whose interest in Amazonia is the valorization of public lands in the name of national progress. They make it possible for the occupants of Amazonia to be portrayed as a 'problem', unsightly obstacles to a vision of progress so abstract as to be unformalizable almost twenty years after the 'rediscovery' of the region was officially announced.

The most recent chapter in the rediscovery of Amazonia – that whose central topic is 'sustainable development'[2] – has appeared to many as both a thoughtful and pragmatic approach: if, as has been widely argued, the region is being desecrated because of forces which are beyond immediate control (a development policy that creates more crises than it does obvious benefits), why not mitigate the effects by finding ways of making forest conversion more profitable in the long run? The 'sustainable yield' caucus is a significant one (although it embraces a disparate set of voices) and certainly the most visible at the moment, but it shares with previous proposals for Amazonian development a view of Amazonian peasantries which bodes ill. The forest which is to produce a 'sustainable yield' is already occupied, and the goals of foreign bodies and those of local inhabitants are unequally represented in the new set of prescriptions). Although certainly acknowledged more than they have been in the past, the actual occupants of Amazonia are still not fully recognized as vital actors in the newly reformulated plans for development.

It would be invidious to select an Amazonian society as ideally representative of the high costs incurred through 'modernization'. Most of the victims are not around to be counted. Of existing non-urban Amazonian societies, there are

2. See Goodman and Hall (1990) for a recent survey of sustainability themes in an Amazonian context.

three broad types: (1) aboriginal societies in various degrees of contact with national society; (2) 'traditional' (i.e. *caboclo*) peasantries constituted through the haphazard colonial incorporation of the region; and (3) the new peasantries which, since 1970, have entered Amazonia at the behest of a state whose concern with peasant agriculture has historically been mollified by its dependence on production of export crops (i.e. non-peasant production).[3]

In an important respect, these types, despite great differences, have a crucial feature in common, and this is that they are difficult to see, Amerindians because they are subsumed under 'Amazonia-the-tropical-ecosystem', historical peasantries because they represent the failure of previous integration efforts, and neo-peasantries because they are excluded from the developmentalist masterplan of highly capitalized extractive industries which absorb very little labour.

The Specificity of an Historical Peasantry

This book is primarily concerned with one example of an historical Amazonian peasantry, one which is 'traditional' in a number of senses. Its origins lie in the earliest Portuguese efforts to lay claim to the interior of Amazonia, thus it began with the kind of colonial apparatus characteristic of the region as a whole, a mission and a military fort. It is also 'traditional' in the sense that the broad outlines of the local economy, a mixture of various types of agriculture, pastoralism, hunting, fishing and gathering, and regional trade in foodstuffs and tropical preciosities are characteristic of the region as a whole. Two ways in which Santarém differs from the other major Lower Amazonian settlements, however, are in the extensive use of the *várzeas* (riverplains) for both agriculture and cattle-raising, and in its having been relatively insignificant, compared to Manaus and Belém, during the period of the rubber boom. It follows from these that Santarém was not only less transformed by the commercialization of large-scale extraction (and its concomitant relegation of other production forms), but also, the agricultural practices included in the repertoire of petty commodity forms

3. According to Hecht and Cockburn (1989: 173), Brazil's smallholders occupy only 12 per cent of the land, yet produce 80 per cent of the food.

which constitute the *caboclo* economy, have been, as result of their *várzea* (floodland)[4] location, far less intrusive in ecological terms than have the *terra firme* (upland forest) forms of agriculture typical elsewhere in the region (cf. Anderson and Ioris 1989).

One of the distinctive features of Santareno peasant production, a result of having an oblique trajectory in relation to the rubber industry, for example, has been that Santarenos depend on a variety of production locales access to which has been – until the contemporary period – relatively unproblematic. With the increasing valorization of land, however, it is significantly more difficult for peasants to achieve the kind of geographical mobility which traditionally ensured the maintenance of the repertoire of petty commodity forms. Crucially, then, in viewing the consequences of the *Transamazónica* Highway and subsequent development programmes, one of the striking features is that neo-Amazonian development is, in some senses, doing exactly the opposite of what it claims. Rather than improving the possibilities for the peasantry, it is systematically blocking social reproduction, and in blocking social reproduction in this way, the modernizationist strategy becomes a self-fulfilling prophecy, producing in its wake an amorphous peasantry whose stagnant economy will have to survive on the leavings of a pillaged landscape. In relation to state-subsidized cattle ranching, clear-cutting of forest and other forms of large-scale development in Amazonia, peasant activities appear amorphous. Concentration of political power and economic power in the same class fractions results in the promotion of an 'offical' Amazonia – one in which the forces of development, however much their activities might be widely criticized, are seen as legitimate – and an 'unofficial' (or invisible) Amazonia – one which in the classic formulation of economic dualism is viewed as retrograde and debilitating from the point of modernization ideologues. These dominant forces are in their own ways invisible, literally in the sense that absentee-landlords use speculative land investment as a hedge against inflation, and somewhat differently in the sense that Grand Carajás (which along with Calhe Norte) accounts for half of Brazilian Amazonia) (Hall 1989: 39) is a large state/corporate/MNC project which is effectively an enclave economy.

4. See Prance (1977) for a typology of várzeas.

Although this book is basically about some aspects of Amazonian peasants, it is also, indirectly, about the way modern ethnography is presented. The publication of *Writing Culture* (Clifford and Marcus 1986) drew together a number of arguments critical of the alleged transparency of anthropological writing and established a new benchmark for self-consciousness and reflexivity in the preparation of anthropological texts. In a field notoriously burdened by a surfeit of ethnographic material yet to be systematically evaluated (except, in most cases, by the original, individual authors), and one in which the absence of core theoretical concerns has been long and widely remarked upon, appeared the claim that there is in fact a central anthropological problematic: anthropological authority is not authoritative in any substantial sense, but is a literary device for encoding representations of others.

In many respects this is neither an original nor a striking claim. As Clifford himself notes in his introduction to the volume, anthropological discourse has historically been preoccupied with theorizing the limits of Western representations of others, and he acknowledges the many sources of the new orthodoxy of textualist critique, but more contentiously, the critique is presented not as the most recent rewriting of what 'Vico called the "serious poem" of cultural history' (Clifford 1986: 10), but ' "tectonic" [scare quotes in the original] in its implications' :

> There is no longer any place of overview (mountaintop) from which to map human ways of life, no Archimedian point from which to represent the world. Mountains are in constant motion. So are islands: for one cannot occupy, unambiguously, a bounded cultural world from which to journey out and analyze other cultures. (Clifford 1986: 22)

The 'ideology' of 'keeping good field notes, making accurate maps, "writing" up results' had crumbled (Clifford 1986: 2), and '[e]ven the best ethnographic texts – serious, true fictions – are systems, or economies, of truth' (Clifford 1986: 7). This is talk certain to tax the resolve of any neophyte waiting to board the plane and it gives pause to those about to write: the best they get will be 'serious, true fictions', and at worst, presumably, 'trivial, false truths'; or something.

Whether or not the practices noted above constitute an 'ideology', as asserted, the statements that only now have the manifold shortcomings of ethnographic writing become subject to a critical scrutiny worthy of the name and that the ethnography addressed is not writing done by anthropologists, but a new genre – 'an emergent interdisciplinary phenomenon' (Clifford 1986: 3) – represent an anthropological remit perhaps deserving of the charge of narcissism. Clifford writes that:

> It has become clear that every version of an 'other', wherever found, is also the construction of a 'self', and the making of ethnographic texts ... has always involved a process of 'self-fashioning' ... Cultural *posesis* – and politics – is the constant reconstitution of selves and others through specific exclusions, conventions, and discursive practices. (1986: 24)

And while anthropological recognition of the kinds of reciprocal relations and responsibilities which obtain between studied and analyst have undoubtedly enhanced the field as a whole, one wonders if this particular (although casually generalized) conception of the other ('wherever found') is not actually a retreat from the world of one kind of other, the one say, in which 80–100 million native Americans were decimated by Conquest or the one in which 500,000 Indonesians were killed in the name of returning Indonesia to the 'free world', to a world in which anthropological discourse itself decides who is to qualify as an appropriate other.

Those for whom anthropology might as well give up attempts at explanation (too scientistic, too locked into Westernness, too formal, etc.) argue that anthropology is fundamentally about inner quest, not especially from the individual practitioner's point of view, but from the point of view of the culture which practises anthropology. By looking at others, the argument goes, a culture reflects therapeutically on itself. A corollary of this is that objectifying others is a bad thing. Because outer quest involves an appropriation[5] of the other – the argument goes – and the anthropologist cannot really 'bring them back alive', as it were, or 'get there in one piece', better to reflect on the

5. Appropriation is a vaguely specified metaphor. It is most commonly used to imply a kind symbolic theft, e.g. the authenticity of a particular account derives its character from the imputed qualities of the object under scrutiny.

Other kinds of appropriation are, although hardly less visible, certainly now less frequently depicted. Analogously, Marx noted that 'primitive' or 'primary' accumulation is a euphemism for plunder, theft, pillage, etc.

dilemma that the more anthropology pursues a cross-cultural, comparativist strategy, the more it diminishes the unique and untranslatable qualities of different cultures by constantly bracketing them. So, for those still interested in doing anthropology, but wishing to escape from the tendency to preserve others as unsatisfactory renderings, the solution proposed is that anthropology should acknowledge that it is trapped within the infinite regress of the interpretation of interpretation of interpretation ... etc.[6]

There must in other fields be analogous forms of the brow-knitting and hanky-twisting which have accompanied the more narcissistic aspects of the 'literary turn' in anthropology (of which *Writing Culture* is least typical) and cognate fields. There must be some comparable sense in which structural engineers, for example, are stalked by large doubts and spend more time than is customary staring into space. Perhaps they find solace in catastrophe theory and reintegrate themselves by rephrasing personal doubt as a normal feature within the new macro-system as do, for instance, a respectable number of medical doctors who seek comfort in substances which simply present themselves in the course of work. But while the unities of engineers/collapsing buildings and doctors/morphine sulphate, etc., have a ham-and-cheese kind of logic, anthropological salvation through writing seems to follow a different logic, seeking an outlet in a representational medium which is by definition foreign to many if not most of those to whom anthropologists have conventionally directed their gaze, non-literate peoples/cultures, and a medium the employment of which actually confirms anthropological discourse in an unchallenged position of power to represent.

The elevation of the text is presented as a concession to the other (no longer will you be objectified), yet it achieves the opposite effect: the other is confirmed in a structurally subordinate position. If anthropology is at all concerned with the study of societies other than those for which anthropology is a practice, what is the point of factoring the historically precise other out of the equation and replacing it with a generalized, abstract other?

6. Two very positive presentations of this view can be found in Shweder (1982) and Sass (1986). A central irony of both is that relativism is rated so highly while historicism is not.

Earlier anthropological terms for other peoples – or simply various generics, the 'savage', the 'primitive', the 'African', the 'Indian', the 'tribalist' and so on – were clearly problematic, frequently offensive and ideologically loaded, and were inadequate short-hand representations which served equivocally in anthropological discourse's mediating role between expansionary social systems and subordinated social systems. Generalized otherness is now, for some, the ethnographic equivalent of ether, permeating anthropological space, but indicating the presence of anthropological activity, not the lives of particular others.

The leap from colonial designations of otherness (the 'savage', 'the primitive', etc.) to the preferred post-colonial designation (generalized otherness) may well serve to preserve the coherence of anthropological discourse and illustrate a critical awareness of the representational shortcomings of the past, but it also has the effect of dehistoricizing the other and of dehistoricizing the field itself. Does the 'post-colonial' usage indicate that neo-colonial others are no more? As far as one can tell, the 'post-colonial' world is largely confined to traditional centres of power, and 'post-colonialism' for others is on par with the 'trickle-down' effect. Similarly, the textualist programme within anthropology ignores the periodization of theoretical developments within the field. Clifford (1986: 10), in discussing the critique of colonialism in the postwar period, observes that the limits of representation were theorized in various ways:

> Positions proliferate: 'hermeneutics', 'structuralism', 'history of mentalities', 'neo-Marxism', 'geneology', 'post-structuralism', 'post-modernism', 'pragmatism'; also a spate of 'alternate epistemologies' – feminist, ethnic, and non-Western,

And while he is careful to note that 'there is no way adequately to survey this multifarious critique' (1986: 10), the representation of recent anthropological history given is one of a shopping list. If the periodization were important to the textualist critique, then it would, presumably, be provided.

For students who came into the field in the late 1960s or early 1970s, it seemed that social anthropology was embroiled in a dispute similar to the current one, namely how to resolve the dilemma of anthropology's apparent relevance to people outside the field, yet also its absence of a means for realizing this relevance without seriously undermining the field's social 'science' claims.[7]

Gough (1968a) and Worsley (1970) were among the most direct in locating anthropology's theoretical dilemmas squarely in a domain in which the working out of imperialism's new forays would flavour the field for the foreseeable future. The subsequent collection edited by Asad (1973) drew in equal measure from political and anthropological discourses (unilineal descent meets counter-insurgency), and there followed, for some, a critical engagement of Marxism and anthropology, an engagement that engendered not only a division of loyalties, but also, thanks to the multidisciplinary domestication of structuralism and consequent relegation of its explanatory value in favour of its form of rarified celebrity, the preconditions for an emphatic rejection (again) of what is casually denounced as 'economic determinism'.

'Economic determinism' is obviously code, but just as obvious for those unconvinced by market-led semio-discourse and its various progeny is the fact that an awful lot of what was offered up in the name of the derogated 'economic determinism' has yet to be refuted. If there are sound arguments to the effect that modernization theory, for example – to name but one heavily state-sponsored soporific – offers a better account of what has happened in the post-war Third World than has the generic alternative (dependency theory/articulation of modes of production/World Systems Theory), by all means let the evidence be presented. If the role of profit in the actions of multinational corporations is irrelevant to our understanding of the conditions of existence of anthropological objects, again, may we see the evidence? Instead, we are offered from many anthropological quarters the claim that the world of anthropological inquiry is simply not like other worlds.

The fact that the social landscape where anthropology is (mainly) practised has been transformed by grotesquely unsubtle forces remains a central issue. Delicate, elaborately nuanced interpretive forays are undoubtedly well within the domain of anthropological inquiry, but is everything else to be excluded (those problematics specifically which, according to

7. This was itself a false dilemma as Chomsky (1979) and others (see Said 1983) have been pointing out for years. The idea that the social science intelligentsia has been free of co-option is a useful fiction maintained most strenuously by those most compromised.

Tyler, hark back to the 'exhausted master narratives of the 19th century – the fairy tales of Darwin, Marx, Freud, and Einstein' (1987: 51))?

The problem, then, is that the fact that some explanations are better than others is taken to be irrelevant in the current climate – that shielded by the awnings of postmodernity[8] – and rather than confront the fact that the comforts of late modernity are more differentially distributed than even early critics had anticipated, some social scientists have chosen to go into what they regard as a principled retreat, seeking comfort in consumer-friendly nihilism and in addition to currying favour with those who view Heidegger and Nietzsche as fonts of therapeutic wisdom, still – and ironically – working things out in a medium (writing) traditionally controlled by priests and not the supposed constituents and beneficiaries of anthropological investigation.

In spite of the very high valuation placed on the notion of internal critique in anthropology, there is less of a relationship between what anthropologists do in the field and how they represent anthropological knowledge once they get home than might be expected of such a wide-ranging 'science of humankind'. Put another way, practising anthropology is something which takes place outside normal experience, worrying about that outsideness is what preoccupies anthropologists at home, and what interests others in anthropologists' work is precisely this sense of worry.

Part of the appeal of Clifford and Marcus (1986) is the fact that it makes a virtue out of a shortcoming: the scientific pretensions of ethnography are chastised on the grounds that they are stylistically defective (and deceptive) and this insight is taken to exculpate practitioners from their traditional (and misguided) attempts to speak on behalf of others. The vexing feature of ethnographic writing (its dessicated prose, the focus of Pratt's (1986) contribution to the volume) is transformed into a new set of textual possibilities. The sleight of hand is that some anthropologists have seized upon this (and cognate) insights in order to produce the following theoretical coupure: anthropology is worthy of attention because it produces fraught other-experienced modernites (if not self-conscious, devil-may-

8. Pfeil (1985) provides a framework for dismantling some of the more exaggerated universalistic claims of postmodernist zeitgeisters.

care postmodernists). The other side of this, however, is that a public to whom the new textualist anthropology is directed is dissuaded from paying attention to what is actually happening (or has already happened) in the place where anthropologists ply their trade and pick up their neuroses, the ecosystem of *Savagery and Its Discontents*.[9]

Take Amazonia, for example. Although Amazonianists regularly note how little is known about the region, by comparison with the educated public this modesty is quite seriously exaggerated. In relation to the impact of recent 'development' programmes (since the mid-1960s, say), Amazonian researchers have had much of interest to report, and few to address. What is of interest to the general public is that which is relevant not for an understanding of Amazonia, but that which has most direct bearing on the lives of North Americans and Europeans, namely the prospect that the devastation of Amazonian forests will result in reduced standards of living for the 'educated public' of temperate climes.[10]

If for simplicity's sake we divide Amazonian research into the anthropological, the ecological, and the political, and compare the thrust of researchers within these broad domains with the impact of their research outside specialist circles, we find a paradox: the more that is known about Amazonia, the more it is allowed to enter our history, the more *natural* it becomes.[11]

To begin with the ethnographic issue: anthropological writing (I am referring primarily to work in English, but the point holds for work in Portuguese as well) about Amazonian societies is mainly restricted to Amerindian societies and that state of affairs is, according to many anthropologists, as it should be. Neo-

9. This is perfectly understandable given the ambivalence of one of the best-known spokespersons for anthropology, Clifford Geertz. In an interview in the *New York Times* (11 May 1988) and commenting on his recent return to sites of his early fieldwork, he observes that, 'For me, it was a rather shaking experience, the reawakening of an imperfectly suppressed conviction that I never have understood and never will understand a damn thing about either of these peculiar places [Indonesia and Morocco], or for that matter, myself.' His judgements are rather more stoutly defended in professional journals, but what is relevant here is the impression of the contemplative, reasonable, schoolmaster who after forty years of professional service declares himself just as baffled by foreigners as, for comparative purposes, S. J. Perelman claimed to be in *Swiss Family Perelman and Westward Ha!*.

10. If, for example, the greenhouse effect were limited to regions where tropical cover once existed (in the way that the 'Sahel effect' is confined geographically and socially), one suspects that there would be much less outcry over deforestation. See Ruckelshaus (1989).

11. Part of the explanation for this is certainly due to the fact that in terms of the cultural conceits of Brazil's major geo-political patron, Amazonia can hardly be represented as anything other than yet another 'new frontier'.

Amazonian (i.e. peasant)[12] societies are, by this conventional view, of marginal interest. Some of the reasons for this disavowal of the anthropological interest of non-Indian Amazonians is taken up in chapters 2 and 3, but the situation is well illustrated by the fact that aside from the standard anthropological work on an Amazonian peasant society, Wagley's *Amazon Town*, published some forty years ago (1953), there is not a lot in the ethnographic collection. Moran's (1981) work on Transamazonica and Bunker's (1985) work on extractivism provide important revisions of conceptions of peasantries (especially the former), and E. Parker (1985a) lays the groundwork for a revised history of the *caboclo*, but these hardly add up to a representative account of Amazonian peasants in the late twentieth century (indeed, one of the points of Moran's book is that no such generalization is appropriate). More recently, the work of Cleary (1990) and Schmink and Wood (1984) (as well as various accounts of Chico Mendes and the RTU, cf. Hecht and Cockburn 1989; Shoumatoff 1991) have significantly enlarged the frame for Amazonian peasantries, but the terms of reference are still by no means clear.

Given the ethnographic lacuna, the claims that we need a rethink which have become pervasive in the climate of ethnographic revision of recent years (see, for example, Clifford and Marcus 1986; Marcus and Fischer 1986; Taussig 1987), appear somewhat premature.[13] Beyond this, however, the postmodernist critique in anthropology almost invariably focuses attention on an idealized Amerindian (the highly styled Other), and in the case of Amazonia the evidence that the idealized Amerindian is the wrong one is compelling.[14]

As to the domains of ecology and politics in Amazonia, they are so closely linked that they should be dealt with as one, as indeed in journalistic (and much scholarly) practice they are, albeit with political discourse at the service of the ecological. Amazonia has produced in many respects a classic Third World

12. There are at least two clearly different readings of 'neo-Amazonian': (1) non-Indian Amazonian (e.g. *caboclo*); (2) new colonist in Amazonia (i.e. post-*Transamazônica*).

13. To say this is not to dismiss the significant body of work undertaken by Brazilians, but I think it is fair to note that the impact of such work in the dominant anthropological culture of the United States and United Kingdom has been undeservedly slight, to say the least.

14. Anna Roosevelt is the major figure here (see especially Roosevelt 1991). It is not hard to see why there is so much hesitancy in taking on board her arguments and evidence: the centrality of gatherer-hunter-horticulturalist Amazonian societies, represented in a large literature fed by many still active researchers, is directly challenged.

stalemate-and-confusion scenario: those who argue for the protection of Amazonians and the environment they occupy are neither numerous nor popular either in Brazil (where they are in serious danger, cf. Chico Mendes;[15] also see Amnesty International 1988) or in the 'Western' countries where, broadly, questions of social justice are subordinate to questions of environmental probity. Further complications are created by the fact that in Brazil the crisis of Amazonian development is part of a much larger national crisis about which outsiders are far less knowledgeable than they are about the ecological crisis. Even in terms of the far more critical coverage of Amazonia which is granted today, what is most often brought to the fore is the fact that Amazonia contains insufficiently exploited resources, insufficiently exploited in two senses: (1) on the one hand, the exploitation which is going on is badly done (i.e. profits going to the wrong people or not enough profits going to potential exploiters); and (2) on the other hand, too many potentially profitable resources are being destroyed casually. A typical article (entitled 'The world's largest lab', *Newsweek*, 20 February 1989), with the title-caption 'Scientists are racing to study the Amazon – before it vanishes') consists of a list of the potentially valuable products which are about to go up in smoke: cures for cancer, AIDS, snakebite, diarrhoea, fever and conjunctivitis. Implicitly, such a report is making a claim which, unsurprisingly, raises the hackles of Brazilians: Amazonia is presented as a global resource, not a Brazilian one, and the idea that the United States or the United Kingdom would permit Brazilians to dictate their respective environmental programmes is obviously unlikely. The environmentalists' claims are important, but hardly exhaustive and tend to subordinate socio-political matters to the status of mere factors.

A consideration of the possibilities for social reproduction of a peasantry in Amazonia entails not only an examination of contemporary societies, but also an analysis of the ways in which researchers (and others) have historically defined Amazonian social objects. *Caboclo* societies are particularly problematic in this regard because they have barely been subject to taxonomic or descriptive study, much less analysis of their internal dynamics and links with wider regional and national

15. Chico Mendes, celebrated organizer and 'forest peoples' activist, was assassinated in December 1988 by agents of ranching interests. See Mendes (1989).

developments. Thus, the study of the particular requires a broadening of the frame of reference, a frame which includes not only Amazonian development (*grosso modo*), but also the internal anthropological debate about the value of acquisition of anthropological knowledge. Prominent in this debate is the status of the anthropological Other (in most respects an unpleasant expression), an issue which is increasingly divorced from concrete historical analysis, made abstract and idealized in a manner which, paradoxically, serves to deny the authenticity of actual historical societies.

There is another reason for the broadening of the issues beyond the concerns of ethnography and this is that Amazonia is a region which appears passive in relation to the actions imposed on it from outside. Much of the dynamic of Amazonian development pathology, for example, comes from a remote state via various fiscal policies, and from the resource strategies of foreign powers and multinational firms, and to pretend that the generic 'Amazon town' is an entirely home-grown product would be to commit oneself to an anthropological trajectory which is manifestly mystifying.

Unlike the disappearing world occupied by pre-capitalist Amazonians, however, the neo-Amazonians' world has a strong sense of immediacy, yet little sense of a past. For many neo-Amazonians it is a world which is being consumed before their eyes, a form of cannibalism far more perverse than any practised in that 'other' disappearing world.

Chapter 2

Invisible *Caboclos*, Visible Nature

The virtual invisibility of Amazonian *caboclo* societies, despite the unprecedented amount of popular and scholarly attention granted Amazonia in recent years, is for those with an interest in the social landscape of the region one of the remarkable and disheartening aspects of the 'rediscovery' of Amazonia. In the popular recasting of Amazonia as the site of a struggle between competing developmentalist forces, the awkward *caboclo* hardly features at all, and when he/she does it is frequently in the role of reprobate. *Caboclos* are not entirely overlooked, but when present they are almost always in the background, heavily shaded by larger, natural features. They are viewable, but rarely viewed.

This is not an unprecedented situation. Aside from ethnographic accounts of Amerindians, the study of Amazonian societies has historically been marginal. Amazonia is projected as a fundamentally natural domain in which society is intrusive. Even in the most recent phase of Amazonian development when, in the modernizationist vernacular, the human resources aspect is unavoidably to the fore, neo-Amazonians are more often depicted as 'populations', migratory trends or inhabitants rather than integral members of real societies.

One of the purposes of this book is to look at some of the ways in which the invisibility of *caboclo* societies has been maintained. A second purpose is to suggest some reasons for the maintenance of this invisibility. The lack of attention paid to neo-Amazonian social formations calls into question – if there are still doubts – much of the developmentalist agenda. Chico Mendes, the best-known neo-Amazonian, is more widely recognized after his death than he was while living, but the society he represented is little more acknowledged now than it was before his death.

While there is a growing body of literature on *caboclos* (see particularly E. Parker 1985a), the main focus is on ethnographic and developmental issues. My concern in this chapter is slightly different. I am less concerned with defining and documenting aspects of *caboclo* culture and society than in focusing on a simple question: why has the study of *caboclo* society been such an overlooked area of Amazonian research?

The work contained in the Parker volume (noteworthy, among other reasons, for its being exclusively concerned with *caboclos*, a rare occurrence) represents a long-overdue survey of what *caboclo* society means in the broad context of Amazonian history and development, but stops short of raising an issue which is particularly compelling in the face of the enthusiastic 'rediscovery' of Amazonia: is Amazonian peasant society really the social void that the modest size of the literature would suggest?

When Parker writes that the 'surge in research has been prompted by profound concern about the fate of Amazon ecosystems and human populations threatened by economic development programs and policies of the Brazilian government' (1985b: xvii), he inadvertently reinforces a view of Amazonia which he and his collaborators refute in their varied contributions. Not only is the surge in research in Amazonia by no means exclusively motivated by a profound concern for the conservation of Amazonia, but in addition, the expression 'human populations' quoted above hardly does justice to the complex social forms represented by *caboclo* societies, evidence for which is amply provided in the volume (Parker 1985a).

The thrust of the argument in this book is that recognition of the significance of *caboclo* societies is not going to be achieved by adding to the current configuration *Amazonian ecosystem/ Amerindian social system/development trajectory* a piebald cousin: *caboclo* society. Rather, what is required is a revision of received wisdom, one in which *caboclo* society is not simply rescued from the land of aporia (not in itself a difficult task: the usual materials of historical and anthropological analysis are available if underutilized), but properly recognized as a society in history subject to the same dynamic as that which has drawn other peripheries into the ambit of expansionary social systems.

In the scholarly literature, two examples of the way in which non-Amerindian Amazonians, neo-Amazonians, are nominally acknowledged yet substantively ignored are the following: in almost all work which attends to questions of peasant agriculture or basic issues of provisioning there is mention of the fact that the *várzeas* – the river plains (and there are different types; see Prance 1977) – have far more potential than *terra firme*. The number of empirical studies which confirm this observation is considerable (see Eden 1990 for review) both for contemporary societies and prehistoric ones (cf. Lathrap 1970; Meggers 1971; Roosevelt 1987). It seems like a strong argument, but if one looks for the consequences – in terms of policy, research, monographs – of what is in fact a quite startling refutation of received wisdom (that Amazonia is and has long been a land of forest-dwellers) there is relatively little to be found. In fact, what is an important observation with many implications for the past, current and future states of Amazonia has largely been relegated to the margins.

The second example: much current research in Amazonia, and certainly that which has found an audience outside specialist publications, is concerned with demonstrating that there are profitable alternatives to the gross clearing of forest. The work of Anderson (1990), Posey and Balée (1989), Fearnside (1983), Hecht (1982), Peters, Gentry and Mendelsohn (1989) and Uhl and Buschbacher (1985), to name some of the better known, has shown that the way in which the forest is currently exploited may be substituted by a profitable, non-terminally destructive alternative. The idea of sustainability, in fact, dominates current discussion of Amazonian development strategies.

What is common to both of these examples is the fact that the Amazonia under consideration is one from which the peoples of the region have largely been excluded. In both cases, the Amazonia considered is one which is largely devoid of structures other than those provided by that thing called 'nature'. The Amazonia considered within both views is a vast resource whose place in the world is narrowly instrumental: how can it be used? Two other questions – How was it used in the past? How is it used currently? – receive far less attention, and as a consequence, the historical peasantries of Amazonia for whom the issue of 'sustainability' of the natural domain has been inseparable from social reproduction tend to be misrepresented. Instead of being social actors, they are mere ciphers.

The Concept of *Caboclo*

Amazonia is a large and complex social landscape and most inhabitants of the region refer to themselves as inhabitants of states or cities and towns (e.g. Paraense or Santareno) or as occupants of a particular eco-zone (e.g. *ribeirinho*). Still, if there is a pan-Amazonian archetype, it is the *caboclo*. Despite wide usage, however, the term has many connotations (including non-Amazonian ones), and the fact that it does so contributes to the difficulty of focusing on the idea of *caboclo* society and culture. For my purposes, *caboclo* refers to an historical Amazonian peasantry which has emerged amdist the abandoned colonial apparatus of empire and state.

Wagley's *Amazon Town* (1953) was not only the first standard monograph on *caboclo* society, it is the only one, a not insignificant reflection on the status of neo-Amazonians in the social science literature. In his discussion in *Amazon Town* and other publications, Wagley subscribes to a number of different notions of *caboclo*: a *mestiço* racial category, a *ribeirinho*, a rustic. He notes that 'the term is mildly pejorative ... it is used by segments of the Amazon population for those lower in socio-economic status than their own. No one, even the innocent Indian, uses the term to identify themselves' (1985: viii).

He observes, in common with other commentators, that the term was formerly synonymous with *mameluco*, the offspring of a European male and an Amerindian female, and that by the mid-nineteenth century it had come to designate an Amazonian rustic, someone who was timid because of a preference for living in isolation, lazy, suspicious, tricky, like an Amerindian in having little body hair, and a number of other fragmentary attributes.

The naturalist Wallace provides a picaresque sketch of the social domain occupied by Portuguese traders and *caboclos*:

> Truth, in fact, in matters of business is so seldom made use of, that a lie seems to be preferred even when it can serve no purpose whatever, and where the person addressed must be perfectly aware of the falsehood of every asserveration made; but [Portuguese] politeness does not permit him by word or look to throw doubt on

> his friend's veracity. I have been often amused to hear two parties endeavoring to cheat each other, by assertions which each party know to be perfectly false, and yet pretended to receive as undoubted fact.(1889: 264)

More recently, the anthropologist Yolanda Murphy, comparing the Mundurucú of the Upper Tapajós with their *caboclo* neighbours has written that:

> As for the cultural differences, the blighted society of the whites offers few attractions ... The mood of the caboclo population ranged from stoicism to despair. They were in debt, impoverished, living at the very edge of subsistence, and they knew it. There was little hope among them, and life stretched out as an endless round of their rubber trees, grinding work, continual insecurity, and no reward or surcease. Only death would liberate them. When a child died, they drew comfort from the fact that he would not have to live in the misery of his parents ... (1974: 40, 37–8).

In a different anthropological context (a study of *batuque*, a version of *umbanda* favoured in Belém), Ruth and Seth Leacock note that the *umbandista* possessed by a *caboclo* spirit is rough, uneducated, and lacking in sophistication and good manners. His tastes are simple and rather crudely physical rather than refined and cultivated' (1972: 165); 'The lower status *cantados*, who do not have noble rank or seem more interested in having a good time than in working, are called *caboclos*' (1972: 156).

Outside the specialist literature, similar accounts prevail. On the dust-jacket of Lucien Bodard's best-selling account, *Massacre on the Amazon* (1971), is written: 'The Amazon basin, rich in minerals, fascinating yet forbidding in its mystery, has over the centuries attracted the dregs of civilization.'

At the turn of the century, representatives of the British rubber industry wrote with reservations about *caboclo* labourers:

> [They] are also recruited from the flotsam of such places as Manaus and Pará (Belém), where criminals, who are already practiced *seringueiros*, are wont to congregate at certain seasons in order to indulge in their natural lusts and wickedness. ... These men can be depended upon to do good work for a time ... but they decamp, possibly after committing a murder or two ... [and so on]. (Woodroffe and Smith 1916: 134–5)

Definitions of *caboclo* in Brazilian encyclopedias and dictionaries concur in portraying the *caboclo* as deeply flawed: a coppery mongrel, backwoodsman, half-breed, cunning, traitorous, despicable and unreliable, a person of dubious origins bred from Amerindians and Africans, a tame Amerindian, 'The *caboclo* is only here for today' – an allusion to the unreliability of the labouring Amerindian – a poor and unhappy individual, a perfidious character, a credulous individual, an imbecile, incapable of taking initiative (cf. Anon 1945; Anon 1957; Faria e Sousa Calvet de Magalhaes 1960; Buarque de Hollanda 1964; Rocque 1968; Fernandes 1974; Anon 1977a; Anon 1977b).

There is a consistency to the characterizations, but there is relatively little space devoted to the *caboclo* in such reference works. Even Roque's six-volume, 1,800 page *Grande enciclopédia da Amazonia* (1968) has only a three-line entry for *caboclo*.

When Wagley remarks in his 1985 *caboclo* discussion that the term is 'mildly pejorative' (1985: xx) he is not indulging in understatement. He is merely acknowledging the fact that *caboclo*'s meanings are varied because the term is commonly used as a distancing device. The usage of *caboclo* by *caboclos* themselves is ambivalent. The ambivalence does not necessarily derive from *caboclos'* unwilling subscription to the official view, but from a recognition that *caboclo* identity has at least two different frames of reference, the region and the nation. In a regional framework, *caboclo* may have an umambiguously positive reading ('I am a *caboclo* and I live in the Pearl of the Tapajos'), while in a national framework it may reflect the fact that 'I am a *caboclo* and I live in the asshole of a turkey'. The disparaged *caboclo com motoserra* (peasant with a chainsaw) may simultaneously be the 'wise forest manager'.

The period during which the contrast between the positive and negative readings of *caboclo* had the greatest revelatory potential was also a period during which it was virtually impossible for Amazonians to voice political views without danger of violent reaction. This was during the construction of the Transamazon Highway and cognate development programmes when the National Security State apparatus precluded the active participation of neo-Amazonians in commenting on much less guiding development. It was a period during which *caboclo* society was most dramatically –

and positively – contrastable with new colonist settlements involving, for the most part, northeasterners. (See Moran (1981) for a comparsion of the adaptive strategies of *caboclo* and non-*caboclo* settlers.) One consequence of the suppression of political discussion was that when *abertura* (redemocratization) was effected in the early 1980s, the reconstitution of political organizations in Amazonia – and the social groups from within which they emerged – appeared to be a novelty. Instead of Chico Mendes and the Rubber Tappers' Union's being compared with the *cabanos*, to take one obvious historical marker, the RTU was treated as an oddity, a new invention without historical precedent. Mendes, in fact, was appropriated by the environmental movement as though he did not represent, as in fact he did, a viable, integral Amazonian society as well as a link between the Prestes Column and post-economic miracle Brazil. While in no way wishing to minimize the significance of the RTU and rural workers' associations, the way they have been treated by the press and some scholars has suggested that they emerged almost from nowhere, by-products of the collapse of the military state. The peasant or *caboclo* society, typically, was merely a silent or invisible partner.

Caboclo Society as an Anthropological Object of Analysis

The opening-up of Amazonia via the Transamazon Highway prompted renewed anthropological interest in peasant societies. The volume of publications since the mid-1970s has been considerable, but a shared feature of the literature (anthropology and human geography) within the Anglo-American traditions is a focus on the incipient possibilities for peasant societies in Amazonia rather than a consideration of actual, historical peasantries in Amazonia. Two of the better known studies, for example, those of Moran (1981) and Bunker (1985), are basically oriented around questions of resource use and the viability of managed environments. Although offering very different conclusions, the two works are similar in beginning their respective analyses with the concept of ecosystem in a privileged position. In Moran's analysis there is a comparison of the adaptive potentials of two kinds of

Amazonian peasantries, those who lived in Amazonia prior to the building of *Transamazônica* and those who entered officially (planned) or unofficially (spontaneous) after 1970. In Bunker's analysis there is an account of a so-called 'extractive mode of production' which narrowly constrains the possibilities for social change. In one case, Moran's, *caboclo* society is absorbed into the natural backdrop and is part of the retrograde Amazonia which is being transformed by the new developmentalists. In the other case, Bunker's, *caboclo* society is similarly naturalized in that it merely represents the obligatory accommodation enforced by the demands of extractivism. In both cases, *caboclo* society is a contingency, something whose structure derives from the character of ecosystemic constraints. Put another way, the study of *caboclo* society may be seen as redundant given an understanding of the broad features of the environment which so narrowly bind the possibilities for social reproduction.

This enforced marginality of *caboclo* society is articulated in other studies. One of more commonly employed metaphors, one with mixed engineering and naturalistic connotations, is that of the 'safety-valve', employed, for example, by Katzman (1976) in describing migration from the northeast during the period of the rubber boom as well as during the period of early *Transamazônica* colonization. The capacity for absorbing surplus population in this way suggests, again, a natural domain yet to be inscribed by society.

These sketches hardly do justice to the work cited and none of these authors is unaware of the problematic status of *caboclo* society, but the point I am arguing is that there is an asymmetry in the relationship between natural system and social system in which the latter is clearly subordinate. Another clear expression of this is provided by Nigel Smith (1982) where he characterizes *caboclos'* prospects in the face of a modernizing Amazonia as being already settled:

> Most *caboclos* have little if any entrepreneurial skills; they are accustomed to a subsistence life or to working for a patron (*patrão*), particularly in extractive industries such as rubber or Brazil-nut gathering.

They are, in sum, already domesticated.

To recapitulate, *caboclo* society, while recognized, has been depicted in such a way as to de-emphasize its social or cultural integrity in favour of its dependence on the environment as its fundamental framework. Its relative passivity in relation to the environment also finds reflection in more specific historical renderings. In Robin Anderson's account (1985) of the mid-nineteenth century *cabanagem* revolt the story is basically one of the struggles among the elites of Belém to transform a regional political crisis into a battle for regional autonomy from the state. This may well be what happened (although see Di Paulo 1985 for a slightly different reading), but the spectator role of the *caboclos* implies a passivity which is too much in keeping with official wisdom. The fact that tens of thousands of 'non-elites' died in the battles (perhaps a third of the colonial population of Eastern Pará) suggests a rather more active role.

More than one hundred years later, in a review of A *Literatura Oficial Sobre a Pesca na Amazônia*, Angélica Motta Maués begins her discussion by noting that fishermen (*caboclos*) 'are always represented as incapable, unproductive, requiring training, irrational in their way of viewing the labour process, unable to take advantage of the natural resources available to them, ultimately, inadequate in conducting their livelihoods' (1984: 103).

Discussion of the *caboclo*, again, must begin with revisions of the standard account. The work of Loureiro (1984, 1985, 1987), Furtado (1981) (with fishermen/women), Gentil (1983) and Motta Maués (1989, see below) all provide similar and welcome revisions all the more striking because of their repudiation of a resilient received wisdom.

There is a striking parallel between the perceived 'marginality' of *caboclo* society and the perceived 'marginality' of the *favelados*, and Perlman's conclusion to the *Myth of Marginality* (1976) could easily be applied to 'marginal' Amazonians: such people conduct lives which are structured by the same forces which structure the lives of the officially normal. *Favelados, boias-frias* and *caboclos* are marginal only to the degree that they reflect the unacceptable face of *desenvolvimento.*[1]

1. The reading of '*desenvolvimento*' varies according to interest group. While many Amazonians certainly relish the prospect of an improved standard of living (and indeed, many colonists have entered Amazonia precisely because the availability of land would seem to afford an entry to prosperity blocked elsewhere in Brazil), for many non-Amazonians *desenvolvimento* simply refers to the propect of lucrative exploitation of a resource-rich frontier.

The Construction of Invisibility I: The Non-equivalence of Amerindian and *Caboclo* Societies

One of the vital historical confusions which sustains the obscurity of *caboclo* society concerns the relationship between pre-colonial Amerindian social formations and the subsequent neo-Amazonian societies. To the limited degree that anthropologists have been particularly concerned with this issue, the received line has been that *caboclo* culture represents a fusion of various influences of the colonial era, an account well illustrated, for example, in the work of Wagley (1953, 1974, 1985). By this argument, *caboclo* society is the awkward, syncretic outcome of the failure of various colonial efforts, and the pathology which is said to characterize contemporary *caboclo* society/culture is therefore the result of a combination of social defect (the withdrawal of colonial and later commerical administrative apparatus) and the restricted adaptations permitted within the humid tropical forest ecosystem.

In this account, the links between pre-colonial Amerindian societies and peasant societies are somewhat obscure and such expressions as 'fusion of culture' do little to explain what happened. In fact, even those like Wagley who subscribe to the 'fusion of culture' explanation accept that two quite different, if related, processes must be acknowledged. On the one hand, Amerindian societies were destroyed en masse.[2] On the other hand, peasant societies were constructed largely as the result of external causes (e.g. extra-Amazonian labour migration during the rubber boom).

The vagueness surrounding the connections between these two processes contributes to the current difficulty in acknowledging the integrity of *caboclo* society. A consequence of adhering to the 'fusion-of-cultures' account is that a naturalized or renaturalized Amazonia asserts itself. Let me try to spell this out by dealing first with the decimation of Amerindian societies.

2. See Dietschy (1990: 17) for discussion of the view that introduction of allocthanous diseases – especially smallpox – by the earliest explorers had such a devastating effect that by the time serious entry of colonial populations began, the Americas were effectively depopulated: 'Thus, there is no longer any controversy among anthropologists that this massive post-contact kill-off of the Amerindian population of the Americas took place. The only controversy that is now going on concerns the magnitude of this kill-off.' By his figures, 80–97 per cent of the North American Amerindian population was killed off in the 100–200 years between initial contact and major migration. It is estimated that 90–95 per cent of the Inca population had been decimated by 1600.

It is not only the case that *caboclo* society descends in anything but a straight line from aboriginal social formations and that what is now regarded as typically Amerindian is only questionably representative of pre-colonial societies, but also that the removal of Amerindians from Amazonia was so abrupt and violent as to be difficult to appreciate.

Even Wagley (who subscribes to a low-end figure for pre-colonial populations of 1–2 million) presents a dramatic picture. (Denevan's (1976) widely accepted recalculation of pre-conquest populations is 5 million, and Hecht and Cockburn (1989: 12) cite a figure approaching 15 million.) The effects of epidemics in the first century of colonial history were marked throughout the colony. According to Wagley (1977), in Bahia, for example, smallpox epidemics in 1562 and 1563 killed half the Amerindian population in the first instance and a quarter to three-fifths of the remainder in the second. In 1621, five years after the founding of Belém, a smallpox epidemic affected the Lower Amazon and had spread to the main upriver tribes by 1651. By the end of the sixteenth century the coastal tribes of Brazil were either dead or had retreated to the interior. In the seventeenth century, similarly devastating epidemics took place and by the mid-eighteenth century the pre-colonial aboriginal sites of choice – coastal and riverbank – had been largely cleared. It is doubtful, writes Wagley, 'whether a single lowland tribe, despite their isolation from European contact, had not already felt the impact of the European presence, directly or indirectly' (1977: 275).

'Contact' is generously euphemistic, covering slave-raiding and murder as well as religious conversion and ethnographic research. It has been impossible to reconstruct with any precision the actual chain of events (see Hemming 1978 and 1987 for discussion), but Ribeiro's widely cited survey of indigenous cultures and languages present at the turn of this century – long after the most dramatic declines had taken place – and present in 1957 indicates the enormity of the collapse and its speed in the modern period (Ribeiro 1967). In 1900 there were 230 groups for which there were good ethnographic data, and of these 105 were classified as uncontacted, 57 as having intermittant contact, 39 as permanently in contact and 29 as 'integrated'. By 1957, of the 105 isolated groups, 33 remained isolated, 23 were intermittently in contact, 13 were permanently in contact, 3 were integrated and 33 were extinct. In other words, of the 230 groups registered in

1900, 38 per cent were extinct by 1957. Of the 105 groups classed as isolated in 1900, 31.4 per cent were extinct by 1957.

If, as common wisdom would have it, the genesis of *caboclo* society and culture is to be found partially in Amerindian societies, the metaphor 'fission' is certainly more apt than 'fusion'. The link between pre-colonial Amerindian societies and *caboclo* societies is not insubstantial, but it is extremely complicated and impossible to reconstruct in any but the sketchiest form. Relatively little is known about the Amerindian antecedents of the *caboclo*; little is known about the non-aboriginal peoples from whom Amerindian-antecedents are claimed. What mainly connects them – too conveniently – is the fact that they operate within the same natural space; it is the continuity of background which provides the ostensible link.

Ethnographic accounts of contemporary Amerindian groups inadvertently contribute to the misrepresentation of links between pre- and post-colonial Amazonian societies. This effect is the result of the fragmentary knowledge we have of the degree to which surviving groups of Amerindians represent their pre-colonial forbears. With the widespread scepticism towards the 'culture type' scheme presented in the *Handbook of South American Indians* (J. Steward 1946, 1948; see Roosevelt 1980 for critique), modern ethnography has tended to present atomized accounts of surviving groups. There are qualified exceptions (Clastres 1974; Maybury-Lewis 1979; Balée 1984), but by and large the emphasis has been on restricted objects of analysis. The composite picture of surviving groups is a matter of accretion of small objects rather than being part of a nomethetically oriented programme. The fragmentary character of the overall depiction of Amazonian societies contrasts greatly with the relative uniformity of the humid tropical forest ecosystem regardless of the fact that researchers are aware of the heterogeneity lurking within the gross 'tropical forest' generalization.

This atomized portrayal prevails, but it is not the only problem. In addition, as noted in the previous chapter, the major alternative approach has hardly received the recognition it is due. For example, there is much published literature (ranging from Palmatary 1950, 1960 to Roosevelt 1980, 1987, and including Lathrap 1970),[3] which convincingly disputes the

3. See Roosevelt (1991, chapter 2) for a detailed discussion of the way in which entrenched interests controlled Brazilian Amazonian archaeology in the post-war period and virtually brought it to a halt.

received wisdom that contemporary Amerindian societies are in a significant sense representative of pre-colonial societies. Archaeological work in Santarém, near Oriximiná at the mouth of the Trombetas, and on the island of Marajó, to name but three of the better known sites, has revealed evidence of forms of Amazonian societies for which there is nothing in the way of contemporary analogues. Large sedentary riverine populations, elaborate and large-scale ceramic manufacture, ranked lineages, funerary urns, *farinha* ovens and other evidence point to a pre-colonial Amazonia far removed from the remote forest-dwelling archetype. The point here is not that such discoveries are overlooked – although that does seem largely to be the case – but that the lack of recognition of the significance of such evidence contributes to the perpetuation of the idea that pre-modern Amazonia was a *tabula rasa* upon which society had failed significantly to inscribe itself (see Irvine 1989).

In this brief discussion of the connection between pre- and post-colonial Amerindian groups all I wish to have put forward is the idea that the conception of Amazonia-as-a-natural-domain asserts itself in two different considerations of Amazonian societies: in relation to the link between Amerindians and *caboclos*, nature is the constant factor as Amerindian society dissolves and *caboclo* society haphazardly replaces it; and in relation to the link between pre- and post-colonial Amerindian societies, even though there is strong evidence of relatively high levels of social evolution in the pre-colonial period, the state of contemporary Amerindian groups is implicitly (in many cases explicitly, cf. the literature on protein capture, e.g. Gross (1975) and Beckerman (1983) as well as Ross (1978)) viewed as a sub-routine of an unyielding natural domain.

The Construction of Invisibility II: Invisible Peasants

In one sense, *caboclos* are invisible to the forces behind so-called development in late-modern Amazonia – and suffer as a result – because the creation of modern Amazonia involved the eradication of Amazonian societies and the emergence of Amazonia as primarily a natural space. In another sense, however, they are invisible because their livelihoods are various and non-specialized. *Caboclos* appear sometimes on the river, at others in the forests (or, not infrequently, cities). They are invisible in this second sense because the extensification of their livelihoods matches the scale of their resource base, a forest and river system which is characterizable as homogeneous at some levels of generality (humid tropical forest, the *várzeas, terra firme*), but which actually disguises a vast and as yet only partially understood array of heterodoxies. For example, exploitation of the various types of *várzeas* available in Amazonia – to note one resource base particularly associated with *caboclos* – implies very different kinds of complementary activities (e.g. depending on whether the *várzeas* are on the estuary, black water rivers, white waters, etc.). One result of this diversity of 'typically' *caboclo* locale is that a feature of generic '*caboclo* livelihood' is its discontinuity. The *caboclo*'s *várzea* ubiquity coupled with differences in the way that *várzea* exploitation is complemented by other activities (pastoralism or fishing, for example) diffuses the focal meaning of the term and leads, I would argue, to a particular kind of invisibility.

In another important respect, *caboclos* become invisible because their priorities are not those of the developmentalists for whom Amazonia is foremost an extractive-resource domain. This is, perhaps, a formal invisibility. No one denies the actual existence of *caboclos*, rather, what is implied is the irrelevance of *caboclos* in terms of various experts' assessments of what is desirable in Amazonia. A typical account of the state of play in Amazonia is the following from a World Bank employee: 'The great problem of the Brazilian Amazon is how to guide its development to further the economic growth and well-being of Brazil and its people without destroying the Amazon's contribution to the well-being of the earth' (Skillings 1984).

In many respects an anodyne and uncontentious statement, this claim invokes a number of simplifying assumptions which are problematic. For instance, the unity of interest imputed for Amazonians and Brazilians – or Amazonia and 'the earth' – is hardly apparent. The acceleration of social conflict in the post-*Transamazônica* period as well as the acceleration of export-focused extraction reveal a growing distance between the interests of Amazonians and others. In the second place, and an issue which is more immediately germane to a concrete discussion of 'development' in Amazonia, the notion of the 'economic' used by Skillings (1984), for example, is too restricted. What is meant by 'economic development' in technocratic usage is in many respects irrelevant to the economic rationality of Amazonian producers. For one thing, *caboclo* producers operate within a largely informal economy, one in which occupational, sectoral and class boundaries are not always clearly marked. For a second thing, many of the resources required for the reproduction of the peasantry have traditionally been non-valorized resources, forest, river, alluvial soils. These aspects of the 'economy', i.e. basic provisioning via non-valorized resources, fall well beyond the model of economic development proposed by developmentalists. Indeed, the insistence that what is meant by 'economic' is that denoted by First World economists has been disputed by a number of studies of sustained yield forest use in which a central point is that major sources of forest income are realized through non-standard and episodic transactions which are beyond the sight of cost–benefit analysts (cf. Peters et al 1989). Again, the effect of invisibility is achieved by applying inappropriate criteria.

The Consequences of Invisibility

It was mentioned at the outset that in spite of the unprecedented amount of both popular and scholarly attention granted Amazonia in recent years, one of the disheartening aspects of the 'rediscovery' of Amazonia has been the way in which peasants and other non-Amerindian Amazonians are still defined as mere guest inhabitants, smaller than trees literally and figuratively. Despite the fact that coverage of Amazonian development issues has become a staple of non-specialist publications – bolstered considerably if frequently uncritically by the growth of specialist publications – the emphasis is usually of only two sorts: despoliation of nature or social pathology. In a typical example (*Observer* 19 November 1989: 39) it is noted that: 'one man and his amphibious saw are proving to big business and the ecology lobby alike that profit and a regard for the country's natural resources can go hand in hand.'

The article deals with a man who has invented an amphibious chainsaw with which he is felling the forest flooded by the Tucuruí hydroelectric dam (the world's fourth largest; located on the Tocantins River). The inventor, Juarez Cristiano de Jesus Gomez, refers to his device as an 'ecological saw'. Optimistically, Gomez claims that he can clear the 18,000 flooded hectares in 10–15 years. The author notes that ecologists are struck by the irony of events at Tucuruí and quotes an environmentalist: 'It's a macabre thought, but if you wanted to log a region of the Amazon, it would be better to flood it first. ... On land which isn't flooded, the loggers hack paths through acres of forest, destroying almost everything around them, just to get the one tree they want. In a twisted sort of way, flooding and then logging is ecologically more sound' (1989: 40).

In the real world, a claim for the ecological soundness of the amphibious chainsaw is a pathetic irrelevance. The 6,000 Parakan displaced by the dam, the destruction of livelihoods of the those downstream from Tucuruí, in Camet for example, and the powerlines which connect the dam to São Luis in Maranhao – by-passing Amazonia – are parts of the story which are left out.

Thus far in this discussion of *caboclos'* apparent absence or invisibility the general theme has been that the natural domain has been granted a priority over the social. The question is, whose interests are served by this relegation of the social – specifically *caboclo* society – to an endnote? This question is all the more pressing now because of the way in which the debate about Amazonia's future has been seized upon by various non-Amazonians as a matter of urgency not just for the region, but for the world as a whole.

Among the most vocal of those who have claimed a priority for their particular prescriptions for Amazonia are the state and international organizations such as the World Bank. From both positions, although, at times, for divergent reasons, the rationale for the current character of development activities largely rests on arguments of scarcity – Amazonia is a repository of resources, supplies of which have been exhausted elsewhere – as well as arguments ostensibly put forward in the name of the greater (global) good.

The latter have a much higher profile and have been the focus of of much widespread concern about the consequences of depleting the 'genetic bank' or destroying the 'lungs of the planet'. Without wishing to play down the seriousness of any such claims, it is important to point out that the 'greater good' arguments have been much more fully aired than have those concerning the more narrow 'business environment'. The depletion of tropical forests in Southeast Asia, for example, has forced importers to turn elsewhere; minerals and hydroelectric power represent other resources whose relative cheapness in Amazonia has enhanced 'environmental concern'. Thus, within rainforest discourse at least two different – and some would say contradictory – aims are presented: to maintain the forests and to maintain the 'economic viability' of Amazonian forests.

It is too early to say whether or not these potentially divergent aims may intersect, but what is almost certain is that those who do occupy the forest will not be consulted. The extraction of Amazonia's resources, as many commentators have noted, does not, indeed cannot, depend on traditional infrastructure in Amazonia. In order to extract such resources profitably, modern enterprises in Amazonia have had – and will increasingly have – to impose themselves on existing Amazonian societies and there are two major consequences for Amazonians already realized: on the one hand, large-scale extraction has forced them to the margins, and on the other hand, such enterprises are by their nature incapable of absorbing dispossessed Amazonian labour. (See Katzman 1976 for an early assessment; there is little, if anything, in recent Amazonianist literature to contradict this view.) If such enterprises can be said to have significant backward linkages, they are either short-term and episodic – construction for example – or pathological, encouraging in the case of Carajás for instance, the accelerated felling of forest for charcoal used in pig iron smelting. In 1989, it was estimated that annual demand for Carajás charcoal was 4 million tons (= 20 million tons of firewood).

From the point of view of these large-scale forms of extraction, Amazonian peasants are at best an irrelevance, hence it is not surprising to find that they are ignored. When peasants and Amerindians do manage to force their way into the discussion of Amazonian development, they can be dramatically disruptive. The postponement of the Xingu hydroelectric complex, a financial blow to the state, the World Bank and the consortium of British banks involved, illustrated how important it is from investors' point of view to exclude Amazonians from consideration. Development agencies' ability to push projects through has similarly been restricted by the attention paid the effects of such projects on Amazonians (as in the case of

Altamira protest), and the high profile of environmental assessment practices attests to the importance which development bodies attach to the public promotion of their role in assessing environmental impact; but as Hall notes in relation to the Carajás project, while 'the company [CVRD] has undertaken a sophisticated publicity campaign throughout the 1980s, professing its concern for environmental conservation within its area of direct jurisdiction' (1990: 181), despite the official objectives, 'a question mark must be raised over the probable effectiveness of such policies in significantly reducing environmental degradation' (1990: 182). What is most important, it seems, is that environmental concern be expressed; implementation of environmentally informed policies is another matter.

The point here is not that there is a systematic exclusion of Amazonians from the considerations of large-scale investment – that is not news – but that when protest is successful, it reveals that the plans for large-scale projects are not infrequently indifferent to the needs of *caboclos*, Amerindians and other Amazonians and that indifference or uninterest is in important respects sustained by the promotion of Amazonia as a social void or as a place occupied by the socially irrelevant. Overwhelmingly, the offical development of Amazonia has been concerned with large-scale projects (mineral extraction, hydroelectric power, roads) and with forms of land valorization (clearing forest for cattle pasture whether or not the land is actually used seriously for ranching) which impinge directly on the livelihoods of small-scale producers in direct and indirect ways, direct in the sense of expelling documented and undocumented smallholders from their plots, indirect in the sense of failing to absorb displaced labourers in the extractive and pastoral projects and thereby forcing them into migratory and marginal livelihoods. Land-use under pastoral regimes, for example, is profoundly inimical to peasant livelihoods. The amount of land required per head of cattle, for example (1+ ha) would sustain a family of agriculturalists.[4] Uhl (1989) has estimated that each hamburger produced in Eastern Amazonia requires the transformation into pasture of 6.25 m^2 of forest (= one half ton); the same amount of cultivated land could produce

4. Shane (1986: 18) notes that 'as soil fertility and the nutritional value of grasses decline, as much as seven hectares per animal may be required'.

(in money terms) 70 times as much *farinha*, 20 times as much maize or beans, or 30 Kg of brazil nuts.

Such considerations have a bearing on the way in which the state collaborates with foreign investors in pursuit of what we may call the ecology of business. At the national level, the maintenance of the 'nature domain perspective' draws attention to what is arguably the major underlying problem in contemporary Amazonia, land reform. The plan for agrarian reform put forward by the government in 1985 was radical in ambition, proposing the redistribution of 43 million hectares of land. These proposals led to the creation of the UDR (*União Democratica Ruralista*), which effectively killed the plan in the National Constituent Assembly. The strength of this reaction – which is itself indirectly responsible for the murder of Chico Mendes and other union organizers – indicates the importance for large landowners to maintain the status quo, a version of 'natural Amazonia' which is the child of Hobbes.

In the international debate centring on forest management as articulated in the World Bank's Tropical Forest Action Plan, The International Union for the Conservation of Nature and Natural Resources on one hand and in the pages of *The Ecologist* on the other (see Shiva 1987; Renner 1988) and elsewhere (Pearce 1989a), one can clearly see the importance of keeping *caboclos*, *ribeirinhos*, and other traditional forest-users off the agenda. The World Bank – to cite a major agency involved – argues, basically, that the forest is too important to be left under the supervision of its inhabitants or indeed the state. According to Fred Pearce:

> The bank ... believes that it is only by taking charge of the tropical forests, and by allowing companies to make money out of them, that the world can save the rainforests. With the exception of reserves set aside for their unique biological features, the forests must cease to be a common resource. They must be fenced, owned and managed for profit if they are to survive. (1989a: 42)

Critics of the Plan have put forward two main objections. On the one hand, they claim that commercial logging cannot be profitably carried out with the kinds of environmental safeguards promised by the Bank. On the other hand they draw attention to a political and moral issue which underlines, from the Bank's perspective, the importance of keeping the *caboclo* invisible: the forests are not simple resource domains, they are inhabited by people, and not only that, people who manage to make a living out of the forest without destroying it in the process.

This seems a simple, not to say banal, point, but it is one which is consistently passed over in much of the debate about Amazonia, and its major implication is, again, the following: whose interests are served?

There are various categories of beneficiaries: at the local level, estate owners and land-speculators would prefer that their access to public land not be impeded by members of local societies, invariably described as squatters, migrants, invaders, mere peasants and the state has used Amazonia as a source of rewards for its various fractions of supporters (cf. Velho 1972; Foweraker 1981); multinational capital and the World Bank, more susceptible to international pressure, would clearly not like to see the developmentalist programme complicated by having to acknowledge that large-scale projects in Amazonia have immediate social as well as environmental consequences (cf. Arruda et al. 1975; Branford and Glock 1985).

The meeting at Altamira in February 1989, and the prominence given the assassination of Chico Mendes – the former adding an unwanted 'human dimension' to criticism levelled against the Bank and the latter allowing the world to recognize an Amazonian with a name, a family, a trade union – have been unwanted intrusions on a landscape fictionally maintained as bereft of any significant social activity.

From most modernizationist perspectives *caboclos* represent complications and it should come as no surprise that efforts should be made to manufacture a formal invisibility the success of which can lead only to real invisibility should the commercial management of Amazonia succeed. The importance of *caboclo* society may well be indicated by the degree of suppression it has endured. If it were really as insignificant as the literature would lead one to believe, the efforts to maintain the fiction of Amazonia-the-nature-domain would be hard to understand. Social movements in Amazonia threaten to reveal that fiction and undo a package of conceits which may be very difficult to recontain.

Images of the Other in Contemporary Amazonia: *Caboclo* and the Anthropological Other

In terms of anthropological discourse, *caboclo* refers to a kind of other which falls outside the terms of reference of anthropology's idealized pristine other, a position of some obscurity if not invisibility.

Three versions of the other which are commonly drawn out in anthropological essays may be characterized as follows: (1) the primordial reflecting surface which serves the anthropological *flaneur*, as in Taussig's *Shamanism, Colonialism and the Wildman* (1987); in his account of the other, an attempt is made to dissolve anthropological authority and obliquely depict the other using devices borrowed from film: montage, flashback, and so on; a number of complementary views are found in Clifford and Marcus (1986) and Clifford (1988). (2) the foreign object constructed by and reinforcing and legitimating the discourse of European social theory, as in Said's *Orientalism* (1978) and Fabian's *Time and the Other* (1983), in which the other is viewed as a construct symptomatic of the West's self-serving rewriting of history. (3) the other as a paragon of a different cultural outlook.

This list is hardly exhaustive, but serves to mark out recognizable positions even for those who eschew the implications of designating the object of anthropolgical investigation as a necessarily romanticized or naturalized other.

The other is positioned at various distances from the milieu of the culture of anthropologists, yet while the realms which are entered by researchers, that of the *gastarbeiter*, for instance, or that of gatherer-hunters in the Arctic, are qualitatively different, the glossing abstraction – 'the other' – serves to reduce the heterogeneity of studies of others to a compact formal object in which difference – the mark of the other – is rendered uniform. Paradoxically, then, the abstract notion of the other provides a unified field despite the fact the otherness has been most forcefully venerated as a theoretical construct by those who have announced the extinction of metanarrative. A further paradox is provided by the fact that the discussions around otherness have tended to focus almost exclusively on high-profile examples of the other, high-profile in the sense that they are archetypes (e.g. Orientalism) or major Enlightenment artefacts (e.g. Amazonian noble savages).

The rise of the other as a touchstone of anthropological debate has served to reinvigorate discussion, but it also excludes by implication a lot of the empirical work done in the past forty years, work carried out amongst peoples difficult to describe convincingly in terms of either the remoteness or idealization evoked by the label 'the Other'.

Despite the appearance that the issue of otherness has extended anthropological discourse into new realms (in collaboration with variants of literary theory, for instance), it could be argued that the idealized other is in fact highly restrictive and that far from opening up the field, other-dependence has contracted the range of anthropological inquiry, reducing a heterogenous set of historical problematics to a univeralizing formula in which the Turkish *gastarbeiter* is formally equivalent to the Rondönian rubber-tapper.

As Fabian has argued, 'As soon as it is realized that fieldwork is a form of communicative interaction with the Other ... a contradiction had to appear between research and writing because anthropological writing had become suffused with the strategies of an allochronic discourse' (1983: 148). He goes on:

> To maintain and renew these relations [with the other] has always required coeval recognition of the other as the object of power and/or knowledge; to rationalize ideologically and justify these relations has always needed schemes of allochronic distancing. The praxis of field research, even in its most routinized and professionalized conception, never ceased to be an objective reflex of antagonistic political relations and, by the same token, a point of departure of a radical critique of anthropology. (1983: 149)

One current emphasis, as in Fabian's writing, draws attention to fundamental ways in which the other is constructed and in spite of the potentially critical results for a reflexive anthropology, this emphasis has tended to reify the distant object, or as Fabian puts it, 'the primitive assumption, the root metaphor of knowledge remains that of a difference, and a distance, between thing and image, reality and representation. Inevitably, this establishes and reinforces models of cognition stressing difference and distance between a beholder and an object' (1983: 160). In other words, the re-ascendency of the other as conceptually central to anthropology marks a retreat to a classic position rather than a theoretical move forward.

Second, in terms of the negotiability of the other, those doing research in unremote areas are viewed with a degree of skepticism hard to overcome even with interesting results. The problem here is that an upclose other is out of focus, not because it can't in principle be seen, but because it can't be seen without the inclusion of a lot of detritus – the *Kentucky Fried Chicken* wrappers, a culture industry soundtrack – which both distracts from and, apparently, trivializes the main object. The other too close at hand, it seems, is too impoverished, its difference eroded by familiarity.

Third, even research among those who ostensibly satisfy the 'remote other' condition (i.e. entailing fieldwork in out of the way places) may still run foul of the problem of intactness. Are their others in possession of a sufficient quantity or quality of otherness or difference? Intactness may be measured in a number of ways: linguistic, ethnic, economic, bizarreness ... the list is long. Peasants are notoriously likely to slide into the trap of non-intactness. In Amazonia, for example, the intactness clause is effected against peasants in a straightforward manner because of the proximity of 'genuine others'. In a region characterized to a very high degree not only by 'genuine others', but by the epitome of otherness, the Noble Savage, there would appear to be little discursive space for those who stand outside the class of pristine others.

According to Fabian, the discursive construction of the other, and the maintenance of that construction through a systematic denial of the coevalness of anthropologist and other, is the crux of the matter, and while his work is a very important critical step, it too can be faulted for subscribing to a conception of the other which is remarkably consistent with that held by the numerous positions he criticizes, in spite of his commending the work of Duvignaud and others for 'reminding us [that] the "savage and the proletarian" are in equivalent positions *vis-á-vis* domination' (1983: 155).

The central question here is: what lies between or beyond the boundaries of otherness as these apply in Amazonia?[5] The suggestion here is that the gap between the pristine other and the researching community is not only an aporia – that which in Fabian's terms impedes coevalness between anthropologists and other – but it is also a domain relinquished to an erstaz other

5. See Alan Campbell's *To Square with Genesis* (1990) for a good, if gnomic, commentary.

typified by the *caboclo*. The *caboclo* is portrayed – when portrayed at all – as the incomplete other (if not, more brutally, simply polluted or pathological) and is an unsuitable anthropological other because the very existence of *caboclo* society subverts the formal distinction between the other and observer. *Caboclo* societies represent ersatz others and not 'real' others both because they are the outcome of conquest and not, as it were, 'local society', and because their existence is testimony to the depredations of 'civilizing' influence. They are reminders not only of what was lost in the conquest of Amazonia, but also the living representatives of those responsible. From this perspective their relative exclusion from social memory is not surprising. Just as certain domains of capitalist culture are by undeclared consent anthropologically unsuitable for investigation, branches of the culture industry, for example (see Huyssen 1986, esp. chapter 3) so are the domains of partial, ersatz others left to be the objects of intense entrepreneurial scrutiny and anthropological oversight.

Pristine Amazonia and the Perfect Other

Caboclos are regarded as ersatz in relation to two sets of imagery which, upon examination, are less intact than they first appear. The first of these concerns conceptions of Amazonia as, overwhelmingly, a natural system. This representation has been enhanced in recent years by the attention granted Amazonia as a privileged site of environmental concern despite the fact that, simultaneously, anthropological and ecological research has been drawing attention to the ways in which the Amazonian environment bears the marks of long-term social manipulation (see, for example, Roosevelt 1980; Irvine 1989; Posey and Balée 1989; Anderson 1990.) In general, the social has been overwhelmed by the natural.

The second set of images which marginalizes *caboclos* concerns the 'natural' inhabitants of Amazonia, Amerindians, contemporary examples of which are, paradoxically, highly unrepresentative of pre-colonial Amazonian societies. *Caboclos* are compared unfavourably with Amerindians, yet those Amerindians, archetypal noble savages who today exemplify 'the lost world' represent a tiny fraction of those present at the time of conquest (and therefore represent a distilled – and as a result, more accessible – object). Thus, even the pristine other with which *caboclos* are unfavourably compared is known to be a heavily qualified exemplar of 'normal' Amazonian society, its otherness in part a product of ignorance about the historical conditions under which Amazonian societies came to lose their social character and became a part of the naturalistic imagery of the tropical forest.

Taking into account this wilful fiction, however, and recognizing that contemporary Amerindian groups have been forced to accommodate themselves to a political situation in which their shared Indianness overrides internally recognized differences (in the form, for example, of the Forest Peoples Alliance), there is a more intractable problem having to do with what precisely contemporary Amerindian groups represent *vis-á-vis* their antecedents. The remote-forest ideal typification – mandatory for noble savage persona – dissolves in the face of evidence of substantial, sedentary riverbank settlements. A 1542 report by the missionary chronicler Carvajal of an attack on Orellana's expedition by 200 Tapajós canoes (each with 20 to 30 warriors) – which also notes that the riverbank was heavily populated for a distance of 150 km – is but one of the numerous observations concerning the profusion of riverine Indian societies (see Hemming 1978 for review) in the sixteenth century, but such accounts are noteworthy not only for what they reveal about pre-modern Amazonian societies, but also for the fact such observations have elicited so little interest among modern ethnographers.

Two consequences, then, for contemporary representations of the pristine Amazon and Amazonian other: (1) neither is pristine; and (2) apparent pristineness is a matter of complex negotiation. A comparison of image and reality (small-scale forest-dwellers versus more complex social forms) reveals that the stereotype is partial if not simply wrong. Those Amerindian groups which survive in Amazonia are most likely those which are *least* representative of the pre-colonial Amerindian reality, those which were forced into interfluves away from the comparative advantage of river bank settlement either by competing Amerindian groups or as a result of flight from European slave-raiders and colonists. It is ironic that while anthropological discourse has been largely fixated on one stereotypical noble savage other, it has been left to soil scientists to recognize the anthropogenic black soils of large and persistent

Amerindian settlements and register them as a taxonomic unit for their own purposes (see Sternberg 1975: 33).

Even if one were to accept the 'fusion-of-cultures' account of the genesis of *caboclo*, the evidence is mounting (see especially the work of Roosevelt 1990) that the Indian from whom the *caboclo* is descended is itself a seriously compromised candidate for the focus of origin myth. Indeed, if there are significant continuities between Indianness and *caboclo*ness (and few would deny any relationship between Indians and *caboclos*), these are continuities which obtain in a far more complex manner between Indian social formations undergoing a dramatic (if geographically uneven) conquest, and a neo-Amazonian peasantry which emerges despite the carnage around it.

If we look at the ways in which neo-Amazonians, *caboclos* in this case, are portrayed subsequent to the defeat of the Indians, there are several themes which are quite prominent and what they all speak to is a pathology intrinsic to the *caboclo* him/herself. Rather than credited as survivors, *caboclos* have tended to be regarded as marginally adaptive hybrids. *Caboclos* in the conventional portrayals are beyond otherness, but not in the sense of being an underclass or simply milling around in a state of permanent subalternism. They are beyond otherness because they are Amazonians made over in the image of Europe in a way which reflects poorly on the influence of civilization.

Aspects of Caricature

A major thrust in attempts to retrieve *caboclo* society from historical oblivion has taken place in the context of the modernizationist rediscovery of Amazonia as a domain of cheap resources, a tendency exemplified in Parker (1985a), and has consisted mainly of the insertion of what is known about *caboclo* society into a standard account of Amazonian colonial history. Important though this effort is, there is a significant missing dimension, that defined by Brazilian national racial ideology.

A recent contribution to the latter issue is provided by Motta Maués (1989), who considers *caboclo* cultural and ethnic identity not as an exclusively Amazonian matter, but as a construction which reflects the enormous importance which modernist ideologues placed on the process of *branqueamento* or whitening.

Citing in particular the work of Agassiz (1868), Gobineau (who served in Brazil as a diplomat) (see Skidmore 1976), and da Cunha (in preface to Rangel 1927), Motta Maués illustrates how the issue of invisibility as it pertains to *caboclos* is in part the outcome of a concerted effort to maintain the 'myth of three races' (1989: 196–7). The crucial debate, according to Motta Maués, occupied Brazilian intellectual life in the late nineteenth and early twentieth centuries and was largely concerned with how to overcome the undesirable effects of miscegenation by implementing massive European immigration, *'a salvação de patria'* (1989: 200).

What is particularly striking in the racist pronouncements offered by those who wished to save Brazil from miscegenate degeneration is the contrast made between the beauty and luxury of tropical nature and the reprehensible face of its inhabitants. Gobineau, for example, wrote that the 'frighteningly ugly' *mulata (mestiço)* population was fated to disappear and that: 'then, the race will be reborn, public health will improve, the moral temperament will be reinvigorated and the best changes possible will take place in this admirable country' (quoted in Skidmore 1976: 47). As Motta Maués notes, the 'admirable' of which Gobineau speaks refers to nature, not people.

Euclides da Cunha, writing in the preface to Rangel's *Inferno Verde* (1927), provides a similar contrast between the desirability of nature and the blight conferred on it by *caboclos*:

> It is a maiden land, infant land, a land without being, a land which is still growing .... In Amazonia there is taking place right now a cruel contradiction: above the full land, in the smiling plentitude of its existence there moves miserably a society which is dying. (quoted in Motta Maués 1989: 200)

From this perspective, it is possible to see another reason for the relative invisibility of *caboclos*: within nationalist ideology they were regarded as unworthy intrusions. Beyond the southern states of Brazil where immigration policies could partially achieve the goal of *branqueamento*[6] lay a region in which the racial purification of the population could not be achieved.

Motta Maués argues that Brazilian racial ideology decrees that those who occupy Amazonia are undeserving and that Amazonian *caboclos* are recognized in national terms not as

6. The process of 'whitening' a population.

people in society, but as ethnic symbols: regional cuisine, folklore, crafts (especially ceramics with motifs harking back to an 'Indian' past) (1989: 203), and such a prejudice is evident as well in the way in which *caboclos* are portrayed as passive (i.e. mere objects) in contemporary developmentalist discussions of 'populations', 'inhabitants', etc.

One of the most common themes encountered in discussions of *caboclos* is that they are to blame for the economic backwardness of Amazonia as a whole. This is due not only to their unreliability as workers for others, but also their failings as independent peasant producers. Due to their alleged propensity for turning their backs on the temptations of agrarian capitalism, they resort to an extensive and relatively unproductive system based on petty commodity forms of production. The result is that the 'stagnancy' of the Amazonian economy generally and the agricultural sector in particular is portrayed as clearly their fault.

This theme at least has the virtue of being clearly enough stated that it can be tackled directly and, I think, easily refuted. Other common themes, however, are less easily approached. The charge of moral turpitude, for example, is hard to unravel, not because the charge is just, but because it is simply nonsensical. There is no '*caboclo*' personality; there is no '*caboclo*' morality.

The concern here is less with the defence of the *caboclo* against the many charges leveled against him/her, than it is with looking at the apparatus which makes possible this sustained marginalization, but one example will indicate the way in which the pathological tendencies of the *caboclo* have been consistently (mis)-represented.

The failed attempts in Amazonia to recover from Southeast Asian rubber competition have traditionally been blamed on neo-Amazonians, both because of their reluctance to work and because of their incapacity for sustained work under a wage-labour regime. One of the problems with this assertion (which reflects as well on the alleged shortcomings of the regional bourgeoisie; *caboclo* defects do not always recognize class boundaries) is that it simply does not fit the facts. 'Under similar conditions', writes Dean, 'the coffee-planting bourgeosie of São Paulo imported nearly two million immigrants at modest expense, and the cacao-growing bourgeoisie of Bahia hired northeasterners, apparently the very same migrants who allegedly could not be persuaded to accept a wage labor regime in the Amazon' (1987: 50). Furthermore, the wages on offer at

Henry Ford's rubber plantations (in Fordlandia and Belterra, on the Tapajós River), the major post-boom plantation sites, were three times those available in Belém at the time, and working conditions were far superior. The point here is that the culpability of the *caboclos* (and *caboclos*-in-training, Northeasterners) is not a reasonable explanation for the failure of plantation rubber in Amazonia, yet the *caboclo* idiom is so deeply internalized that mere matters of fact are not allowed to dissolve unwarranted prejudice even in matters of Amazonian history as well researched as the rubber era. The Amazonian rubber industry found labour to be quite up to the task for almost one hundred years. Between 1827, when Brazilian rubber export data were first recorded, until 1911, when Southeast Asian rubber entered the market in volume, Brazilian output increased inexorably and, given the apparently intractable technical obstacles to improving productivity, increased directly as a result of allegedly recalcitrant Amazonian labourers. A comparison of Brazilian and Souteast Asian data shows not only the steady rise of Amazonian output, but also the overwhelming speed with which plantation production overtook extractive production.

Table 2.1 Brazilian and Southeast Asian rubber exports, 1827–1911

Year	Tons
1827	31
1837	289
1847	624
1857	1,800
1867	5,826
1877	9,215
1887	13,290
1897	21,256
1902	28,631
1907	36,490
1909	39,026
1910	38,546
1911	36,547
Southeast Asian rubber exports, 1901–1911	
Year	Tons
1901	5
1906	646
1911	12,000

Source: *Associação Commercial do Amazonas* (1912: 42–3).

A further point underlined by these data is that the so-called 'boom' – with all the connotations of *ad hoc* frontier development – actually looks quite stable in retrospect, stretching over almost a century. While the system of plantation production achieved in ten years what had taken sixty years in Amazonia, the role of *caboclos* in the failure of the Amazonian rubber industry is almost irrelevant, yet this failure is portrayed as somehow reflecting intrinsic properties of Verissimo's '*caboclo indolente*' (Verissimo 1970).

In a sense, too much emphasis on the under-representation of *caboclos* in Amazonianist discourse may unintentionally have overemphasized their role in the larger scheme of things as Amazonia is depicted in both recent and historical writing. In fact, the *caboclo* is not often a main topic, more an occasional reminder of an Amazonian reality which lurks at the edges of various texts. In some writing, however, even excellent peripheral vision is not enough. An INCRA (the former National Institute of Colonization and Agrarian Reform) document of 1972, citing the familiar theme of 'demographic void' announces that unoccupied Amazonia requires development with the objective of: 'marking by the presence of the Brazilian man in Amazonian lands, the conquest for himself and for his Fatherland of that which was always theirs, so that no one may ever dare dispute them in this objective' (see Sternberg 1975: 58).

In trying to characterize this ersatz otherness, one way of avoiding the misrepresentations incumbant on viewing it as a non-pristine version of 'real' Amazonian otherness is by viewing it not as a version of Amazonian society, but as a version of Western, metropolitan society. This may not do much in terms of clarifying exactly how the other is composed, but it does have the virtue of drawing attention to the extent to which modern Amazonia is explicitly a European/North American invention rather than simply the unanticipated issue of fecund, Amazonian naturalism. I think it also usefully draws attention to a common misrepresentation of Amazonian societies' relations with the rest of Brazil.

That Amazonia is peripheral to Brazil is not an unusual observation, but there is an assumed corollary – that Brazil therefore stands between, mediates between Amazonia and the rest of the world – a claim which is not only erroneous, but makes possible the maintenance of a number of fictions useful to those for whom Amazonia is, conceptually at any rate, a durable frontier yet to be sufficiently exploited. These fictions include (1) a social vacuum, (2) an imagery of tropical rusticity, (3) an inventory of 'limitless natural resources', among others.

In fact, (1) the social vacuum fiction is maintained by portraying Amazonia as containing only two types of social formation: Amerindian, subsumed by and large under nature, and peasant, rarely granted the 'society' suffix, rather portrayed as mere populations; (2) most Amazonians live in large towns if not cities rather than dispersed throughout the river-forest network; (3) many Amazonian natural resources are not only now vastly depleted, but those few which have been profitably extracted have been produced at the cost of the destruction of many other unmarketable resources not to mention the network of interdependent biological systems about which far less is known than might be imagined (see Anderson 1990 for discussion).

One regional, *caboclo*-associated feature which reveals the formative influences of unambiguously external factors, but which is now regarded as distinctively Amazonian, is the pyramid trading network – *aviamento* – in which direct producers (classically, rubber-tappers) are linked through debtor–creditor relations and which culminates in the import–export houses so prominent in the major entrepots of Manaus and Belém. With the collapse of the rubber boom, these trade networks remained more or less intact (if significantly scaled down) dealing in a wide variety of low-volume tropical produce and preciosities. The 'stagnant economy' of the *caboclo* is conventionally rendered as somehow inherently bound up with such a system in spite of the fact that the system was the apparatus which ensured the transformation of petty commodities (i.e. the products of many independent producers) into bulk product supplied to large commercial consumers. The '*caboclo* economy' was the outcome of this commercial system rather than its genesis, yet its frailties are seen to derive from – and of course reflect badly on – the traditional scapegoat. This rendering of the *caboclo* as somehow responsible for the abandoned colonial-extractive apparatus is, if not unusual, certainly perverse and of a piece with that tendency which would seek to blame the poor for the failings of the economy.

What seems to make this misallocation of blame not only possible but commonplace in Amazonia is the fact that the extractive economy appears more naturalistic than it actually was or is. The naturalism which makes this possible is initially baffling, but explicable: if any non-specialist knows anything about Amazonia, such knowledge is almost certainly based on data which are both inconsistent and of a scale which is beyond the limits of normal discourse. When one reads that Brazil is X size and Amazonia is not only the largest tropical forest but also Y per cent of X, and the deforested area is equivalent to Z times the arable land available in Belgium, Wales and Switzerland, or that the amount of water flowing from the mouth of Amazon could fill Lake Ontario in about three hours, etc., it is not surprising that it is difficult to get one's bearings. Images of Amazonian naturalism are constructed not only around the familiar contents of Central Casting, but also a set of quantified, scientific or pseudo-scientific generalizations, which are largely dehistoricized. Even the gloss used to describe the prevalent peasant livelihoods in Amazonia is shorn of a social reading: extractivism, as though humans directly engage nature without benefit of the mediation of social forms.

I have referred to two ways in which the ersatz other is kept in place: on the one hand, by being burdened with the debts of a bankrupt colonial apparatus, and on the other, by disappearing behind a screen of naturalism. In both instances, the denial of integrity to this ersatz other is presented as springing from a flaw which is identifiably Amazonian. There is, in other words, a process of naturalizing as well as a naturalistic backdrop, and it is an almost obsessive feature of writing about Amazonia that nature be mythologized (the challenge of the tropics), anthropomorphized (Mother Amazon), and granted a heightened sensuousness (e.g. Gilbert Phelps' (1964) description of disembarking at Belém: 'The heat that met me the moment I stepped off the gangplank was like an oven door opening or an animal breathing in my face'). In the presence of an overdetermined naturalistic imagery the ersatz other who lives in Amazonia is a rather faded, marginal character who is neither of nature nor adequately representative of the idealized European conqueror. S/he may have the marks of the European appropriation of Amazonia, but has failed to synthesize, and is instead the imperfect ambassador, the half-breed, the failed colonist who no longer has a claim on the mother country and yet has not quite gone native either.

While some recent anthropological discussions of the penetration of consumer culture into the periphery have argued that there is now a homogeneity of artefacts and imagery which makes possible the addressing of a capitalist global village, it may be countered that the appearance of similarity – via, in the main, mass global consumption of, primarily, culture industry products – is just that: appearance. An example from Amazonia of the way in which European/North American imagery comes to be instantiated in the ersatz Amazonian other is via the appropriation of minor culture industry iconography in the form of the T-shirt with a message:

Modern Concourse Nudity USA
Pank Pieces in Your Tasting
On the atomic laboratories we make the nergie
Competition of life Mascot Competition
Ghetto Dog Quicksilver
Risk primitive water for the world direction in colors
This land is Surf vitamin.
Feeling Makes Science Memory
Spatial Ligation

Some of these shirts are worn by people interested in displaying their access to the metropolitan good life, but for the majority of wearers, the connection between message and the reality of their situation is remote at best.

The consumptionist implications of such displays seem to me a minor point. That people would choose a particular imagery by way of identification is an unpursuable issue: the messages are not in any rigorous sense 'chosen', in the first place, and they do not scan in the second.

Their significance is that they contribute to the ersatz imagery which confirms neo-Amazonians in their out of focus position, the worst parts of two worlds, impinging on that of the pristine other and representing the most uncouth and vulgar of that of the pursuer of the other: naturalism and civilization, an extension of us, the defects of which (e.g. the ludicrousness of the messages) are almost unfailingly attributed not to us, but to the realm beyond, that bordering on the true other, the one with a penis-sheath and Ray-Ban *Wayfarers*.[7]

The image of the ersatz Amazonian other, in general terms, is situated around a number of ambiguities generated by the three footed nature of the relevant social space, the feet represented by Amazonia, Brazil, and the generic 'West'. One ambiguity is illustrated by the partial nature of Amazonia's inclusion within mainstream Brazilian culture and the fact that the resource potential of Amazonia is realized by foreign corporations with only minimal mediation through Brazil *per se*. Another ambiguity resides in Brazilian usage of the term *caboclo* itself: regionally commendable (perhaps; it is negotiable), nationally pejorative.

One thing suggested by these ambiguities is that the irony in Wolf's title, *Europe and the People Without History* (1982), is perhaps unavailable for *caboclos* precisely because they *do appear* to have a history. They are not victims of exclusion, but victims of inclusion, albeit inclusion as products of Europe's failure to make them over into an acceptable image, and one of the consequences of this downgrading of the authenticity of such history is evident in the way some Amazonians have internalized the contradictory images as in, for example, Santarenos' dual subscription to identities of relegation and identities of success.

The anthropological discourse on the other in Amazonia both acknowledges and avoids a class of other which is problematic, namely that of those whose origins appear to be remote and exotic, but in fact are close to home and mundane. That the ersatz Amazonian is overlooked reflects on anthropology's studied avoidance of what Fabian has described as the problem of coevalness, the recognition that objects of anthropological scrutiny are necessarily and, in his terms, dialectically embraced by and embracing of the terms of reference of the observer. That such Amazonians are not so much faded versions of 'real

7. Gjertsen (1989: 75) provides an interesting example of an analogous form of abstruse messages in his discussion of two computer programmes, one – named Racter – designed to produce rambling monologues and the other – Eliza – designed to mimic the queries of a psychiatrist. The programmes were introduced to each other and, 'While Eliza began with its standard request; "Please state your problem", Racter unpredictably excused itself to attend to some other business. On its return Eliza could get nowhere, as Racter began to respond with questions of its own: "Is it better to need or despise?" and answering inconsequentially: "Because electrons are brave".'

others', but ersatz versions of European conceits, is an idea I have tried to illustrate in the course of arguing that the idealization of the other is a distracting heuristic.

I have criticized a tendency towards idealization of the other, referring specifically to Amazonia, and by implication have drawn attention to what is excluded from that ideal typification. That is one problem for anthropology: according to what – other than endlessly relativized, i.e. arbitrary – criteria is one an other and another a non-other? A further and related problem is: why is the ersatz other conceptually suspended between the observer and the pristine other? One suggestion is that the erstaz other is an awkward reminder of the lack of distance between Europe and its effects. Adorno described the culture industry, 'mass culture', as the 'threatening other', and though he resisted conferring integrity on this 'threatening other', he did draw attention to the fact that this other was present not in remote places, but at home, literally at the feet of the observer. It is not coincidental that the ersatz other of the periphery, the lumpen version of the pristine other – the peasant, the misaligned victim of the demonstration effect, the Amazonian bar-girl emulating Joan Collins – is so easily mistaken for the post-punk urban Indian, but while the post-punk urban Indian is taken to be symptomatic of a legitimation crisis, the remote ersatz other is taken to be merely bathetic and pathological.

I have tried to argue in this chapter that the equivocal position of *caboclo* society is the result of a number of constructions placed on Amazonia in the course of its representation within those intellectual and political domains for which Amazonia is a significant object of scrutiny. The prominence of ideal typifications of 'natural systems' (with the convenient and appealing distraction of the 'green hell' designation) and 'the noble savage' account for much in that they are expressions of an apparatus within the terms of otherness are given and relatively unexamined (e.g. temperate forests are 'normal'; 'tropical' forests are 'exotic'; Europe/the West is normative; non-Europe is 'different').

Caboclo society is formally invisible because it straddles incommensurate domains: *caboclos* are Amazonians, but not intrinsically 'of Amazonia'; they are like Amerindians in terms of their livelihoods, but not at all like Amerindians in terms of the social space within which their livelihoods are articulated;

they are Brazilians, but to the degree that Amazonia is, for most Brazilians, a remote and unknown region, they are marginal citizens. While there is general agreement about the out-of-focus quality (or, to push it further, invisibility) of *caboclos*, the significance of this invisibility is a matter of dispute. The argument developed in subsequent chapters is that the standard characterization of *caboclo* society as a passive, stagnant, enfeebled peasantry is awry and that the real pathology has been the dismantling of *caboclo* society realized in the course of the developmentalist 'rediscovery' of Amazonia.

Chapter 3

Social System as a Function of Ecosystem: The Ecological Idiom in Amazonian Studies

The distinctiveness of the humid tropical forest ecosystem is a major theme – overtly or covertly – in most work on Amazonian societies and the prominence of eco-discourse in anthropological writing has provided a naturalistic backdrop against which society is commonly depicted as highly contingent and to a considerable degree subordinate to the structures of biological systems.

In recent years, Amazonian eco-literature has changed in two important ways: first, it is much more comprehensive and authoritative; and second, it has revealed a heterogeneity within the humid tropical forest (expressed in terms of well-articulated sub-systems whose relationship to the system as a whole is still poorly understood) previously ignored. The increase in eco-literature is a direct result of *Transamazônica*-related schemes (and subsequent schemes such as *Pôlonoroeste*) and refinements in ecological models have been associated with critiques of the schemes as well as with developmentalist proposals and has provided one of the major referents in the emerging global perspective on environmental conservation.

While the association of ecosystem and social system has been particularly close in anthropological studies in Amazonia, in recent work the interest in ecosystems *per se* is strongly influenced by the explicitly instrumentalist concerns articulated within the globalist perspective: how to achieve commercial exploitation of a 'vast resource domain' and how to do so in a sustainable manner.

There is a consensus among Amazonianists that there are compelling reasons to take account of ecology in a way far more comprehensive than is usual in social anthropology (although see Ellen 1985 for a parallel Southeast Asian example and Richards 1984 for West Africa). The major reason put forward for the privileged status of ecological considerations is that the Amazonian tropical forest ecosystem is more rigid (in terms of its capacity to accommodate social systems) than are other ecosystems, therefore (the argument goes) it has more of a determinative effect than is the case in other socio-ecocomplexes.

The relationship between social formation and ecosystem in Amazonia has, roughly, been presented in two main ways: (1) aboriginal social formations are depicted as having had to submit to nature in particularly direct and mechanical ways, low population density and absence of advanced (i.e. politically centralized) social formations being taken as evidence of this (cf. Meggers 1971); in particular, the debate about 'protein capture' (Gross 1975; Ross 1978; Beckerman 1983) has drawn attention to the kinds of ceiling on social evolution which the Amazonian environment is said to impose (also see Meggers 1971); (2) in the context of neo-Amazonian studies, nature is widely presented as a 'management' problem (part of 'the challenge of the tropics', etc.). In this context the rigidities of Amazonian ecology are to be accommodated through the application of appropriate technological measures. Both views take as given limitations on the possibilities for social evolution, limitations mainly attributable to intrinsic features of the ecosystem, but as noted above, there are two quite different reasons for pursuing an 'ecological' trajectory. From within anthropology, the concern has been mainly to account for the fit between social and biological forms; from the developmentalist perspective, the purpose has been to explore ways in which natural resources can be effectively (i.e. profitably) exploited.

There are a number of well-documented objections to the conventional accounts which portray Amazonia as, fundamentally, a natural landscape whose rigidity has blocked significant social development, but here, only two observations will be made: first, as noted in chapter 2, there is considerable evidence which suggests that the idealized conception of pre-contact aboriginal social formations is incorrect. On the one hand, Amerindian societies were not all of the same type and the conception of migratory, forest-dwelling groups is not exhaustive of social forms: in Santarém itself the evidence suggests that there was a large sedentary population, extensive manufacture of ceramics, use of funerary urns, and extensive warfare and slave-capture, aspects which contradict the standard view (Palmatary 1960; Roosevelt 1980; also see Lathrap 1970; Meggers 1971). Furthermore, recent evidence of the heterogeneity of ecological features previously elided under the gloss 'tropical forest ecosystem' shows that several kinds of comparative advantage provided the preconditions for differentiation within Amazonian tribal social formations taken as a whole. Evidence of trade in food (and other goods, cf. Lathrap 1968), slave-raiding, and links with Andean societies, incipient state-formation (Clastres 1974; Balée 1984) are among the facts which dispute the conception of stereotypical forest hunter-gatherers. The significance of the misrepresentation of pre-historical Amazonian societies in relation to the prospects for peasant societies' viability is great if, as Roosevelt (1991) has argued, the models of resource use cited are based on the ethnographic recored alone.

Second, the 'conquest of the tropics' (the 'management' approach) mounted under the auspices of *Transamazônica*-related (and derived) schemes has not been achieved in terms of establishing a smallholder peasantry with an agricultural base. What has emerged as a result of the large-scale, extractive enterprises which succeeded the initial agricultural trajectory is social conflict on a large-scale (see Foweraker 1981; Branford and Glock 1985; Hecht and Cockburn 1989 for discussion).

It could be argued that the recent assault on Amazonia has not been so much a grappling with a rigid ecosystem as it has been a *de facto* rejection of the notion of ecosystem in favour of the more conventional (and as many planners would have it, 'realistic') notion of 'natural resources'. Social planning in Amazonia, spearheaded by the recolonization programme of the early 1970s, has been rapidly overtaken by 'resource management' and the prime focus of developmentalist attention in Amazonia is, yet again, extraction (see Bunker 1985). In other words, the kinds of intimate, intersystemic relations said to be particularly delicately balanced in Amazonia are relations which have been largely pushed aside in favour of short-term commercial goals. For example, while the evidence suggests that large-scale human habitation of the *várzeas* is a productive and rational form of resource use (and there are significant historical antecedents), the actual – and allegedly ecologically-informed – development schemes of recent years have ignored the *várzeas* in favour of forms of exploitation which are manifestly environmentally destructive (clear-cutting, cattle pasture, hydroelectric; see Friends of the Earth 1988). The current large-scale extractivist activities are ecologically sensitive only to the degree that environmental protection is technically appropriate for immediate commercial needs and they draw very little on well-documented historical examples of the ways in which Amazonian societies have been able to sustain themselves without significant environmental degradation.

As we saw in the previous chapter, one of the consequences of this present-and-future orientation of environmental concern is that those who have pursued environmentally rational livelihoods are rendered invisible, and it is an invisibility which is functional from the point of view of the ideologues of modernization.

The two conceptions of ecosystem (that associated with previous social forms and that associated with modern intervention) are linked: aboriginal societies are presented as having been incapable of overcoming environmental contraints (they represent, after all, the purest ideological examples of pristine noble savages), constraints so rigid that the ecosystem is shown to be unmanageable as a system *per se*, although it can be managed 'selectively'. As many critics have shown, however, such selective intervention is not only environmentally destructive on a large scale (see Goodland and Irwin 1975; Fearnside 1979b, 1986a, 1986b; Smith, N.J. 1982), but provides little in the way of backward linkages or labour absorption while at the same time forcing small producers out of the way. In other words, such selective 'management' does not accommodate the 'ecosystem', as much as it ignores it.[1]

1. The criticism of aboriginal social formations implicit in the developmentalist proposal is a familiar contemporary ideological precept: development is basically altruistic, we are helping those who cannot help themselves. The post-war record, however, shows that the beneficiaries of such aid have less often been the ostensive recipients than the donors themselves, as anticipated by Lenin and Luxemburg, among others, and discussed at length in the contemporary period by Hayter and Watson (1985), Hayter (1989); Payer (1982); Lappe, Schurman and Danaher (1987); Branford and Kucinski (1988).

The Peasant Landscape and Modern Amazonia

In terms of the discussion about environmental determinants of possible social forms, thus far cast only in relation to the evolution of aboriginal social formations and the intervention of modern developmentalists, peasants occupy an awkward position in the sense that not much is known about historical peasantries in Amazonia and in the sense that until recently and in spite of having been overlooked by developmentalist patrons, they have endured. In what follows I review some of the ecological issues which have particular bearing on peasant production.

The fact that the *caboclo* has 'adapted' is a minor point. Of greater interest is the fact that *caboclo* society has transformed and it has done so by virtue of the particular kinds of social relations maintained between an enclave economy and remote structures. The environment presents certain constraints, but these are not given, nor are they in themselves 'systematic'. Their 'systematic' character varies historically and not simply in relation to the structures of local societies, but in relation to the way in which local societies are affected by social forces originating beyond the region.

As noted earlier, discussions of the Amazonian tropical forest ecosystem are united in arguing that the ecosystem is particularly rigid in the sense that it is, among other things, delicately balanced (e.g. high species interdependence), depends on the rapid recovery of scarce nutrients, and is characterized by high species diversity and low species density. Goodland and Irwin (1975), in an authoritative compendium of Amazonian ecological research, and Sioli (1984), in a more recent overview, place emphasis on a central feature, the short nutrient cycle. The major implication of this feature is that seemingly minor interventions by social systems may have extensive ramifications: clearing the forest results not just in the removal of biomass, but in the removal of those structures responsible for cycling nutrients. Fittkau writes that:

> It is true that, biohistorically speaking, [man] arrived very late on the scene and his presence can easily be counted in thousands of years. Furthermore, up to a few centuries ago, surrounded by an extremely diverse and impressive nature, he played a relatively modest role.These difficulties (colonization effects) are perhaps most

> strongly shown as large-scale modifications to the natural scene, mostly disadvantageous (e.g. disaforestation, erosion soil degradation, karst formation, catastrophes due to weeds and pests and so on) which, stemming from the environment in question, affect economic and social conditions. (Fittkau 1969: xiv–xv)

In the face of such cautions, attention has been drawn to technological solutions to Amazonian fragility. In Wagley's introduction to a volume surveying a range of Amazonian themes, the technological 'solution' is presented in bare form. After restating the theme of 'natural obstacles' to socio-cultural development, Wagley states: 'I do not believe, however, that Amazonian potentiality is so limited. We are no longer dealing with a neolithic technology but a highly complex atomic age technology which most certainly can be adapted to a specialized physical environment' (1974: 13).

It is not, however, technology which is adapted for Amazonia. On the contrary, it is the Amazonian environment which is 'adapted' to 'atomic age technology' in spite of the wide recognition that in crucial respects, major features of the Amazonian environment are not 'adaptable' unless that term is rendered devoid of precision and becomes simply a euphemism for 'altered'.

One of the main features of the environment, for example, is the closure of energy cycles, particularly in relation to the nutrient cycle of plants (Richards 1973: 63; Goodland and Irwin 1975: 28). This is a consequence of the fact that the *hyleia* (tropical forest) is the oldest of the earth's environments of this scale and is therefore the most elaborate in terms of the interdependency of natural forms. Richards (1973: 59) describes its clearing as a major event in the earth's history, larger in scale, for example, that the clearing of North American and European forests (1973: 59). Because of its age, the forest floor 'rivals a cave or laboratory growth room in uniformity of conditions' (1973: 59); there is greater diversity of plant and animal species than there is in any other major ecological community, yet there is a very low density of plant and animal species. The age of the ecosystem and the absence of Ice Age interference with plant and animal reproduction have allowed speciation to continue without interruption for a longer period than is true of other environments (Richards 1973: 61, but see Meggers 1985). As a consequence, there are highly particularistic relationships between and among various flora and fauna, and extreme host-specificity which has tended to produce diffuse rather than aggregated plant populations. Within this sort of delicately balanced system, the indirect effects of disrupting a species population may be extensive because of the complex interdependence of many species. Within the ecosystem in an ideal state (which is to say in the absence of large human populations), Richards notes that plant rather than animal species have tended to prevail:

> The degree to which plants have succeeded in this competition is perhaps indicated by the surprisingly low total mass of animal life in the rain forest compared with the mass of vegetation ... The low ratio of animal to plant life (when measured as weight) confirms a suspicion, derived from other observations, that there is a shortage of edible plants in the rain forest. (1973: 62)

The question of scale of human intervention is obviously crucial in light of the peculiar evolution of the Amazonian environment, and this renders the expression 'adaptation' subject to modification (see Crosby 1972). Environmental features of Amazonia are historically specific. When Wagley writes (of *Amazon Town*) that it is:

> a study of a region and the way of life of its people. The region is the Brazilian Amazon where a distinctive tropical *way of life* has been *formed by the fusion* of American Indian and Portuguese *cultures* during the last three centuries. In a larger sense, the book is a study of the *adaptation* of man to a *tropical environment*. (1953: 2)

it is necessary to add that *adaptation* is not a matter of reciprocity between *ecosystem* and *social system*, but rather is a matter of social systems acting upon ecosystems. In Amazonia, with the advent of large-scale colonialization, the ecosystem has shown itself to be resistent to *adaptation*, and its resilience has not meant an adjustment in terms of the social systems which have emerged, but a predatory expansion with extensive and negative ecological consequences.

One example of *adaptation* will illustrate both a peculiarity of Amazonian ecology (one which illustrates the character of a nutrient cycle) and a commonplace of post-colonial resource use. Fittkau's analysis of crocodile extermination in the late 1940s also shows some of the paradoxes of scale noted earlier when Richards' discussion of species interdependency was mentioned, and it illustrates how seemingly minor disruptions of species populations may have far-reaching effects.

The principle which Fittkau is concerned to demonstrate is one which 'determines the structure of a tropical ecosystem with a low, but balanced supply of nutrients' (1973: 129). The stability of such a system increases with the abundance and diversity of its species biota: 'higher abundance and diversity enable the system to take up the available allocthanous nutrients, to conserve them, and to continuously hold them in shortened nutrient cycles as efficiently as possible' (1973: 129).

In the late 1940s, near Manaus, there was a concerted effort to kill caymans which, it was thought, were impeding the develoment of the fishing industry. The results of the slaughter were the opposite of those intended, that is to say the fish crop declined as the cayman population was reduced.

Fittkau discovered that it was not simply the case that the decimation of caymans removed an element of a food cycle, but that caymans have a special capacity to release chemicals essential to the maintenance of nutrient cycles even when the caymans themselves are starving and are passive members of a food chain. Starving caymans in Berlin aquaria and analysing their faeces, Fittkau showed that the animals continued to release N, P, Ca, M, NA and K in quantities sufficient to maintain the links in the supply of allochthanous organic matrial which, during the annual flooding of the river, was drastically reduced. The low levels of electrolytes in Amazonian water (the consequence of long-term impoverishment of *terra firme*) reduce primary production and lead to the aquatic food chain's dependence on allocthanous material. Reduction of one element in this tight chain, caymans, had unexpectedly extensive effects (see Goodland and Irwin 1975 for comparable examples).

This example illustrates not only some esoteric features of Amazonian ecology, but also a typical pattern of scientific inquiry (and one especially well revealed in Amazonia): the ecological implications are realized after the damage has been done. Comparable examples are provided by the failure of *Transamazônica* settler recolonization schemes (see Moran 1981) and the subsequent failure of large-scale cattle-raising, projects for which there is now much published research documenting the general unsuitabilty of such forms of *terra firme* land use (Fearnside 1979a; Hecht 1982; Uhl and Buschbacher 1985).

Agriculture as a near-exclusive livelihood is a relative novelty in Amazonia. Not only did aboriginal populations for whom horticulture/agriculture was a major activity depend heavily on complementary extractive activities, historical peasantries in Amazonia have rarely been exclusively agricultural. In part, this is because of the limited market within Amazonia, but it is also a consequence of the contradictory demands implied by sedentism combined with agriculture: the level of exploitation of primary forest (*terra firme*) required to sustain a primarily agricultural settlement leads to dispersion; thus, it seems inappropriate to discuss agricultural use of land as though it could be separated from other forms of land and resource use. None the less, attention is particularly drawn to agricultural land use because of the internal economic and political priorities of the state (attempts to incorporate marginal lands for food production while reserving productive areas for export agriculture), and because in spite of the ambiguities which inhere in the term 'peasant', attachment to land is a universal criterion. In Amazonia, however, it is important to distinguish between two broad categories of peasant: those newer ones for whom agriculture is the primary activity (not only in terms of its being the central activity, but also in terms of providing the structure within which supplementary activities take place) and those for whom agriculture is one instance within a repertoire of production forms the priority of any one of which is negotiable.

In this context, agriculture in a place such as Santarém displays a major contradiction: it is the major peasant activity and at the same time it is a marginal (or marginalizing) activity in the sense that it depends on predatory expansion in the exploitation of a non-renewable resource – cleared forest land. With agriculture's emergence as the major activity (providing the basic framework of peasant production generally) in a setting of exaggerated demographic growth, the character of soils has received not unexpected scrutiny. The consensus is that with the exception of occasional pockets, Amazonian soils are incapable of sustaining large-scale permanent cultivation of annuals (food crops). This is hardly a new discovery, but it is important to underline it by way of noting that whereas this has dramatic implications for the durability of the new Amazonian colonists, it appears not to have blocked the transformation of historical peasantries in the pre-*Transamazônica* period.

The infertility of Amazonian soils is widely reported (Falesi 1974; Goodland and Irwin 1975; Hecht and Cockburn 1989: 34), and although there are locations with considerably better soils, they are, in Falesi's despairing comment 'scattered in the midst of the ocean of senile, lixivated latasol'. Amazonian soil is not only relatively infertile, but the consequences of infertility have been registered slowly. Schwabe points out that the idea of a lower critical ceiling on the mineral cycle in tropical land has probably been slow to take hold because of its not being so immediately obvious in other major landscapes outside of South America:

> It is not usually directly noticed until it is accelerated by the cultivation of soils which are already impoverished of their minerals. On the removal of the original vegetation, especially of the natural forests which are still capable of maintaining a narrowly balanced cycling of minerals under minimal conditions, it is as if a brake were released and the abiotic process of mineral extraction were immediately accelerated. These circumstances are of crucial importance for large parts of South America. It is thus no coincidence that the phenomenon which Boerger called demineralization was first discovered in eastern South America. (1968: 126)

A parallel argument is presented by Goodland and Irwin (1975: 28), who point to the special features of the plant life of Amazonia by way of illustrating the relative unimportance of soil *per se* in plant growing cycles. Soil in this environment is relieved of certain functions which it commonly performs in other environments, namely as a source and storing place of nutrients necessary to the reproduction of the constituent flora. It neither contains a high proportion of the nutrients available, as is indicated by the impoverished condition of water which has leached the soils (especially in the 'clear' tributaries of the Amazon River where water purity is said to approach that of distilled water), and by the predominance of plants which reproduce by vegetative growth rather than through seeds.

Even if it were the case that nutrients were available, it is thought that the soils would not be capable of retaining them, hence the questionable utility of fertilizer use. Goodland and Irwin cite a study undertaken in 1973 into the effects of swidden agriculture on soil fertility. Researchers 'studying soil nutrients before and after the forest was burned showed that in slash and burn operations great quantities of nutrients are rapidly lost by leaching as the nutrient capacity of the plants is not sufficient to absorb the great quantity of rapidly released; nutrients are thereby irrevocably lost' (Goodland and Irwin 1975: 110; see also D. Harris 1971).

Even on a modest scale, the implications for *terra firme* agriculture meant to sustain sedentary populations are quite clear: most of the nutrients available are lost merely in preparing to exploit the soil and continued production entails the extended appropriation of mature forest.

Rainfall and temperature contribute to the impoverishment (*vis-à-vis* colonial/European notions) of soils. Not only is rainfall high, but also a large proportion of it comes in sharp bursts which have more erosive effects than do moderate patterns.The absolute amount of rainfall is not that great, 1,500–2,000 mm/year, but generalizing, Meggers says that for the region, 20 per cent of the total rainfall comes in bursts which have the capacity to release at least 0.1 mm/minute for a minimum of 5 minutes. The erosive effects on cleared land are very pronounced.

Temperatures are consistently high enough to inhibit severely the growth of fungi which are the major producers of humus. Meggers (1971: 15) summarizes the findings of various soil scientists that temperatures above 77°F discourage fungal growth and aid bacterial growth, which speeds the decomposition of humic material (i.e. bacterial decomposition exceeds fungal formation).

The combination of high temperature and high rainfall results in what is broadly referred to as laterization, the process whereby soil is leached of the phosphorous necessary for plant growth, but retains oxides of iron and bauxite. Once the process begins, it is irreversible, and while an average rainfall of 2,130 mm/year removes (over a three-year period) less than a quarter ton of topsoil/ha from uncleared forest (in a study in which the slope was 12–15 per cent), 45 tons of topsoil are lost from a denuded hillside only half as steep (Meggers 1971: 17; see Eden 1990; Jordan 1989 for up-to-date surveys).

It should be emphasized that under ideal conditions, which is to say when land is not extensively cleared for cultivation, the sorts of process described above – humic destruction, erosion, laterization and leaching – occur as *regular features* of the ecosystem. These processes which militate against sustained agricultural production, are the fundamental ways in which nutrients are transferred in the environment. The ideal nutrient cycle does not appear to be flexible enough to accommodate large scale cultivation of *terra firme* of the sort which could sustain highly commercialized agriculture, and the possibilities for adapting agricultural practice to accommodate the peculiar features of the Amazonian environment have thus far produced disappointing results. There is not, for example, much hope to be found in the application of fertilizers which, according to Goodland and Irwin (1975: 34) are inadequate in replacing what nutrients are lost through the process of erosion (and in any case represent a level of investment denied most Amazonian peasants although see Subler and Uhl 1990 re: Tomé-Açu). Fertilizers are typically leached because there are few colloids in the soil to retain them, the same problem noted earlier in the study which showed that the soil was incapable of absorbing, in swidden agriculture, nutrients released in burning. Goodland and Irwin note that what fertilizer is salvaged from leaching is ineffective, an echo of Falesi's pathologist's tone, 'sequestered by toxically high amounts of aluminum and iron' (1975: 34).

An important and suggestive exception to this generalization about the inherent obstacles to permanent agricultural activity is provided by the example of Tomé-Açu, a Japanese settlement founded in the late 1920s in Eastern Pará (see Staniford 1973; Subler and Uhl 1990). There, under an *ad hoc* agroforestry regime, permanent cultivation of 'uncultivable' land has been achieved, but as Subler and Uhl note (1990: 164–5), this permanence has been achieved at relatively high input costs (for fertilizers and labour) and against a background of institutional support (a co-operative) and security of land-tenure denied the majority of Amazonians who might seek to emulate the Japanese example. In addition, Tomé-Açu incomes are largely derived not from annual food crops, but from black pepper (1990: 157). In a breakdown (by value) of the products sold by the Tomé-Açcu co-operative in 1987, nearly 80 per cent of income was derived from black pepper, 10 per cent from *cacao* and 7 per cent from passion fruit. Of the other products listed (numbering 11), none could be said to qualify as a staple.

In this sketch of a few points concerning Amazonian ecology, one of the issues which is of most concern is the way in which the concept of *adaptation* has been used. In considering the difference between, say, Amerindian societies' effects on the ecosystem and contemporary colonists' effects, the term *adaptation* has been treated as though it means the same thing in both contexts. While swidden agriculture is certainly a major feature of the 'distinctively tropical way of life', its adaptive significance is clearly not the same for all who use it. For pre-contact gatherer-hunter-horticulturalists, swidden agriculture was mainly practised on alluvial soils and deforestation was not a consequence. By contrast, immigrant colonists, especially in the last twenty years, also dependent on swidden agriculture, have contributed to a significant amount of deforestation (although an amount inconsequential by comparison with the effects of commercial clearing for timber and and cattle pasture). It is not the case, however, that the latter are less well 'adapted' to the tropical forest ecosystem. On the contrary, it is the immigrants who have been 'adapted' for the purpose. Agricultural clearing has been the first step in land valorization in conjunction with clearly non-viable forms of land use (mainly pastoral) (see Velho 1972; Foweraker 1981; Hecht and Cockburn 1989 for discussion). Immigrants in Amazonia who have not had to contend with large predatory, competing enterprises of scale (e.g. those immigrants who preceded the rediscovery of Amazonia in the 1970s) did not, and indeed could not, restrict themselves to agricultural acitivities. The derided *caboclo* whose livelihood is based on the combination of agriculture and (primarily) riverine extraction, is testimony to this. In a survey of land use in six Eastern Amazonian municípios, Anderson and Ioris (1989) show that there is significantly more forest destruction in newer settlements and in those without floodplain (i.e. non-*caboclo* settlements).

This discussion, then, is less about ecosystems than it is about arguments within an ecological idiom. The abundance of ecological research in Amazonia in the past fifteen years has produced largely negative projections for the viability of peasant systems. These conclusions are shaped by a variety of political sensibilities. The position of the state is not univocal, but effectively it is that Amazonia represents a repository of natural resources whose value can best be realized through non-renewable extraction. With few exceptions, the scientific community has been highly critical of rampant exploitation of Amazonian resources, one of the central arguments in this critique being that the highly specialized features of the Amazonian environment preclude benign, piecemeal exploitation. If these two positions may be taken to represent the general terms of the debate (glossing over, admittedly, a great number of other views), the ecological idiom *appears* to provide the framework for a critique of developmentalism, but in fact, achieves just the opposite effect. Because ecological arguments feature so prominently in Amazonian social scientific research, there is an apparently virtuous association whereby developmentalism manages to be cushioned by informed, environmental safeguards. The record of hydroelectric construction, forest clearing for pasture, mining and timber extraction illustrates that the association between environmental conservation and development enterprise is more formal than substantial (see especially Fearnside 1986a 1988a; Treece 1987; Hall 1989). Examples of the discrepancy between professed concern over environmental impact and reality are numerous. In the Greater Carajás project, for instance, environmental impact studies featured prominently in the promotion of the project, yet deforestation in the region – especially on the margins of the railway line – is extensive (mainly in the service of pig-iron smelting). In 1988, it was reported in the Belém press that charcoal consumption in nine pig-iron smelters in Carajás would be 1.1 million tons per year. Other examples include the appointment of Jose Lutzemberger – the most visible Brazilian green critic – as Environment Minister, an appointment from which he resigned after claiming that his own subordinates in IBAMA (Environment Institute) were conniving at the activities of the very timber interests they were supposed to regulate. The *Nossa Natureza* (Our Nature) programme instituted by (now ex-) President Sarney was widely ridiculed as a cynical public relations exercise typical of offical concern for the environment. As Susan George notes (*Guardian* 22 May 1992: 33), agencies responsible for funding environmentally unsound projects (the World Bank is the major example) are conscious of the importance of seeming to be environmentally sound, yet the effects of such consciousness are hard to detect in terms of changes in practice.

One of the ways in which eco-critique enhances the developmentalist position is through its treating of ecosystem and social system as directly comparable systems, systems which can be analysed in similar ways. In order to achieve this level of comparability, however, real social systems have to be ignored. What we get in their place are 'populations', 'settlements', 'resource users', and so on. In other words, we do not get a system at all; we get a list of features or variables whose valences are revealed only in relation to ecological effect. One obvious consequence of this is that the actual effects of historical social systems in Amazonia are extremely muddled and the efficacy of the ecological advocacy arguments is seriously undermined. It is obvious, for example, that the Amazonian environment is capable of supporting many people; the historical and archaeological record shows as much. What Amazonia does not seem capable of sustaining are social systems whose conditions of existence are largely determined in external social spheres, i.e. social systems producing commodities embodying values which can be realized on the world market. The destruction which faces Amazonia is not something intrinsic to local social systems, rather it is specific to a kind of social system in which the value of things is determined by market utility. Furthermore, and to recapitulate, the environmental depredations in contemporary Amazonia are somewhat mistakenly attributed to 'human intervention' in a lumping together of all forms of resource use, implying a unity of purpose of what are in fact class antagonists. Peasant and multinational are presented as allied in a manner which, if it were true, would indeed be an exotic discovery. As the literature attests, however, it is large enterprises which not only present the gravest threats, but which also create the conditions under which depredation attributable to peasant production is possible, encouraging, for example, the felling of forest for short-term financial gain (such as charcoal production in Carajás; see Treece 1987; Hall 1989) and, in the longer term, valorization of large estates controlled by non-residents.

The history of Amazonian ecological studies is mainly focused around one debunking point: in spite of the appearance of luxuriance, the tropical forest is actually quite impoverished. What is at first taken to be a garden is in fact a fossil-like structure whose dramatic episodes have long passed (excepting, of course, its possibly imminent demise as an integral system). While the weight of evidence suggests that the system – once tampered with on a large scale – is not highly adaptable (as an example of this argument which considerably pre-dates *Transamazônica* eco-arguments, see P.W. Richards 1952), it is precisely such kinds of large-scale resource extraction which are being promoted in Amazonia. These kinds of resource extraction are the most 'viable' not because of intrinsic features of the ecosystem, but because current development is directed by enterprises whose notion of economic rationality is strongly determined by considerations of scale. This is the ecology of business.

I began this chapter by arguing that ecological arguments have played a, perhaps questionably, exaggerated role in the study of Amazonian social formations, yet much of the material cited actually supports the view that ecological considerations have a privileged status in this setting. That this appears an unsupportable contradiction is understandable, but only if several crucial facts are ignored. One of these is the fact that the ecological characterization of Amazonia is most frequently posed against a highly fragmentary literature on Amazonian social formations and arguments concerning the long-term viability of particular societies (about 'protein capture', for example) are not necessarily generalizable. In addition, the ecological idiom within which the justifications for the form of contemporary development are cast by and large ignores the fact that Amazonia has sustained large (or larger than popularly claimed) pre-colonial populations. The notion of 'ecosystem', therefore, needs to be recast in terms of relevant concrete social formations, not an abstract notion of 'society'. Relatively little may be known about Amazonian social formations, pre-historical or contemporary, but more is known than can be adequately filed away simply as 'populations' of the region.

The Managed Ecosystem

The most noteworthy shift in prescriptions for the 'appropriate' exploitation of Amazonia is presented in the claims made for agroforestry (see King and Chandler 1978b for early programmatic account), an approach within which the yields of annual (primarily food) and perennial (primarily extractive) products are calibrated in terms of the specific constraints of the ecosystem. The dynamic limits of such a humid tropic system are neatly summarized by Ewel: 'The plant's photosynthetic energy may be allocated to either harvestable products or to the ecological functions that sustain complex ecosystems, but not to both simultaneously', (1986: 260)

In practice, the outcome of this recognition of the dynamic limits of the humid tropical forest has been registered in an increasing sensitivity to the fact that forest management practices of the type outlined by biological researchers are – or have been – conducted for many years by Amazonian Indians and *caboclos* (and others). As a number of recent studies have shown (Irvine 1985; Hiraoka 1985a; Anderson and Posey 1987; Anderson, Hecht and May 1988), the structure of succession forests manipulated by agriculturalist/extractivists may represent an ideal mix of species complementarity. Whereas forest cover consisting of adult species is more uniform in terms of demands on nutrient resources (as well as wavelengths of solar radiation, Ewel 1988: 256), managed succession forests combine plants at different stages of maturity as well as plants that differ in phenology and differ in terms of their nitrogen-fixing properties and overall are therefore complementary rather competitive in relation to resource availability.

This shift in approach represents a considerable revision of received wisdom, most importantly in acknowledging the significance of aspects of the social construction of viable ecosystems and, by implication, the rejection of crude notions of 'human adaptation' to the environment. It also, if as well only by implication thus far, introduces an historical dynamic to the study of what has previously been held to be a combination of biological systems.

Early proponents of agroforestry defined the sub-field as follows:

> sustainable land management systems that combine the production of crops including tree crops, forest plants and/or animals simultaneously or sequentially on the same unit of land, applying management practices that are compatible with the cultural practices of the local population. (King and Chandler 1978b: 8; also see King and Chandler 1978a)

As Hecht (1982: 331) has noted, such an approach implies a substitution of existing practices by 'appropriate' ones when in fact such practices may already be in place, and indeed the further revision required of the agroforestry view may be that the apparently 'natural' structure of forests bears the marks of knowledgeable intervention not by 'local populations', but social systems.

Although it may – perhaps with premature optimism – be argued that the relevant social agents, *caboclos* and other forest-users, are increasingly depicted as ecological *bricôleurs* with as yet insufficiently recognized compentencies, there remains a vast distance between new research results and the social policies which they might inform. Some measure of the distance is provided by the distribution of SUDAM funds in the period 1967–71 when *Transamazônica*-related policy was formulated and it was clear that extractive activities were regarded as anathema to the modernization of Amazonia. Of the funds made available by SUDAM and BASA, 0.1 per cent were earmarked for extractive activities; 1.4 per cent went to colonization programmes; 12.1 per cent were directed to social projects; and 57.4 per cent were devoted to infrastructure (SUDAM 1967, cited in Bakx n.d. : 2).

Consequences reflecting the priorities of SUDAM-administered development have been widely and well documented (see especially Hecht and Cockburn 1989; Fearnside 1986a) and the implementation of policies reflecting a generic agroforestry approach have paled by comparison. According to Allegretti (1989: 32), the 2 million hectares of extractivist reserves established by 1989 supported 3,700 families (= c. 20, 000 people); by her estimates, 400,000 Amazonians are primarily dependent on extraction (1989: 33). Two million hectares is considerably less (35 per cent) than the forest cleared by SUDAM-approved cattle ranches up to 1982. Currently, 73,000 hectares of forest are cleared annually just for charcoal (= 1.7 million tons/annum) (Hebette, Dall 'Agrol and Souza 1989: 6).

The agroforestry argument (and those more generally concerned with sustainability) are dealt with in chapter 8. The purpose in bringing up the matter here is to underline one argument, that the increasing sophistication with which ecological matters have been dealt in Amazonia has little improved the position (or visibility) of those who live in societies which are characterized as being more or less environmentally compatible with their surroundings. The shift afforded by the agroforestry approach to evaluating ecosystems, while leading to recognition of *caboclos*, tends, as argued earlier, to renaturalize them: instead of being regarded as functioning social systems, *caboclo* societies are treated as a new resource, an opportunity to find out more about the forest and its utility from the point of view of non-Amazonians.

Crocodile Tears: Modernization in Amazonia

While the study of Amazonian social formations has traditionally stressed the complex interplay between biological and social systems, in the late twentieth century it is necessary to recognize that a major addition to the social landscape is the apparatus of modernization represented by both the state and international development agencies. One of the major effects of the heightened developmentalist profile in Amazonia is that the unfolding of knowledge of biological and social systems is increasingly administered by extra-Amazonian agents for whom Amazonia is less a coherent social field than it is a management problem. This perspective is most obviously revealed in the now global debates about the fate of the forest, a debate in which a prominent theme is the continued viability not of Amazonia *per se*, but of Amazonia as a durably exploitable resource domain.

As has been argued thus far, neo-Amazonian – *caboclo* – society is in crucial respects a reconstituted society (or societies) and in the current period, modernization ideology and policies have had an overwhelming impact in transforming the basis upon which *caboclo* society is again reconstituted in the name of 'national integration' and the 'global community', but while research in Amazonia over the past twenty years has contributed significantly to the demystification of what has long been a refuge of exoticism (and continues to be), there is very little in Amazonian studies which makes clear the relationship of the region to that body of critical social science literature in which 'Latin America' has featured so prominently in the post-war era: regardless of one's judgement of its explanatory value, dependency theory (used here in a generic sense to designate a broad body of theory critical of modernization theory, but see C. Kay 1989 for a pointed survey), can hardly be excluded from an assessment of modern social science anywhere in Latin America – except in Amazonia. In fact, the frequently remarked upon anomoly of Amazonia's size in relation to that of the Brazilian state is matched by the anomoly of Amazonia's marginality in the dependency literature. Bunker (1985), Foweraker (1981), Velho (1972), Branford and Glock (1985) and Davis (1977) are notable exceptions to this sweeping claim (as are the less widely cited Ianni 1979; Arruda et al 1975; Weinstein 1983; Cardoso and Muller (1977), but by and large, Amazonia has been a mere footnote in the analysis of *subdesenvolvimento*. Two volumes with explicitly anthropological trajectories, Forman's *The Brazilian Peasanty* (1975), which provided a welcome and long overdue survey, and Goodman and Redclift's *From Peasant to Proletarian* (1981), a comparative study of European and Latin American debates about agrarian structure, are both notably bereft of reference to Amazonia. Hall's more recent *Developing Amazonia* (1989) is an astute analysis of the centrepiece of modern Amazonian development – the Carajás programme – which requires little reference to the assault posed by critiques of modernization bolstered by association with dependency literature.

Given the relative youth of this new body of research and given the array of specialist disciplines drawn to Amazonia, as well as the impact of relatively new sub-fields such as ethnobotany and agroforestry, is not surprising that in many respects social science research is somewhat cloistered. Given the relative poverty of local research institutes, the politically volatile character of Indianist research (the major area of social scientific contribution), and the stultifying effects of years of National Security State repression, it is not surprising that large, foreign-supported research and development projects guided by the precepts of modernization/developmentalism have come to be seen as representing a new and stable basis upon which to proceed with the 'conquest of the tropics'. In the absence of critical approaches which have informed the discussion of development theory elsewhere in Latin America, and facing little resistance, proponents of modernizationist policies in Amazonia have been able operate in a remarkably unencumbered way.[2]

2. David Price's *Before the Bulldozers* (1989) offers a highly detailed, insider's account of work within one such agency, the World Bank.

One consequence of the rapid increase in research undertaken in an ill-defined context (a large region with a poorly provisioned research infrastructure and little institutional support) has been that a new consensus on general historical and sociological features of the region has been set aside in favour of a provisional agenda based, in the main, on the results of research into biological systems. Because recent undertakings have displaced many earlier misconceptions, there has been a tendency to overlook generalizations which might hark back to an era of gross and misinformed overstatement (e.g. uniformly poor soils, deforestation through predatory expansion of small-holders, and so on).

Laudable though this approach has been in many respects (not least in encouraging a modesty in extrapolating from narrow case studies), certain general features of Amazonian social formations should not be neglected, even if the baldness with which they may be presented appears somewhat out of touch with current trends in which technical expertise reflects an increasingly detailed academic division of labour. Among these are the fact that the modern phase of Amazonian development has occurred under the auspices of a National Security State; that it has depended heavily (as indeed has the Brazilian 'economic miracle') on foreign capital encouraged by the 'improved investment climate' accorded by the generals; that a progressive programme of agrarian reform is no closer to being realized than it was twenty years ago. These are general features of which Amazonian researchers are all aware, yet such seemingly significant factors are generally appended to the research literature rather than situated at the centre of arguments (although see, in particular, Hall's detailed critique of the Greater Carajás Project 1989).

One reason for drawing attention to the neglect of the political and economic climate of Amazonian (re)development is that much current research views the tragedy of state policy as deriving from inefficiencies of management, that is what has gone wrong in Amazonia was an unintended consequence of the too rapid drafting and implementation of development programmes. This argument is strongly evident in a number of authoritative works generally critical of what has passed for 'development' within Transamazônica-related planning schemes (see Kleinpenning 1975; Bourne 1978; Moran 1981; Bunker 1985; Hall 1989; Hecht and Cockburn 1989).

An alternative reading of the manner in which modern Amazonian development has gone awry depends on distinguishing between two quite different ways in which Amazonian development was conceived by planners. On the one hand, there is the well-known conception of Amazonian development in which the state put forward a programme of national integration among whose elements was the provision of an infrastructure which would encourage the emergence of a smallholding peasantry whose dynamic would largely be determined by national market structures. The failure of this programme is widely documented (see Kleinpenning 1975 for a concise, early review).

On the other hand, however, there is a level of development which has taken place in spite of the failure of the state policy of integration. This development has been largely concerned with organizing the extraction of minerals, hydroelectric power and timber from Amazonia, possibilities as much incumbent on the state provision of infrastructure as were the failed colonist resettlement schemes.

From this second point of view, the dilemmas of Amazonian development are neither particularly Brazilian (or Amazonian) in character (i.e. the relevant frame of reference is not the state), nor are they particularly unusual. Brazil is a client-state of the United States and thereby pursues policies which are by no means legitimated by the state alone; the major beneficiaries of Amazonian development are those for whom the investment climate can best be exploited, absentee and multinational capital by and large. The provision of raw materials (and policies concerned with ensuring such provision) has been, in both vulgar and sophisticated analyses, the focus of studies of colonialism and imperialism (and their neo-variants) since such studies began. In this sense, then, what has happened (and is continuing to happen) in Amazonia is hardly remarkable in the sense of being unique, yet the uniqueness of Amazonia in an ecological context has tended to overshadow the geopolitical context as an arena for debate.

Brazil as Client-state

Brazil's long-standing alliance with (and, crudely, resemblance to) the United States is so well documented as to elicit little interest as a topic in itself. Melting-pot pluralists have long drawn parallels between the two nations in terms of ethnic composition; the role of African slave-based plantation systems has provided a basis for much comparative work; the role of European immigrants at the turn of the century has provided another common focus. The role as gendarme of Latin America outlined in the Alliance for Progress (see Gordon 1963), the active participation and/or connivance of US officials in the coup of 1964 (see Black 1977; P. Parker 1979; R. Leacock 1990), the inordinately high levels of US bank lending to Brazil (and crippling debt thereby incurred; see especially Branford and Kucinski 1988); the US training of military and security personnel (Langguth 1978; Herman 1982), and the generous terms according to which, periodically, US firms have been able to dominate the modern Brazilian economy (Evans 1979), all speak to the intimate connections that exist between Brazil and the United States.

Given the extent of United States penetration of Brazil it would be astonishing if Amazonian development policy were found to be formulated in an independent realm. A number of works have drawn attention to this aspect of Amazonian development (cf. Arruda et al. 1975; Davis 1977; Price 1989), yet most attention has been directed towards the most dramatic, and perhaps unrepresentative, cases of foreign usurpation of Amazonia, such as Ludwig's Jarí project (see Ianni 1980) and the Volkswagen and Liquigas cattle ranches. Important though these examples are in illustrating the improvements in the investment climate which accompanied the coup, they are not representative of the major features of Amazonian development as it has diverged from the initially stated aims of recolonization.

The State as Broker

Foreign investment in Amazonia is mainly focused on the extraction of raw materials for export without significant processing of such materials within Brazil. Projects concerned with the extraction of iron ore at Carajás (see Treece 1987; Hall 1989 for discussion), manganese at Amapá and bauxite on the Trombetas are among the major recipients of multinational attention. The heightened participation of foreign capital is hardly unique to Amazonia, but rather has been a general feature of post-coup Brazil, and as Alves has noted:

> [A] reduction in the effective protection level and an end to subsidized credit during liquidity crises made it easier for foreign – especially American – firms to acquire bankrupt Brazilian companies. The resulting denationalization of the economy has been a major characteristic of the Brazilian economic model. (1984: 50)

These policies, largely credited to Octavio de Bulhões and Roberto Campos, also included repeal of the Profit Remittance Law passed in 1962 and generous incentives with regard to taxes and importation of machinery (Alves 1984: 51).

The significance of the US–Brazilian clientage relationship has been analysed in a number important works, but the role of Amazonia within this relationship has not drawn a great deal of attention. It is worth looking briefly at a number of critical accounts of United States–Brazilian relations before proceeding to locate Amazonian development in this international context.

Peter Evans' *Dependent Development* (1979) is the most thorough account of the way in which the alliance has developed. What is emphasized in his work (which draws heavily on a wide range of critical analyses including, perhaps especially, those of Cardoso and Muller 1977) is the way in which the character of the modern Brazilian state can only be defined by reference to its dependent relations with multinational capital backed by the United States (and to a lesser degree other core nations). There is not, in this analysis, so much a concrete entity called 'the Brazilian state', rather there is a structure of dependency and alliance within which one of the elements is a bureaucratic regime whose legitimacy is in large part derived from its brokering role in establishing external links. The character of these external links has long been treated in the literature. In political terms, Stepan (1973), for example, presents a number of detailed studies of the important institutional links (especially military) which obtain between Brazil and the United States. Langguth's *Hidden Terrors* (1978) examines the way in which these institutional (and, need it be said, ideological) links have been extended when, for example, Brazilian policing expertise is employed in other Latin American nations. In Herman's (1982) study of the National Security State, it is noted that Brazil was among the first of Latin American

National Security States to accept a death squad organization for which the United States was largely responsible (1964), that Brazil has the largest number of US-trained military personnel (8,659, 1950–80), and has been a major Latin American recipient of US military aid ($US 640 million, 1946–79) (1982: 116).

A number of recent works have begun to situate Amazonia in terms of the transformation of the authoritarian-dependent state (Velho 1972; Foweraker 1981; Hecht and Cockburn 1989), and although the focus in these works is by no means the same, an argument common to all of them is that recent development in Amazonia has been widely destructive in ecological and social terms and has done little to improve the lives of Amazonians despite official claims to the contrary. Amazonian development, however, continues regardless of the demonstrable unsuitability of many of the specific features of development programmes (e.g. extensive agricultural and pastoral exploitation of *terra firme*) and regardless of the failure of export-oriented production to provide significant backward linkages which might provide some basis for local development of the productive forces. One obvious question raised, then, is: why does Amazonian development continue in spite of its numerous ostensibly irrational features?

One explanation, noted earlier, which has been put forward frequently in analyses of the planning apparatus responsible for implementing *Transamazônica* development within the programme of national integration is that there is something about bureaucratic organization in Brazil that has made the efficient implementation of Amazonian redevelopment impossible. Moran's (1981) discussion of the official recolonization attempts at Altamira, virtually a pilot programme for *Transamazônica* colonist resettlement generally, illustrates the inadequacy of the basic features of the agrarian reform programme. More recently, Bunker (1985), who has concentrated particularly on bureaucratic structures, has argued that:

> Rural development programmes for the Amazon were distorted by private-sector penetration of the state apparatus and competition for its resources; bureaucratic inefficiency associated with excessive complexity; lack of effective governmental control and coordination; the accumulated residues of past political and adminisrative arrangements; and discontinuities of government commitment caused by shifts in the relative power of different segments of the government itself. (1985: 117)

He goes on to argue that within the patrimonial state, it was impossible to modernize the administrative apparatus in a manner appropriate for the special demands of the development programme as conceived for Amazonia.

Similarly, Moran (1985), in a review of colonization programmes in Amazonia, argues that the relative failure of *Transamazônica* colonization was due to problems of implementation:

> The most serious constraint to the develoment of the Amazon is not the absence of adequate soils, nor is it the lack of labour, or even an insufficient amount of capital. Rather, the lack of management capacity at all levels of institutional functioning makes the process of Amazonian development extrememly hazardous from both an environmental and a social point of view. (1985: 98)

There are many strengths in both Bunker's analysis and Moran's, but there is a compelling alternative explanation, and this is that there is nothing disorganized about recent Amazonian development, that the objectives of the planners have in fact been achieved, these objectives being, in the first instance, the establishment of an infrastructure appropriate for the extraction of raw materials from Amazonia.

One reason for doubting explanations for inefficiency in Amazonian development based on the nature of bureaucratic organization in Brazil is that in other realms of national life, the bureaucratic state has showed itself extremely capable when attempting to implement policy. The notorious Institutional Acts served to centralize state authority within the idiom of National Security State ideology; internal opposition was successfully suppressed for almost two decades; trade unions were abolished; an indexed wages policy was implemented in the face of drastically declining standards of living; blatant manipulation of the skeletal parliamentary apparatus was a pronounced feature during the rule of the generals. In short, in a number of significant respects the National Security State was anything but inefficient when it came to implementing policy.

Another reason for doubting received accounts of the disaster of Amazonian development, i.e. that the carnage has been an unintended result of poor planning, is that Amazonian development has, from the outset, been carried out with the direct assistance, supervision, and collaboration of international development organizations such as the World Bank, FAO and USAID, and although there have been well-publicized disagreements over specific issues (the permeability of Indian lands, to name one notorious example), the participation of such organizations has been a regular, not to say crucial, feature of Amazonian development. According to Nigel Smith (1982: 14–15), 'Funds for construction of the *Transamazônica* were drawn from PIN and USAID', and 'USAID donated $10 million to Brazil in the form of PL–480 wheat, the proceeds of sale to be used on the highway project'. World Bank participation in the early stages was less direct. Rather than funding the *Transamazônica per se*, between 1970 and 1979, the World Bank loaned Brazil $629 million for improvement of highways, and through the IBRD (International Bank for Reconstruction and Development) has made available a further $132 million for integrated development projects which include the building or recuperation of roads, and '[t]hese generous allocations of money have allowed the Brazilian government to shift road construction funds to Amazonia that would have been spent in other regions' (N.J. Smith 1982: 14–15; Bourne 1978: 66–7).

A further reason for critically examining the 'disorganization' thesis is that the unevenness of development within Brazil itself obscures the fact that economic relations between sub-regions of Brazil, Amazonia, say, and foreign nations may be more significant than indicated by such economic activities' measure in national accounts. Amazonia, for example, although contributing relatively little to national accounts (5 per cent of GNP according to Myers 1980: 120) contains considerable quantities of strategic minerals. As Kolko (1969) and Kolko and Kolko (1972) have argued, US industry's high level of consumption of imported raw materials has provided a compelling motive for ensuring reliable and cheap supplies, noting further that: 'Imported raw materials in American industry have a value and role which superficially appears quite slight, but their value far exceeds either their weight or cost' (1972: 624).

Increasing dependence on mineral imports is indicated in Tables 3.1 and 3.2:

Table 3.1 Import contribution to US consumption

1930	%
copper	65
bauxite	64
lead	9
1950	
iron ore	8
bauxite	76
copper	48
lead	43
zinc	40
1960	
iron ore	32
bauxite	98
lead	35
zinc	60
copper	46
1975	
aluminum	84
iron	29
lead	11
manganese	98
tin	84
tungsten	55
zinc	61

Sources: 1930, 1950, 1960: Kolko and Kolko (1972: 624–5); Kolko (1969: 51). 1975: Hoogvelt (1982: 61).

Table 3.2 US dependence on imports of strategic minerals

Imports from all foreign sources (%)					Imports from LDCs (%)
	1950	1970	1985	2000	1971
Bauxite	64	85	96	98	95
Iron	8	30	55	67	32
Manganese	88	95	100	100	57
Tin	77	98	100	100	94

Source: Barnet and Muller (1975: 126)

Hoogvelt (1982: 60–2) argues that 'precisely because the number of Third World countries that possess these resources is limited, direct foreign investment in extractive industries generally is concentrated in a limited number of countries', noting in addition that in the list of developing countries which receive the bulk of overseas investment, all such countries are either mineral exporters and/or newly industrializing, and that of the twenty-three principal hosts (recipients of $65,482 m, 1977), Brazil itself absorbed $10,700 m.

Three points may be summarized here. One is that in the past decade there has been a marked concentration of direct foreign investment in selected peripheral/semi-peripheral nations – Brazil being a prime example; much of this investment has been concerned with the provision of raw materials – strategic minerals being among the most important; and the strategies of foreign aid and foreign policy have parallel structures.[3]

Amazonia has major reserves of gold, manganese, cassiterite, iron ore and bauxite, and much *Transamazônica* activity is unabashedly concerned – now that peasant recolonization has been set aside – with presenting the exploitation of these resources as the key to development via such efforts as the Grand Carajás Project). Although some mining projects have been carried out for many years by private Brazilian and foreign-owned firms (and a large proportion of gold and cassiterite production takes place in the informal sector; see Cleary 1991 for discussion), the recent tendency has been for the creation of multinational consortia in which the state participates. The bauxite reserves on the Trombetas River, to give some idea of the scale of operations, produced 4.7 million tonnes in 1984 of which 3.9 million tonnes were exported (Branford and Glock 1985: 116). Iron ore exports from Serra de Carjas are, depending on projections of world demand, expected to be 35 million tonnes/annum by 1988 a quantity equal to one-seventh of world iron exports. Even at these high production levels, the mines would have a life of 350 years (Branford and Glock 1985: 117). It is widely agreed that in spite of the scale of such operations, the benefits likely to be accrued locally, in

3. See discussion of Resources for the Future in Kolko (1969). An aerial survey of Amazonia (RADAM) was undertaken in the early 1970s and was explicitly concerned to reveal sub-soil resources (which, according to Brazilian law, do not belong to surface freeholders). The survey was made using radar equipment rented to Brazil by the United States for the sum of $1 (Bourne 1977: 74).

terms of labour absorption, for example, and backward linkages with local economic structures, will be minimal. Instead, the most obvious results will be (and some are already realized) displacement of local populations (including Indians on 'reserved' lands) and the establishment of the by now familiar enclave economy (cf. Roberts 1978).

The focus on mining (and to a lesser extent, timber extraction) follows on the widespread failure of large-scale cattle-ranching. While Amazonia has as yet provided little scope for the development of export agriculture, the pastoral use of cleared tropical forest has at various times been promoted as a likely spur to local development. In part, the motivation for this form of land use (one universally condemned by serious researchers; see especially Hecht 1985; Uhl 1989) has been derived from Brazil's increasing dependence on foreign exchange earnings to mollify the crushing external debt and Amazonia's possible contribution to debt repayment is largely restricted to the extraction of raw materials (its rather modest comparative advantage). The prominence given this possible contribution of Amazonia to Brazil's debt burden is quite out of proportion to its actual potential export values (unless the landscape is to be denuded). The debt issue if of most direct relevance to Amazonia in relation to the prescriptions which have emerged in globalis eco-security arguments: debt-for-nature swaps (in which debts are written off in exchange for debtors' commitments to environmental conservation) and increasing demands that in the face of potentially global environmental disasters, sovereign resources be considered as global resources (cf. Pearce and Myers 1990).

From 1971 to 1976, and with considerable financial support from SUDAM, the agency empowered to oversee regional development in Amazonia, export-beef potential was highlighted in view of the projected growth of the US food industry as a whole, with fast-food chains growing at 20 per cent per annum in the mid-1970s two and a half times faster than growth in the restaurant industry as a whole. This stimulus for 'non-inflationary beef' resulted (in the period 1966–78) in the conversion of 80,000 km^2 of Brazilian Amazonian forest into ranches, 336 of them supporting some 6 million head of cattle under the auspices of SUDAM (Myers 1980: 44). Although Myers' claims for the role of Amazonian export beef are widely disputed (see Hecht and Cockburn 1989: 98; Hall 1989:25–6; Shane 1986) the point here is that whether realized or not, the rationale for gross conversion of forest for cattle pasture was articulated within a plan for regional development structured by extra-regional concerns. Although the levels of economic expansion in Amazonia are relatively modest in national terms, they may have considerable significance in terms of needs fulfilled outside of Amazonia, particularly with regard to strategic minerals. In addition, the effects of such extraction have been shown to have important ramifications in terms of the displacement of Indian and peasant societies (Davis 1977; Foweraker 1981; Branford and Glock 1985; Bunker 1985;) and in terms of ecological effect (Goodland and Irwin 1975; Sioli 1984; Eden 1990). The infrastructural provisions of *Transamazônica*-related development have not been equitably realized by Amazonians. The major beneficiaries are those enterprises operating economies of scale, which is to say enterprises unrepresentative of Amazonians as a whole. In addition, the specific kinds of economies of scale operating within Amazonia are little engaged with local economies, but rather are primarily concerned with exploitation of local resources to be processed outside of Amazonia (and Brazil in many cases).

One example of the way in which infrastructural provision, in this case roads, has locally transformative effects the benefits of which are not realized locally, yet which have durable and largely negative consequences for Amazonians, is provided by timber extraction. Until the modern period, timber extraction concentrated on firewood (mainly adjacent to waterways) and exotic hardwoods and, according to Myers (1980: 126), the absence of transport infrastructure meant that less than 1 per cent of the dense forest zone was susceptible. He goes on to say that 'With improved technology, logging areas are expected to expand to about 500 m. on either side of rivers and roads, making some 430 000 km^2 of Amazona, or 15 per cent, accessible'.

In Myers' discussion of the role of foreign corporations and tropical forestry, he makes a number of points which underscore the importance of infrastructure in creating an appealing investment climate. Foresty is both dependent on rapidly expanding technology and is exceptionally capital-intensive. Citing an example from Indonesia, Myers notes that for the exploitation of each kilometre of forest, timber extractors had to construct as much as 4 km of road. The appeal of Amazonian resources to such MNCs as National Bulk Carriers, Georgia Pacific, Atlantic Veneer, Eldal, Bruynzeel and Brumasa – with concessions as large (in the case of Georgia Pacific) as 4000 km2 (Myers 1979: 191) – indicates that the modern provision of infrastructure within *Transamazônica* development has had at least some obvious beneficiaries.

It has been argued in recent years – by Myers among others – that the aid agencies responsible for supervising multinational expansion in such regions as Amazonia are increasingly committed to the 'rational' exploitation of such resources as timber, hydroelectric power and minerals, that is to say that even though such forms of extraction might yet be some way from permitting benefits to trickle down, the more destructive effects of large-scale extraction are mollified by sound environmental provisions.

In practice, however, and although there is a great deal of talk about environmental assessment and monitoring, development programmes have largely been effected despite environmentalist critiques (cf. *Balbina, Tucuruí, Transamazônica* itself, Carajás). Some insight into the degree of obfuscation generated by the apparent concern for environmental impact is provided by the World Bank. The Bank, a major participant in the rediscovery of Amazonia, has maintained a very high environmental profile. The substance of this interest, however, may be less than it appears to be. According to Bruce Rich, in a statement made before the Subcommittee on International Development Institutions and Finance of the Committe on Banking, Finance and Urban Affairs of the US House of Representatives, the Bank's actual devotion to such matters dissolves under scrutiny. The Bank's Office of Environmental Affairs employs only three full-time professionals (out of a total of 5,250 Bank employees) to review approximately 315 projects per annum. He notes that:

> Agriculture, the single largest lending sector, is regulated in only one area – pesticide use – and by guidelines that are obsolete. In fact, the Bank's sole mandatory environmental procedures call for the review of projects long after they have been chosen and designed, and just before the initiation of loan negotiations. (Rich 1983: 10)

The argument put forward in this chapter is quite simple: the conquest of Amazonia succeeded in so far as the objectives of the state and the overseas business community are concerned. For Amazonians, of course, and those technocrats who attempted to carry out the recolonization policies, the consequences of the past twenty years of development bear little resemblance to what was envisioned. In this discussion, emphasis has been placed on the fact that the upsurge in Amazonian research has mainly been focused around issues relating to the *Transamazônica* and that there is an argument to be made for situating *Transamazônica* itself within a larger framework, namely that defined by the compelling presence of foreign investment (whether in conjunction with the state or not). The overview of The Alliance for Progress, the programme which outlined official US views on what constitute desirable relations between the United States and Latin American states, provides a very succinct – although partial – description of what has actually occurred in Amazonia, and in *New Deal for Latin America: the Alliance for Progress* (1963), Lincoln Gordon, then US ambassador to Brazil, notes the 'three keys to genuine progress' which are embodied in Alliance prescriptions:

> an intensive and well-planned program of public investment to supply both the economic and social infrastructure (such as roads, power, water, education and public health) required for rapid development ... special incentives to attract private investment in order to get over the hump of initially low returns which create a vicious circle of stagnation. There are many types of such incentives. Tax concessions, market guarantees, government assistance and credit on unusually favorable terms have all proved their usefulness ... and perhaps [the] most important key is full economic integration with the wealthier regions of the nation. (Gordon 1963: 65-6)

These prescriptions, anodyne though they are, bear quotation for a simple reason, and this is that they are ambiguous as far as identifying the beneficiaries of these 'keys to progress'. Gordon's outline – a gloss on Rostow's (1960) prescriptions for modernization – is a description of the programme's advantages from the point of view of investors, the underlying assumption being that what is good for 'Latin Americans' is that which is good for the United States.

The 'economic miracle' conceived within the prescriptions outlined in the Alliance for Progress has, of course, been realized in a variety of ways by Brazilians of different classes and by those for whom the investment climate has proved so alluring. A decade after the installation of the authoritarian regime, the Brazilian Labour Minister reported (*New York Times*, 25 January 1976) that 151 hours of labour were required to meet basic needs for a month (food, clothing, rent) while in 1965, 87 hours of labour were required. According to the US Tariff Commission, multinational corporations in Brazil account for only 8 per cent of total employment yet control almost half of all manufacture (Hewlett 1980: 154). While the amount of total foreign investment and reinvestment (with the United States being the largest contributor) reached $17.5 billion in 1980, Brazil had the second lowest minimum wage in Latin America (after Peru) with the minimum being earned by 31 per cent of (formal sector) workers; in real terms these wages are lower than they were at the start of rapid industrialization in the late 1950s. With Venezuela, Brazil had the longest standard working week in Latin America (48 hours), and the infant mortality rate, one index of economic progess, is the second highest in the continent. These are consequences of clientage no less intimately related to policies that was the brief period of the 'economic miracle'. These are the results of an unfettered hand in shaping the 'development' of Brazil (see Cleary 1991).

The Social Object

In reviewing some points concerning the role of aid policy and projects as they have constructed an investment climate amenable to outside interests in Amazonia, the purpose is not simply to argue that two quite different notions of *development* are being pursued, but also that the coexistence of these two trajectories/conceptions of development have important consequences for the way in which the social reproduction of local formations is structured. On one hand, the reconstruction of Amazonia at the behest of agencies and their corporate and state allies is occurring without account being taken of local societies. On the other hand, the conditions of existence necessary for such societies to reproduce are being shaped by factors quite external to the control of such societies. This is not by any means a novel circumstance, the transformation of Amazonia historically having been more a matter of foreign imposition than autochthonous development, but what is novel is that with heightened research interest in Amazonia and manifestly more authoritative literature, the cardinal features of the geopolitical context in which Amazonian development is situated are so neglected. One consequence of this neglect is that the 'failures' of the *Transamazônica* are only treated in terms of a mythical, reified, and exotic Amazonia, one in which it is only to be expected that 'society' is merely an appendage to well-managed resource extraction.

The 'failure' of the *Transamazônica* is old news, but no less interesting for that, and there is good reason to doubt whether the initial goals of *Transamazônica* – the settlement of independent, smallholding producers – was ever taken seriously by those overseeing the various *Transamazônica* programmes. The explicit shift to development of Amazonian resources rather than Amazonian societies did not distract the technocratic gaze, for there is little evidence it was ever focused on anything other than the traditional booty of the periphery, and as Bakx (n.d.: 2) has argued, with the exception of peasant migration to Maranhão in the 1920s, 'movements in to the Amazon are indissociable from the actions of the state as either facilitator or regulator of them'. A 'peasant problematic' in Amazonia is the result of different kinds of structures (*aviamento*, the National Security State), processes (ethnocide, migration), historical factors (marginality in relation to commercial export agriculture), and lacunae in the systematic study of biological and social systems. In this chapter I have looked at two of the most influential areas of research and policy implementation – those defined by the ecological idiom and modernizationist ideology – which serve further to shape the way in which peasantries are conceptualized. Ironically, one of the major sources of knowledge now increasingly cited – the so-called traditional forest manager[4] – is a source directly threatened by the fully administered 'development of Amazonia'.

4. Note that peasant/*caboclo* society has been leapfrogged: once spurned as 'stagnant', peasants are now post-Fordist 'managers'.

Part II

Caboclos in History

Chapter 4

Santarém and the 'Failure' of *Transamazônica*

In the context of Amazonia's having been reintroduced to the national/international development agenda via the *Transamazônica*, Santarém is doubly marginalized. On the one hand, in relation to both the initial and revisionist goals of *Transamazônica* – peasant resettlement and large-scale resource extraction – Santarém lay beyond the the brief of resettlement and its significance in terms of resource extraction is due only to its relative proximity to Trombetas bauxite deposits (prompting some improvements in docking facilities) and the Upper Tapajos goldfields. Second, however, Santarém is marginalized in terms of its having become a dropping-out point for refugees from *Transamazônica* resettlement schemes. As such, it is a monument to two distinctive phases of Amazonian development. It represents both an abandoned peasantry which has endured in spite of the 'stagnation' supposedly typical of Amazonian peasantries, and it is capable of absorbing neo-peasants for whom *Transamazônica* was somewhat less than El Dorado.

It is not surprising given the way in which Santarém has been directly and indirectly shaped by *Transamazônica* that it displays contradictory features, both in terms of itself (a city of peasants) and in terms of Amazonian economic development (Santarenos are little absorbed in the large-scale extractive enterprises which constitute the main thrust of 'development').

As a social object, then, it is the site of a peculiar negotiation: a peasantry which does not officially exist except as an aggregate of undistinguished production figures, a typical *caboclo* mélange, and a peasantry which has historically defied this negative characterization.

While there is a distinctiveness to Santareno society, an aspect of this is its limited autonomy in relation to developments within Amazonia overall. If anything, Santarém confounds the purposes of *Transamazônica* revisionism (the resources strategy) because of its relative autonomy. Having adapted to neglect, it barely notices that the spotlights are playing elsewhere in the region.

The boundedness of the Santareno social formation is in large measure not a result of something special about Santarém *per se*, but a result of its position within the modernizing apparatus which prevails in Amazonia, a modernizing apparatus which is by and large unconcerned with Amazonian societies except in so far as their existence has implications for the extraction of raw materials. As Santarém features little in this regard, it continues to expand as a trading centre, a wide place in the road.

The Modernization Landscape

Much of the current discussion of peasantries in Amazonia centres around questions of context. Is analysis best approached through considering the character of ecosystemic constraints? Should Amazonian peasantries be treated as intrinsically different, or are they merely extensions of the heterogeneous set of peasant types characteristic of Brazil generally? Is the question of peasant formation best discussed in terms of class and agrarian structure? And so on. Another dimension, however, concerns the impact of modernization strategies not only as they alter the conditions under which Amazonian peasantries reproduce, but as they are implicated in the structure of anthropological research. The development of Amazonian peasant studies is parallel to the development and implementation of modernization strategies, and anthropology in Amazonia – as has been increasingly common in sectors of other newly industrializing countries – has performed a crucial ideological function in this implementation.

It is commonly supposed that theory is, if not dead, then at least exposed, denounced and put back on the shelf. There are two realms of anthropological practice within which this characterization holds. In the teaching of anthropology, modernization theory has been confronted for many years by critiques posed under the rubrics of dependency theory, articulation of modes of production and world systems theory. With the failure of universities to absorb academic anthropologists, the consultancy field is now better represented by anthropologists than has ever been the case.[1] For the former, theory is an intellectual artefact. For the latter, theory is not a theory at all, it is simply the set of assumptions according to which technical expertise is employed in the administration of lending and investment.

The ideology of modernization subscribed to in the core nations is generally not regarded as ideological. In the crudest accounts it is merely manifest destiny, the right of core nations to extend their planning to include others. In slightly more sophisticated accounts, the ideology of modernization is a matter of *noblesse oblige*: it is incumbent on the core to extend a helping hand to the obviously inadequate on the periphery.

The detachment of anthropological practice from broader political processes has long been a disputed issue, but the controversy about the role of social scientists in the more general political process of legitimation has largely been limited and centred around the realization of overt imperial aims (cf. the responses to Asad 1973; Gough 1968b). Recent suggestions that the increase in applied anthropology's participation in development projects demands discussion of the the political implications of such activities are treated in a variety of ways. One frequently noted position is that it is better to have anthropological consultants on the inside of such projects than merely criticizing from the outside. More often, however, the raising of such issues is countered by applying putatively dismissive labels (e.g. 'neo-Marxist'), by designating such suggestions as coming from the fringes of anthropology, the labelling of a critical anthropology as a new sub-field (e.g. a 'political economy' approach, that is to say, not 'normal' anthropology), or, most commonly, by simply brushing it off as uninformed, unrealistic and naive (cf. Hoben 1981: 362 in which the arguments in Hymes (1974) are dismissed as 'naive' positions).

1. To give some idea of the scale of the field to which the anthropological consultancy gaze is increasingly drawn, Edwards (1989: 116) notes that in sub-Saharan Africa alone there are more than 80,000 expatriate workers engaged in 'development' at a cost of $4 billion/annum.

What is represented here is the – according to some – excessively overworked argument between those who make claims for a 'value-free' social science and various opponents who regard 'value-freeness' as a frequently insidious and politically self-serving concept, ideological in several of that term's many pejorative senses, and especially so when coming from those whose livelihoods are ostensibly based in great part on the discovery and analysis of 'values' whose truths are not necessarily apprehendable within the terms permitted by the culture of 'normal science'.

The claims of 'value-freeness' of modernization theory (another – reputedly – excessively flogged dead horse) is cynical in the extreme. The anthropologist Hoben, in a review article championing the contributions made by anthropological consultants in a variety of development projects, writes that: 'In the World Bank anthropologists and sociologists have made effective contributions in rural development, agricultural production and extension, social forestry, Indonesian transmigration' (1982: 363). The fact that anyone would crow about the 'effective contribution' made to Indonesian transmigration can be understood (perhaps), if not appreciated, in light of what Hoben views as the very narrow limits within which anthropology should operate. Far from being a discipline with a sufficient body of distinctive features, anthropology is merely a service industry:

> Despite the often polemical and morally contentious burden of much anthropological commentary on development, it appears that the discipline's theoretical contribution lies in the elucidation of means–ends relationships, rather than in the choice of ends themselves. It is not evident from the literature that anthropologists, by virtue of their professional training or knowledge, have a distinctive or even a shared vision of degree, direction, and pace of social, technological, economic, or political change that is to be desired. (Hoben 1982: 366)

Leaving aside the question of whether such duties have ever fallen within any 'discipline's' brief, we can only observe that if, as Hoben asserts, the experts should be left to get on with the job (the masterminds of the Green Revolution, Project Camelot and other social engineering efforts) and that, as Hoben recommends, development anthropologists submit to the judgements of these expert others, he will agree, as must his peasants in the field, to let others choose his 'ends' at home where he will no doubt quietly submit to whatever his expert superiors advise.

While development-oriented anthropologists keen to play Tonto to the Lone Rangers of develoment agencies are, as it turns out, free to do so, it is presumptuous to claim that by relinquishing judgement to technocratic superiors, development anthropology (or anthropology for that matter) is a benign technical practice without implications except as these are drawn out by development planners.

These remarks are not intended particularly to condemn anthropological participation in development work (although there is clearly much to be condemned). The point, rather, is to underline the fact that the claims of some anthropologists to 'value-freeness' are as suspect as those put forward by developmentalists, and even more so when anthropological practice takes place at the behest of the modernizers. In spite of claims to the contrary, modernization theory is – in Amazonia, to take only one notable example – a fundamental feature of the social landscape and is thereby necessarily subject to the same scrutiny accorded other significant sociological and anthropological phenomena. When treated as something detached from the dynamics of local social formations – as is the case in much of the treatment of contemporary Amazonia – the logic of theory's intervention in local social formations is disguised. In particular, the centrality of aid provision in the commodification of peasant production and in encouraging the valorization of land have had dramatic effects in terms of transforming the basis upon which local social reproduction depends, but more than being merely the agencies of particular 'effects', such provisions, linked as they are to wider regional, national, international strategies of development, curtail the possibility of speaking sensibly in terms of conventional anthropological objects of analysis because the terms according to which such peasant formations reproduce are increasingly set beyond the scope of any conceivable local control.

New kinds of Amazonian peasantries have been (and are being) created through the application of aid policies in which the correctness of modernization dogma is taken for granted or merely accepted as an aspect of *realpolitik*. Modernization theory is portrayed by its adherents as not having any ideological content. It is portrayed as being a management procedure, or as being informed, scientific common sense. To challenge modernization policies is, apparently, effectively to impugn the character of its practitioners: if, as its adherents would have it, the theory is not an ideological one, then any attacks on modernization must be nothing more than thinly disguised attacks on its practitioners (since there is no content to the theory to be attacked).

Amazonia is in some senses a special case of developmentalism and therefore of particular interest. It embraces stereotypical, pristine social formations and it is the focus of interest of among the most modern of state/corporatist alliances. The exoticism of Amazonia, however, has not served the interests of Amazonians particularly well, the exoticism being used as a metaphoric buffer to the grimness of the well-documented consequences of development from above. In the end, the imagistic superstructure of tropical exoticism is no match for the unbearable ordinariness of 'development'. In a sober overview, Kleinpenning distills the implications of the less-than-magical Amazonian development:

> Up to the present, the business community has shown the greatest interest in the exploitation of natural riches which can be easily utilised and yield good profits in short time. Mining, forestry and extensive livestock farming are now the activities most capable of ensuring rapid economic growth. It is therefore not improbable that these sectors will continue to play a dominant part in the develoment process in the future, in which case the North will acquire an increasingly neo-colonial status both within Brazil and in relation to other countries. (Kleinpenning 1975: 139–40)

In Amazonia, it must be stressed, modernization policies have operated in a largely uncontested field. If the consequences of twenty years of 'development' have significantly unpalatable aspects – as most observers to a greater or lesser degree would concede – the modernization strategists must be acknowledged as having had a central not to say determinate role in this outcome.

Some of the material in this book is based on fieldwork carried out in 1975 and 1976. Since that time a number of important developments have occurred in Amazonia. Most dramatic has been the increase of violent land disputes, an increase which while highlighting the seriousness of social conflict within Brazil and Amazonia generally, has also enhanced one of the major myths about Amazonia, namely that it is a vast and lawless frontier yet to be drawn into the administrative apparatus of modernity.[2]

This depiction of Amazonia – like other myths – is accurate in some respects, but hardly exhaustive, and the prominence of this mythical depiction serves to disguise the fact that social conflict is the result of modernization policies, not an original feature which modernization serves to eradicate.

Heightened social conflict, mainly concerned with control of land, may draw attention to the fact that the reoccupation of the region has involved not the conquest of a social void, but a confrontation between, roughly, two different kinds of land and resource use: petty commodity production for which land and resource use is significantly non-valorized, and land and resource use motivated by the possibility of primitive accumulation or speculation.

In Santarém, levels of violence were far lower than those reported elsewhere at the time (e.g. Tocantins/Araguaia) and subsequently notorious in Western Amazonia, especially in Acre and Rondonia. There are several reasons for this. One is that Santarém, being somewhat removed from the main *Transamazônica* colonist resettlement sites, was not subjected to an immediate influx of migrants. Although the population rose significantly as a result of *Transamazônica* attrition, it did so gradually and did so not in the context of a frontier assault – as might be said to have been the case in Acre and Rondonia, but in the context of a well-established, historical peasantry. Second is the fact that few Santarenos depended entirely on *terra firme* agriculture, while most agricultural migrants did. This meant that the impact of migration was not a direct challenge to local producers, but oblique. Third is the fact that in Santarém was based the army corps of engineers (*8* BEC*) responsible for supervising completion of the road connecting Santarém to

2. It is noteworthy that despite the nominal recognition that social forces are at the root of Amazonian conflicts, there is still a strong tendency to resort to a simple environmentalist idiom rather than one more explicitly political. The *Guardian* report (2 March 1992: 24) of the quashing of the sentence of Darly Alves – a conspirator in the murder of Chico Mendes – began: 'Brazilian environmentalists expressed outrage ...'.

Itaituba (on the *Transamazônica*), and for all practical purposes, Santarém was under the direct political supervision of the army, thus the possibility of overt confrontation was dampened (by comparison with Tocantins/Aragauia, for example, where eventually it was necessary to introduce an interventionist agency, GETAT).

In this chapter I situate the Santareno peasantry in relation to some of the literature bearing on other peasantries in Lower Amazonia. I use the term peasant in a loose fashion and in lieu of a better term (although 'petty commodity producer' is one strong analogue). Santarenos themselves use terms with the meaning 'peasant' only rarely (*campones; peão; riberinho; caboclo*) and then mainly to indicate extremes of rusticity and poverty.

Peasants as a Default Category

In anthropological discourse peasants occupy a contradictory position: on the one hand they represent a reference point for a variety of active theoretical debates[3], but on the other hand, the term 'peasant' is generally acknowledged as being of little value as more than a descriptive category which is the starting point for analysis. In addition, the sense in which the term's relevance to European debates about the agrarian question may be transferred to other geohistorical spheres is a matter of some disagreement especially as such efforts raise the question of forcing others – yet again – into the European mould. Even as anthropology's traditional objects of analysis have disappeared, however, and ethnography is increasingly dependent on what are – for want of a better term – late-capitalist peasantries, the conceptual clarity of the peasant has hardly improved. While the pathological character of peasants is increasingly downplayed (few, for example, still explicitly blaming peasants for their own misfortune), peasants are nevertheless mainly portrayed in negative terms, usually defined by reference to what they are not – indigenous tribalists, fully alienated modernites or a class – rather than being accorded a place of their own. Even when peasantries defy expectations and mobilize to effect major socio-political transformations (cf. Wolf 1969) the success of peasant or

3. See, for example, the symposia in *Labour, Capital and Society* 1986: 19 (1) and *Social Analysis* 1986: 19.

peasant-based movements is still generally attributed to a variety of conjunctural relations, e.g. external (i.e. non-peasant) political leadership (cf. Roxborough 1979: 95–9).

In spite of peasant societies' increasing usurpation of the position previously held by classic anthropological objects of analysis, in the literature the lack of consensus over the definition of such concepts as 'peasant' and 'peasantry' has tended to reproduce the negative connotations which peasantries have borne historically. In terms of the archaic, but still widely employed, contrast between tribal and non-tribal societies (complex, urban), peasantries occupy a default category, one bounded by these ideal typifications which, while generally acknowledged as having some (merely) heuristic value, are at least granted some analytical status. The interstitial peasantry lacks even this.

The increasingly historical focus of much recent social anthropology has produced clearer notions about how to approach peasant societies. The main emphasis has been on characterizing the kinds of transitions in which peasantries are implicated; thus peasantries, instead of being shunted into an interstitial category, have emerged as the sites of particular kinds of transformations, ones entailing in most cases the appropriation of non-valorized labour within commercial economic structures. Many of such recent studies, however, implicitly subscribe to a tribal–peasant–modern typology, not, it appears, in order to shore up this anthropological received wisdom, but because most of the peasant societies studied were historically grounded in indigenous social formations, thereby providing at the least a 'properly' anthropological reference point (an important exception here is Mintz's treatment of 'reconstituted peasantries' 1974;[4] see also Pearse 1975; Wolf 1982). Such studies have improved matters by making the theoretical status of the previously vacuous peasant category commensurate with that of the categories which bound it, and such approaches preserve the conventional anthropological

4. Mintz's concept of the 'reconstituted peasantry' marks a great advance in the study of New World peasantries on several counts, but is generally confined to discussions of the Caribbean. Given that the 'reconstituted peasantry' is not a transitional form between indigenous pre-capitalist social formation (relatively few examples of which survived conquest) and a peasantry defined in relation to an increasingly commercialized agrarian structure, but is an artefact of colonial plantation apparatus, the kind of diaspora against whose backdrop his notion provides such insight has analogues elsewhere.

notion of primordial social formation as the starting point for the incipient peasant society.

Coexisting with this brand of benign evolutionism is a body of work which has sought to demonstrate the ways in which the structures of peasant societies are not only compatible with both pre-capitalist and capitalist relations of production, but also may be said to have been creations of capitalist relations of production, in other words that peasant societies do not constitute an evolutionary stage, but rather an abrupt shift in which the terms of local social reproduction are determined externally, largely through incorporation within the global market.[5] The proliferation of petty commodity forms of production during the period of dominance by merchant capital has been one such area of study, and work on the so-called informal sector has tended to emphasize the ways in which peasant/petty commodity production is functional for capital accumulation elsewhere in the system.

These brief points on some aspects of peasant studies are meant to highlight two aspects: the emphasis on the character of transformations and the situating of the question of transformation in the context of an altered indigenous social formation.

Such studies have a built-in comparative basis given that there is, in most cases, a primordial social formation from which the peasantry in some sense emerged. In Lower Amazonia, however, there is not such a convenient base line. Peasant societies in Lower Amazonia do not represent transformed indigenous social formations, rather they are creations of colonial and post-colonial expansion.

To some, the disjunction between indigenous societies and historically subsequent Amazonian social formations may appear a small point (and it is hardly an observation exclusive to Brazilian Amazonia), but it has important implications for the analysis of the transformation of peasant societies in Amazonia for several reasons. In the first place, the allocthonous origins of Amazonian peasantries make it impossible to separate an

5. I have largely left aside discussion of Chayanov on the grounds that peasantries in Amazonia – whether or not they have eventually been left suspended in a state of producers = consumers stability – originated at the behest of commodity-producing effects of colonialism, but see comments later in this chapter. Ayres (1992) provides a Chayanovian analysis of *caboclo* society in her study of communities near Tefe.

anthropological problematic from questions of historical process. Second, it is difficult to define a local object of analysis. While it may be claimed that the concept of 'local society' has some integrity, it is hard to argue that the structure of that society is easily separable from external constraints. This is only to say that the fiction of 'local society' be recognized for what it is: an object of analysis whose internal structure is defined as much by external structures as by local ones. Third, the Amazon region's historically marginal position in relation to Brazilian development as a whole has meant that the study of Amazonian peasantries has lagged behind the study of peasantries in other regions of Brazil. The structural marginality of Amazonia has contributed, among other things, to Amazonia's having continued to be treated as a vast natural resource in which society is a relatively small and insignificant feature. One striking consequence of this is that Amazonians have been acted upon by foreign and Brazilian interests with a brutishness unmollified by national political representation. Amazonia is still widely conceived of as a frontier, passive and available, in which social formations are incidental. In the context of peasant studies generally in which peasantries have a second-class anthropological status, Amazonian peasantries are relegated even further.

Attention paid to Amazonian peasantries has increased greatly in recent years largely due to Amazonia's role as a focus of environmental debate rather than because of an interest in peasants or *caboclos per se*. The recasting of *caboclo* societies as major features of the social landscape (as, for example, 'wise forest managers') is an issue taken up in chapter 8, but for the moment it is sufficient to note that the change in the conceptual status of the *caboclo* is mainly due to a shift in the way in which the region's resources are viewed by global markets.

There are two main emphases in the section of the book concerned with Santareno society. The first concerns aspects of social organization in Santarém, and these matters are presented in an ethnographic context. I am particularly concerned to show that there is a distinctiveness to the Santareno social formation which belies the characterization of Amazonian peasantries as stagnant and astructural, a kind of discarded 'natural economy'. The second concerns the question of the social reproduction of a peasantry. By social reproduction I mean those structures and processes according to which local Santareno society shapes the form of its incorporation within a larger system. The purpose here is to argue that the recent attempts to reconquer Amazonia entail serious misrepresentations of Amazonian society generally on the part of developmentalists. The assumptions challenged here include the notion cited above, namely that there really is no social structure of consequence in Amazonia, that Amazonia consists of a vast natural arena within which a few peasantries manage to eke out an unpromising existence. While much attention has been paid the colonist enterprises introduced under the auspices of *Transamazônica* development, the relative lack of attention paid historical peasantries in Amazonia has been part of a legitimation process according to which the rapacious redevelopment of Amazonia has been justified by non-Amazonians.

Peasantries in Amazonia have a special place in the anthropological literature, although they do not take up very much room. There are several factors which may account for the relative paucity of ethnographic accounts of Amazonian peasantries. First, Amazonia's special status as both the source of fundamental notions about the archetypal noble savage and as one of the few areas of the world where – although in precarious circumstances – such peoples continue to exist, may help to account for the disdain in which Amazonian peasants appear to be held by many anthropologists because peasants on the one hand symbolize the corruption of pristine social formations (or as *mestiço* relics – damaged goods – represent the outcome of such corruption), and on the other hand, Amazonian peasantries are widely seen to be the vanguard colonists in exploitation of virgin areas within Amazonia, exploitation which in the first instance frequently involves the abuse of Indians. Although both Indians and peasants are manifestly victims of similar sorts of external forces, at the local level they are frequently antagonists, with peasants the unwitting, although for that, no less destructive, agents of 'national progress'.

Another factor which may account for the relative paucity of Amazonian peasant literature is the historic marginality of the Amazonian region in relation to the general trajectory of development in Brazil. Brazil's insertion within the world system has a number of unique features, one of which is the scale on which colonial society was built and the degree to which that colonial society came to epitomise a particular colonial phase, one in which monocultural export agriculture based on African slave labour prevailed. The main features of the agrarian structure of colonial society are not as apparent in Amazonia as they are in other regions of Brazil where the cycles of plantation-based export agriculture were focused, and in spite of the national prominence of rubber production in the late nineteenth and early twentieth centuries, the transformation of local Amazonian economies did not provide the basis for insertion of the region within the national economy as did occur to a greater degree for other regional economies in Brazil.

Recently, the number of studies of Amazonian peasants has increased, not, however, because of a revival of interest in peasants *per se*, but, as noted above, because of an increased awareness of the environmental consequences of rapid deforestation and because of the research possibilities afforded by the construction of the *Transamazônica*. The *Transamazônica* focus of much of the recent research on Amazonian peasantries tends to obscure the fact that the history of Amazonian peasants did not begin in 1970. In the comparative treatment of 'spontaneous' versus 'planned' colonization of Amazonia, for example, a contrast around which much current discussion of agrarian structure is focused, there is little explicit acknowledgement that the conditions of peasant existence in Amazonia do not derive exclusively from the structure of *Transamazônica* recolonization.

While the ignoring of pre-*Transamazônica* agrarian structure and peasant livelihood is a marked feature of recent work, there have been some attempts to justify analytically this separation. One of these is provided by Moran (1981), a major contributor to modern Amazonian peasant studies, who argues that generalizations about an Amazonian peasantry are not possible (desirable) because of the variey of ecological constraints (and resulting forms of peasant adaptation) apparent in Amazonia. His argument is that until the specificity of local conditions is appreciated, the scale at which anthropologists can operate is restricted to, for instance, community studies. This approach has much merit and as noted above there is a shortage of comparative material which may no doubt be overcome by pursuing this particular approach and it seems clear that the studies of sustainable forest use by botanists and agro-foresters confirm the insight that intra-regional variation is extreme (Anderson 1990). In addition to the literature available in English, there is a growing Brazilian literature largely unrecognized outside Brazil (cf. Furtado 1981; Sousa Santos 1982; Gentil 1983; Loureiro 1985, 1987), which attests to the heterogeneity of Amazonian peasantries.

This book, however, proceeds from rather different premises. Peasantries in Amazonia are not simply social groups adapting to local conditions, rather they are societies which have been *adapted for* Amazonian conditions. Another way of putting this is to say that Amazonian peasantries have been created by forces external to Amazonia; thus while one may agree with Moran that intra-regional variation is so great that one may not generalize on the basis of an archetypal peasantry, the conditions under which peasantries have emerged in Amazonia have been structured at a level above that at which ecological variation conditions the types of peasant adaptation which have occurred. This point would be more obvious if, as in the cases discussed by Mintz (1974: 146–56) in his elaboration of the concept of 'reconstituted peasantry', Amazonian peasantries had been part of a plantation system. In Amazonia, however, such attempts at plantation production, although numerous, were by and large unsuccessful, but such peasantries as did emerge were in no sense less 'reconstituted' despite the absence of a plantation system base. Such peasantries are the fragmented legacy of a system which chronically failed to become a significant force in Amazonian colonization.

Among the factors germane to an appropriate level of generalization are the type of early colonial settlement pattern (riverine mission settlement) within which the transformative effects of an extractive economy produced a relatively undifferentiated and fragmented set of petty producers; the private and Imperial modes of labour extraction which resulted in the depopulation of the accessible regions (see MacLachlan 1972, 1973, 1974); and the institution of *aviamento* trade relations during the period of intense rubber extraction (see Wagley 1953; Dean 1987). In addition, in the relatively recent past the availability of land (however unsuitable for sustained cultivation it has turned out to be) in Amazonia has meant that the effects of changes in the Brazilian rural economy generally have been frequently realized – in indirect fashion (cf. Velho 1972) – in Amazonia; regardless of the relative unsuitability of much Amazonian land for intensive cultivation, in ideological terms the availability of land has led to the whole region's having become an institutionalized frontier and one whose significance nationally in terms of provision of cheap foodstuffs may be greater than realized (cf. Velho 1972).

For the moment I only wish to note that the context in which my discussion of Santarém is located is one which I take to be defined both by local conditions and by an historical process in which local society is firmly subordinated to external causes. The character of Santarém society is singular, but the conditions under which that singularity has been realized are not.

As noted, it is only relatively recently that peasant societies in Brazilian Amazonia have received much anthropological attention. The basic reference for those interested in such societies was Wagley's *Amazon Town* (1953), a work which, although dealing with one Amazonian settlement, has served as a standard account of the region as a whole. Material available to a non-Portuguese-speaking audience was scarce (although Murphy and Steward's (1956) 'Tappers and trappers' discussion and Riviere's *The Forgotten Frontier* (1972) drew attention to what was being overlooked), a condition which prevailed until assessments of the impact of various projects (as well as those more directly related to national transformation of agarian structure; cf. Foweraker 1981) began to appear in the 1970s.

The long gap between the appearance of the standard work and Transamazônica-related work has had a curious effect on peasant studies in Amazonia. It is as though peasants were reinvented in conjunction with the rediscovery of Amazonia, and their history is the history of the way in which they were reintegrated into Brazilian national society. Another consequence of having so few fixed points of reference within Amazonian peasant literature is that any new additions are seen to fill gaps which they are in fact incapable of credibly occupying. New material takes on a significance whose luminescence is mainly a function of the extreme opacity of the backdrop.

Santarém is neither a product of *Transmazônica* nor a version of Amazon Town. The distinctive features of Santarém's development from a mission to a tropical forest city illustrate extension – from the north and south respectively – and the city lies on a shallow promontory bound on two sides by the Amazon and Tapajós Rivers. Immediately behind the city (to the south) rises a plateau some 150 metres in height. Until the *Transamazônica* period the edge of the plateau was the effective limit of other than scattered settlement.

Historically, rural satellites were for the most part located on the river plains (*várzeas*) across the Tapajós, e.g. Lago Grande do Curuaí, and across the Amazon, e.g. Costa de Tapara. Since the late 1950s, however, Santarém's rural satellites have included plateau (*planalto*) communities based on *terra firme* agriculture, and these now comprise a greater proportion of the Santareno rural population.

The mission village of Santarém was elevated to the status of town (*vila*) in 1758, around the time when the Jesuits were expelled from Brazil. Municipal boundaries had been established in 1754 and were extended in 1911. Reclassified as a city in 1848, Santarém became the capital of a municipality which included four districts: Santarém, Boim, Alter do Chão and Curuaí.

Although there is considerable disagreement about the size of the size of the Tapajós population at the time of conquest (see Palamatary 1960 for summary of historical records), there is general agreement that Santarém was a large settlement. The decline of the Indian population, however, was precipitous, and by 1820 the Tapajós were extinct. According to Palmatary, the Tapajós were last cited in a list of tribal names in 1779. From the perspective of modern Santarém, 'local Indians' are represented by the Mundurucú, many miles upstream on the Tapajós. The *muiraquitão* frog image is one of the few widely cited connections between Santarém and Tapojônica civilization (see Nimuendaju 1952).

Santarém is the metropolis for a number of important towns lying outside the municipal boundaries – Oriximiná, Obidos, Alenquer, Jurutí, Prainha – and is the entrepot for such Upper Tapajós communities as Itaituba and Jacareacanga, although its significance as an entrepot has diminished as the *Transamazônica* network has improved overland access.

There are two roads leaving Santarém, one running parallel to the main course of the Amazon and ending, after 80 km, at the Curua-Una hydroelectric plant, the other, BR 165, running to

Itaituba and joining Santarém to the *Transamazônica* network. There are secondary roads splitting from the two main ones, joining Santarém with its main plateau satellite, Mojui dos Campos, in the case of the Curua Una road, and Belterra, the site of Henry Ford's second attempt to establish a rubber plantation. There is scheduled airline service to Belém and Manaus, and small planes service the gold fields to the South. In spite of the growth in overland transport, much of the area is dependent on a range of boat services.

The basic division upon which the colonial mission was based was that between the Centre (*o centro*) and the Village (*aldeia*). These terms also represent two of the thirteen *bairros* (neighbourhoods) of the city and along with Prainha constitute the old town, to which have been added in recent years a number of residential and commercial areas and squatter sections. Except for the older three neighbourhoods which contain examples of colonial architecture, the city is built of a mixture of wood, brick and wattle and thatch. Aside from the more desolate fringes of the city, there are fruit and palm trees, much seconday foliage, extensive gardens and a mixture of residential, commercial and productive forms of land use.

There are at least three senses in which people live in Santarém: as permanent urbanites, as cyclical rural–urban migrants and as inter-/intra-regional immigrants for whom residence in the city is one phase in a chronic migratory trajectory. I refer to all of these people as Santarenos. Recent changes in the definition of what it means to be a Santareno reflect changes in the region's relationship with the rest of Brazil. Until the completion of the *Transamazônica* (c. 1974), Santarém for most people was only accessible by river. The riverine focus of Santareno society has been altered by the opening of the hinterland, and the *terra firme* settlements of the past ten years constitute a radical departure from what had been, until the early 1970s, 'normal' processes of occupation in Amazonia.

The periphery of Santarém, by and large those parts of the municipality which are occupied on a regular basis by Santarenos who oscillate between town and country, is of two sorts: the pre-*Transamazônica* periphery is mainly riverine in combination with *terra firme* agriculture and extraction of an extensive rather than intensive sort; the new periphery is on *terra firme*. The bifurcation of interests of those who occupy these two peripheries is explored more fully later. Three basic terms of reference, then, are *a cidade* (the city/town), *o planalto* (the plateau/*terra firme*), and *as várzeas* (the riverplains).

Residential areas or settlements are referred to by a variety of terms. In the city one lives in a 'neighbourhood' (*bairro*) indicated by a proper name or street name; in the country, one lives in a named settlement, or simply 'on the river/on the plateau', on a smallholding (*sítio* or *roça*), or simply in the interior or forest. These different terms indicate important, if casual, distinctions in a society in which a high proportion of residents are recent immigrants and in which a previously unified notion of peasant (*caboclo*) has been challenged by *nordestinos* many of whom are scornful of *caboclos* (a feeling which is reciprocated). The distinctions are not recognized by all Santarenos as equally important (some will stress their affiliation with a rural settlement, some ignore it as unimportant), but most people will stress their affiliation with Santarém itself in view of the very low status accorded *Zé Ninguem* (Joe Nobody, the habitual drifter) and anybody who is simply 'from the forest/interior'.

The People of Santarém

Ignoring for the moment marginal groups such as the Japanese and the North American members of religious orders, Santareno notions of identity are largely shaped primarily by distinctively regional features (*caboclo* versus *nodestino*; *comerciante* versus *produtor*) and secondarily by national ideologies (people of the interior versus 'nationals'). In general, people tend to identify themselves in terms of where they live rather than in terms of the numerous categories offered within the lexicon of Brazilian racial discourse. Explicit identity with ethnic groups other than those marked by the terms *caboblo* or *nordestino* (or other regions of Brazil, e.g. sulista) is unusual. Overt connections with Portuguese, for example, are minimized (the Portuguese being most often portrayed as bumbling, ineffective, small-scale merchants) as are those with Indian groups (Indians being widely regarded as uncivilized forest-dwellers who are, in many Santarenos' opinion, little better than animals). Blacks' contribution to Santareno ethnic identity is slightly different from that of either Indians or Portuguese. In the first place, Indian and Portuguese ancestry are assumed (even if Indianness is glossed over), while black antecedents are ignored if possible. Second, blacks in the area were less often imported slaves than they were runaway slaves who lived in remote communities (along the banks of the Trombetas River, for example). Schematic accounts of ethnicity are not matters of major discussion among Santarenos. Although racial distinctions are widely used, a greater preoccupation *vis-à-vis* physical appearance has to do with what appearance indicates about class position. A 'healthy' person, both physically and socially, is one who is 'well put together' (*bem feito*) and well-fed (*gordo*). Period of residence, in short, conferred identity far more significantly that did claims for ethnic or cultural identity. This is not to deny the existence of a complex racial code according to which, for example, someone would be likely to claim to have had a 'white' grandmother and deny having had a 'black' one, for example, nor to deny the complex manipulation of codes involving skin colour, hair texture, and the like.

There are categories of Santareno, however, with fixed dual-identities, although it is not obligatory that this dualness always be recognized. Japanese colonists, for example, Lebanese merchants and *gringo* members of religious orders were seen, under certain circumstances, to be positioned somewhat outside the Santareno mainstream, but as with other ethnic identities in Santarém, the significance of the ethnic qualifier varied according to circumstances.

It may have been the case that the relative fixity of ethnic/cultural identity was being undermined by the demographic consequences of *Transamazônica*. Not only was Santarém subjected to a major wave of immigration (the city's population approached 100,000 in the mid–1970s), but the visible facilitators of this change – the army corps of engineers responsible for completing the road connecting Santarém to *Transamazônica* – were largely drawn from Rio Grande do Sul, an area of Brazil heavily colonized by German immigrants.

Table 4.1 shows the distribution of Santareno immigrants by place of birth (as of 1970). In 1960, of the 91,954 Brazilians in the municipality of Santarém, 79,321 were natives of the state of Pará, and 12,633 were from other states in Brazil, mainly Ceará (83 per cent) (IBGE 1970: 23).

Table 4.1 Place of birth of immigrants in Santarém

	No.	%
North	985	7.8
Northeast	11,507	91.09
Southeast	80	0.63
South	15	0.12
Centre-West	44	0.35
not known	2	0.01

Source: IBGE (1973)

According to official census data (IBGE 1973: 174–5), of the total municipal popultion in 1970 of 132,456, place of birth is as shown in Table 4.2. Although the proportion of Cearaenses and other northeasterners appears slight, note that many of the Santarenos listed under the Pará heading are children of people born in Ceará or the northeast.

Table 4.2 Place of birth of Santarenos

	Male	Female
Rondônia	32	36
Acre	118	126
Amazonas	457	501
Roraima	19	32
Pará	59,702	60,759
Amapá	60	59
Maranhão	415	239
Piauí	102	58
Ceará	6052	5191
Rio Grande do Norte	171	123
Paraiba	97	76
Pernambuco	77	44
Alagoas	20	10
Sergipe	4	3
Bahia	18	7
Minas Gerais	38	31
Espirito Santo	2	1
Rio de Janeiro	11	9
Guanabara	20	11
São Paulo	39	27
Paranã	58	35
Santa Catarina	26	—
Rio Grande do Sul	13	5
Mato Grosso	18	18
Goias	6	15
Distrito Federal	4	1

Source: IBGE. (1973).[6]

6. It should be noted that according to many Santarenos a typical pattern of migration involved entering a region for a year or so, moving on, and perhaps moving back. The IBGE census should be taken as providing only a rough indicator. In general, IBGE data are treated with some scepticism.

Table 4.3 Time of residence of immigrants in Santarém

	Men	Women
1 year	856	713
1 year	300	301
2 years	433	499
3 years	517	556
4 years	464	311
5 years	550	462
6–10 years	1,588	1,481
11+ years	5,961	5,142

Source: IBGE (1973: 223–5).

Of 20,134 immigrants, 7,807 are from Pará and 9,121 are from Ceará. Of the people living in Santarém in 1960 who were officially classified as foreigners, there were 19 Germans, 1 Argentinian, 3 Spaniards, 1 Italian, 28 Japanese, 1 Pole, 39 Japanese, 1 Syrian, 1 Russian, and 60 'others', undoubtedly Canadian and American members of religious orders. The offical designation of 'stranger' is not recognized locally. Almost anyone can 'become' a Santareno in a fairly short time. Priests and brothers, however, are unassimilable at this level in spite, in many cases, of decades of Amazonian residence.

To sum up: Santareno society is ethnically heterogeneous and large portion of the population is represented by recent immigrants. From the point of view of many recent immigrants, longer-term Santarenos are 'more Indian' than Brazilians in general, and such an assessment has, for relative outsiders/newcomers, implications of backwardness, some *nordestinos* treating Santareno *caboclos* with the condescension they feel is appropriate for 'Indians'.

Santarenos are physically distinguished by the features of Amazonian poverty. Most suffer from a variety of intestinal parasites; malaria is widespread; there are many lepers; few people have all their teeth by the time they reach adulthood; and while no one starves, pathological syndromes related to diet are widespread.

It would seem that during the period of fieldwork, matters pertaining to self-presentation (health, appearance in general) assumed a greater significance than had been the case before *Transamazônica* altered the terms of 'national integration'. Santarenos were very conscious of their new visibility, and not infrequently characterized themselves, deprecatingly, as 'little brown people'. I stress the preoccupation of physical appearance because of its manifest centrality in Santarenos expectations for the future. Much of what was known about southern Brazil was learned from photo-magazines and cinema newsreels (television had not yet arrived in 1976) in which physical beauty (mediated through a variety of racial stereotypes) was very explicitly related to the possibilities for social mobility, whether realistic or not.

A Sketch of Occupational Structure

In pre-modern Santarém class structure corresponded to a rural–urban division of society. The city was occupied by a merchant class, artisans and labourers, and domestics; the countryside by smallholding agriculturalists and extractivists. Class structure in contemporary Santarém is far more complex, although for many Santarenos the basic division is between rich and poor.

In the 1960 census, the municipal population was distributed by sector in the manner shown in Table 4.4.

Table 4.4 Population by economic sector

	%
Agriculture-ranching-extraction	75.41
Industrial activities	3.94
Other (tertiary)	20.65

Source: IBGE (1960)

Data published in 1969 (IBGE) show the distribution of agricultural, ranching, and extractive income in relation to gross industrial sector income in terms of the reported economically active population.

Table 4.5 Economic value of primary and secondary sectors, 1969

Primary sector	$CR (1k)	%
Agriculture[a]	5,911	13
Extractive (animal)[b]	1,884	4.42
Extractive (vegetable)	1,320	3.09
Livestock[c]	28,003	65.65
Aviculture	429	1.01
Total	37,549	88.03
Secondary sector[d]	5,105	11.97

a. Excluding fruits.

b. Including fish farm produce.

c. Value of herds.

d. Includes jute processing and rice milling.

Source IBGE (1969).

The tertiary sector has expanded substantially in the subsequent decade and the proportion of urbanites involved in the service sector was 35 per cent in 1975–6. In a survey of households accounting for 843 economically active persons, Wyer (1983) found that 270 (32 per cent) were engaged in services, 42 (5 per cent) in the public sector, 236 (28 per cent) in the private sector. Occupations in the public sector category include teachers, civil servants and sanitation workers; occupations in the private sector category include domestics, prostitutes, entertainers, drivers and stevedores, just to give an idea of the range.

This brief sketch of sectoral participation is meant only to indicate that the rural–urban continuum does not represent a separation of urban and rural activities: most Santarenos live in the city, and most Santarenos are involved in agriculture/extraction, but in the city proper such activities are quite specialized (e.g. seasonal gathering, market gardening). In other words, place of residence indicates little about occupation (or sectoral position) or levels of employment. The ease with which agriculture is pursued by urbanites is achieved through the wide extension of kin groups, a wide variety of land tenure arrangements, and expectations of high rates of intra- and inter-regional migration. Thus in one sense Santarém is a city occupied by people whose position within the urban economy is ambiguous, yet that ambiguity is due less to the character of the urban economy *per se* than it is to the urban economy's contingent character, a contingency comparable to that which characterizes the many forms of petty commodity production in which Santarenos are engaged. The city, in brief, is part of a repertoire of petty commodity possibilities.

Local Society Versus International Culture

Santarém is in no sense a 'traditional' society surrounded by new and threatening influences, rather because it is itself a colonial product it represents a ready ground for the cultivation of new definitions of the boundaries between and among local, regional, and national networks. With the completion of the *Transamazônica*, Santarém's frame of reference was drastically enlarged. In the mid-1970s, while there was much evidence of notions of social status and class derived from earlier periods when the symbolic aspects of patron–clientism were more clearly reflective of merchant–producer relations, embourgeoisement reflecting the shift from 'town on the Amazon River' to 'town in Amazonia' was represented in some novelties. I shall discuss several of these by way of illustrating some of the contradictory tendencies which are the results of the region's rapid incorporation within a wider set of economic relations, economic relations which while having generalized effects (heightened commercialization of production and services) are by no means evenly presented in terms of the local economy: while on the one hand, the appurtenances of developing capitalist relations of production are in evidence, cardinal features of capitalist production *per se*, an index of which might be sought in the proletarianization of agricultural producers, say, are not. These examples, then, are indicative of a particular kind of unevenness of development, one in which the display and consumption of artefacts and practices represents a juxtaposition of internal features of social organization in Santarém and features distilled from the efforts at 'national integration' introduced by the *Transamazônica*.

There is a network of social clubs long established in Santarém. The bases of association are varied and the clubs include football supporters' groups and occupational and political groups. There are cross-cutting ethnic criteria which sometimes apply (e.g. Cearaense) and some clubs are more strictly neighbourhood-based. Clubs have regular parties, attended by family segments and groups of age-mates or work-mates. Membership is not usually required for attendance. During the period of fieldwork, an addition to this set of clubs was a new one, the *Iate Clube* (Yacht Club). Although matched in terms of high social status by a traditional association, *Clube Sociale*, the Yacht Club was taken to embody the aspirations of the most ostentatiously modern fractions of the Santareno ruling clique. Built on the beach facing the mouth of the Tapajós and within sight of the Hotel Tropical, the Yacht Club is approached through an area of squatter shacks. Physically it consists of a fenced compound, a roofed eating and dancing area, and a number of poured concrete moorings. It is basically a country club without many amenities, and differs from other social clubs in being used during the daytime as well as for evening dancing and drinking.

Although the setting is atypical for Santarém (urban fringe and no residential basis for location) and membership is markedly restricted, the forms in which social status are displayed are not (although rather more extreme): hospitality is generous, kinship and fictive kinship relations are revealed, and less permanent members of the Santarém community are welcome guests.

At the Yacht Club, outsiders tend to be representatives of Southern firms, certain technocrats, entrepreneurs in the gold business, and other *vipis* (VIPs). Another departure is that families are attended by entourages of domestics (especially during weekend daytime fêtes). In spite of its name, nautical aspects are limited. A number of members own water-ski boats, and there is a certain amount of game fishing (as well as casual shooting of waterfowl), but the crucial feature of the club is its display of class solidarity. Unlike other clubs in which patron-client relations are acted out in a leisure setting, at the Iate Clube the intense interaction is between intra-class rivals, not between creditors and debtors (symbolic or actual).

In spite of what may have been inadvertantly implied, there is nothing even faintly ridiculous about the Yacht Club. It represents the class fraction which has, if only in the short term, benefited most directly from the specific way in which the *Transamazônica* has effected 'national integration'. The wealth represented in the Yacht Club is derived from commerce, real estate, gold-mining and cattle ranching, none of which (with the qualified exception of commerce), in pre-*Transamazônica* Santarém, provided the basis for such upward mobility.

Members of the Yacht Club represent as well, however, a traditional index of local wealth and power: the extended domestic retinue. This consists of primary kin and more vaguely related kin (in the extended *primo* (cousin) category; see next chapter), as well as domestic servants, drivers, go-fers and specialist employees such as boat crews. What is significantly different about the Yacht Club domestic retinues is the public character of display.

Hotel Tropical (part of a chain built by the national airline, Varig) sits in the midst of a squatter neighbourhood on the Tapajôs side of town. Large and well appointed, it rarely has more than a few rooms occupied, yet in spite of the underutilization of its many facilities (conference centre, cinema, hairdresser, night club, restaurant), these are always available. The air-conditioned cinema shows recent releases, yet effectively restricts its audience by beginning showings so late that the larger potential audience cannot get home by the last bus. Those who can take advantage of Hotel Tropical are, by and large, those who have access to the Yacht Club. The hotel seems to anticipate the possibilities for conspicuous consumption, a vanguard item of *o futuro,* and is widely noted locally as clear evidence of the imminence of modernization-led development.

A different kind of example of the confrontation of Santareno custom and external artefact/practice is evident in birthday celebrations. A number of birthdays have attached to them a particular significance, the first being especially noteworthy. These are generally occasions for gatherings of kith and kin and generous provision of food and drink is typical. Such celebrations are also occasions for the preparation of regional dishes which, for a variety of reasons, are no longer as frequently consumed as they once were. Dishes involving traditional delicacies – *tartaruga* (turtle), for example – are difficult to provide because of the dramatic decline in the turtle population (and the fact that eating turtle is illegal). Other 'traditional' dishes, however, are still possible, *pato no tucupi,*[7] for example. Complementing such offerings, however, are some of the least noteworthy contributions of the tinned food industry, Vienna sausages, for example, served on toothpicks and set on paper plates decorated with various Disney motifs.

The enhancement lent such celebrations by the use of international symbols of prestige is considerable and should not be taken to be presented as an example of the misappropriation of cosmopolitan apparatus, nor are associations with external status items limited to the ruling clique. Representations of the 'developed' world are integral to Santareno notions of culture,

7. *Pato no tucupí* is a celebrated regional dish of duck served in the juice (prussic acid, boiled and sharpened by hot pepper) squeezed from bitter manioc during its transformation into *farinha.* Along with *pirarucú* (large fish, Arapaima gigas) and *tacacá* (a soup made of manioc starch – tapioca – dried shrimp, *tucupi,* hot pepper, and *jambu* – the leaves of which act as a local anaesthetic), *pato no tucupí* epitomises Amazonian cuisine. River turtle (*tartaruga*) (capture of which is illegal) has been largely excised from the menu although it appears often enough on the tables of elites. Exotic entrees tend to be encountered outside commercial settings: *peixe-boi* (manatee), for example, on the *várzeas* and armadillo *(tatu)* on the *planalto.* Unsurprisingly, Amazonian cuisine is a neglected topic. One can hardly present gastronomic codes of people satisfied with 'a bowl of farinha and a fish'. For an interesting discussion of Amazonian folklore and food, see Motta Maués and Maues (1980).

many being used to mark the ascendancy of the new Santarém. The dominance of consumption of international artefacts as marks of status is achieved through various devices. The establishment of the duty-free zone in Manaus – enclave-led development – has made available in Amazonia a variety of luxury goods, 'designer' sunglasses, cameras, and the like, as well as such specialty items as racing gloves (favoured by taxi drivers). In terms of popular media, there is a clear tendency to suppress the local in favour of the more glamorous international, mediated, if appropriate, by more ideologically sound readings: Paul Anka's tune, 'You're Having My Baby' appears in the popular Brazilian cover version as 'You're Going to Be a Mother'. Films, avidly consumed, provide much information about the proper comportment of modernites, and many confirm the suspicions of those Santarenos who see themselves – in national terms – as retrograde and marginal, depicted on the screen through their socially deviant doppelgangers, black or *mestiço*, crippled, poor and outcast.

Santareno notions of the historical present reveal little in the way of gradual transition from isolated agricultural community to national city, rather there exists the superimposition and juxtaposition of different kinds of identity, and though the effects of such encounters may appear at times to be trivial or ridiculous (the cachet of French designer labels), the fact that such different conceptions of social identity do provide coherent alternative versions of what it means to be a Santareno attest to the speed with which (nominal) national integration has been effected. These are examples of the way in which one symbolic apparatus (now regarded as retrograde) is supplanted by another (one redolent of the promise of *o futuro*, a term used obsessively in discussions of local development). What is distinctively *caboclo* is interpreted according to the canons of the emerging elite, and according to this elite, the delay in realizing o futuro is attributable to the 'backwardness' of the *caboclo*, content, as he is, with a fish and bowl of *farinha*. The alternative available in this setting is not the 'cultivation of Amazonian cuisine', but *cachorro quente* (hotdog). The kind of social transformation involved is one in which the basis for the new set of cultural conventions is not located within local society, rather it is abstracted from a set of cultural practices which is partially presented to Santarenos through the example of the ruling elite, mass media, and immigrants. The integrity of a pre-*Transamazônica* Santareno culture is only recognized as a defective melange of peasant practices incapable of sustaining itself in the face of such concerted opposition as that posed by *desenvolvimento.*

Contingency and Permanence in Santareno Peasant Production

Much recent work on peasantries has departed from the previous anthropological concern with the internal organization of peasant societies by concentrating on the way in which the pre-capitalist or non-capitalist features of peasant production are articulated with capitalist social formations. Kahn (1980), for example, has presented an analysis of a petty commodity economy in Minangkabau which through its periodic insertion in the national economy is structured from without (via the price mechanism) and yet sustains a degree of autonomy by virtue of the possibilities of increased self-exploitation through subsistence production of rice. Others, although pursuing different analytical objectives (cf. Banaji 1977; Bernstein 1979; Friedmann 1980; Roseberry 1983), are similarly concerned with the question of characterization of peasant production as contingent – to varying degrees – on the particular mode of insertion within capitalist (or other) relations. As Shanin has argued, however (1985: 165–7):

> [while] the conceptual solution of designing a subsidiary and specifically 'peasant' or 'simple commodity' mode of production that is 'articulated' to capitalism ... has the virtue of enabling the systematic discussion of specific characteristics of peasant economy, [the] limitations of that usage are considerable. (1985: 167)

In particular, there is a configuration of production characteristics in the peasant economy – 'self-exploitation', 'irrational diversification of crops', telescoping of occupational skills, the 'packages' of different categories of employment – which 'means that the impact of the logic of profit-maximization can up to a point be held at bay, qualified or inverted by a peasant economic logic, rooted in the structure of the family farms' (1985: 169).

As Shanin points out, to argue for the economic specificity of peasant production is not to accept an essentialist view by which 'homogenous "interests" or "laws of motion" of peasantry ... serve as predicates from which all else follows' (1985: 168, citing Bernstein 1982 in Harriss (1982); also see discussion in *Labour, Capital, and Society* 19/1, 1986). To argue for this kind of specificity is to help 'explicate its stability as against the many failed predictions of its imminent demise' (1985: 168).

Parallel to this qualified shift in peasant studies has been the development of a set of arguments concerning non-agricultural equivalents to this kind of articulation. The obvious failure of modernization on the periphery to match capitalist development as it occurred in North-west Europe and North America and the acceleration of urbanization without commensurate labour absorption spurred an interest in so-called informal sector activities. The specificity of peasant production was here complicated by the extension of peasant production far beyond rural domains. If the contrast between rural and urban was not wholly dissolved, the continuum at least became a circle as Mangin's *Peasants in Cities* (1970) transformed into Roberts' *Cities of Peasants* (1978).

Peasant production in Santarém is unusual in several respects. In the first place – and perhaps unlike the majority of peasant societies to which anthropological attention has been drawn – it is not one which is based on the partially fulfilled transformation of an indigenous social formation into a marginal, bounded, local society embodying contradictory features of antediluvianism and modernism. The Amerindian societies previously occupying Santarém could not be described as having been transformed into contemporary peasantries: they were abolished in a manner too familiar throughout Amazonia (and Latin America generally, cf. Wolf and Hansen 1972; Hemming 1978, 1987) and although individual peasants have Amerindian antecedents, peasant societies themselves do not. The contemporary peasantry's antecedents lie in particular Crown policies largely concerned with control of trade in tropical preciosities (see McLachlan 1972, 1973, 1974) followed by post-Imperial, large-scale extractive enterprise (rubber being the best example) (see Weinstein 1983; Bunker 1985; Dean 1987;).

Santareno peasant production embodies less the juxtaposition of pre-capitalist and capitalist forms of production, than it does the structure of capitalist development of an earlier epoch, namely that dominated by the circuit of merchant capital. Its particular features are as much symptomatic of the collapse (or failure) of capitalist development as they are clearly shaped by the impact of capital penetration (see G. Kay 1975).

Another difference is that the distinction between town and country is not at all clear. Although one could characterize the Lower Amazonian economy generally as 'peasant', one would also have to note that urbanization is pronounced in Amazonia. On the other hand, the very poor absorption of labour within the city precludes residential stability. For many Santarenos, the city functions as one site within a range tied to a repertoire of petty commodity forms. In discussing this range it is necessary to idealize to some degree, specifying three relatively distinct geographical districts no one of which is adequate to provide for most Santarenos the means of livelihood. While there is differentiation within the Santareno peasantry based on a greater dependence on one particular kind of site (e.g. recent *nordestino* immigrants tend to stay on *terra firme*), in the idealized form presented, the possibilities for the continued reproduction of a Santareno peasantry derive from high mobility among the three sites.

The 'specificity' of peasant production in Santarém, in view of the points above, is as much 'urban' as it is 'rural', and it is a result of (failed or blocked) capitalist development as much as it is an anterior stage of anticipated development. The specificity of this particular peasant system has, in the main, been overlooked, greater attention being drawn to the allegedly pathological features of the system, its 'stagnation', its marginality in relation to the better integrated (in terms of global markets) plantation and *latifundio* peasantries elsewhere in Brazil.

One consequence of overlooking the distinctiveness of such a peasant system is its portrayal as a fundamentally contingent system, one whose basis lies in now defunct efforts at large-scale exploitation of Amazonia, e.g. the rubber boom. The peasantry 're-emerges' in conjunction with the new phase of Amazonian conquest. While this characterization of contingency is valid, it is inadequate in terms of accounting for the durability of peasant production in the absence of concerted, large-scale efforts to exploit Amazonia. The peasant system is not wholly contingent, thus its specificity includes conditions for social reproduction which are maintainable even in the absence of a rationale provided by periodic 'integration'.

The City as Wreckage

> Anthropology, a residual science par excellence, since it has been assigned the 'residue' of societies which the traditional social sciences did not deign to take into account (precisely because they considered them to 'astructural'), cannot, by definition, use any method other than that of residues. (Lévi-Strauss 1967: 323)

Like other cities on the late-modern periphery, the processes of urbanization in Santarém do not include increasing industrialization or indeed the capacity to absorb labour (cf. Katzman 1977: 155). Santarém is large, yet the formal sector is precarious in spite of the existence of a complex bureaucracy, banking system, public utilities and a public transportation system. Santarém illustrates in graphic form what Kay has described as the legacy – on the periphery – of domination by merchant capital: incorporation within global capitalist development, but little local development of the forces of production (G. Kay 1975). The phenomenon most obviously associated with this failure of capitalism to exploit sufficiently – in Kay's paradoxical expression – is the proliferation of petty commodity production forms, that is production of commodities by owners of means of production, yet owners who must subsidize such production through increased self-exploitation in the subsistence agriculture sphere (cf. Kahn 1980).

Given the manner in which Santarém is constituted as a city, as a necessary but insufficient base for local development, an expansion of Lévi-Strauss's comments on 'residues' is suggested, and this is that Santareno society, as an anthropological object, is marked by – and, in fact, is fundamentally derived from – the intersection of two kinds of 'residues': those which have antecedents in the the productive activities (and to a considerably lesser extent, cultural practices) of indigenous peoples of the region, and those which are by and large exogenous, colonial legacies in the most general sense.

In contemporary Santarém, the former assume the character of culturally denigrated 'residues' although the ethnic differences within contemporary Santareno society produce different readings of what is 'Indian' and therefore dissociated. *Caboclos* (whose distinctive feature in this context is their riverine orientation) regard themselves as Amazonian peasants in nominal terms and (remotely) descended from Indians, Europeans, and Africans. To be 'Indian' is to be something not quite human, Indians being widely regarded as the archetypal *bugre mansos* (tame wild men). From the point of view of many *nordestinos,* however, *caboclos* themselves were 'like Indians', in *nordestino* terms committed to archaic hunting and gathering, fishing and horticultural practices which indicated their inferior origins. From this viewpoint (and one characteristic of more recent *nordestino* immigrants rather than veterans), extensive *terra firme* agriculture was the mark of a Brazilian colonist in the interior as opposed to an Amazonian *caboclo* who maintains a varied set of livelihoods. Many *caboclo* Santarenos, however, used a national stereotype in describing *nordestinos* generally: *arigó,* a bird which flits from bush to bush and never settles.

As indicated earlier, for *caboclos,* the coincidence of large-scale immigration of *nordestinos* and the marked presence of federal government apparatus was treated as a unitary phenomenon, one which was by many regarded as the harbinger of, in their term, *desenvolvimento,* and far from there being serious ethnic antagonism, as might be implied in the comments above, there was, rather, a tension generated by the contradictory position in which Santareno society seemed placed: a society with a history, but one marked by the idiom of stagnation according to which Amazonia stands in relation to the trajectory of the Centre-South of Brazil; and a society being very rapidly acted upon by the state which had for so long remained aloof from, if not oblivious to, local societies such as Santarém. The promise of state intervention, then, was regarded with mixed feelings. The construction of new quay and docking facilities in the early 1970s had temporarily provided employment, but upon its completion there was little evidence of a structural change in the urban labour market. The hydroelectric dam at Curua-Una absorbed some labour, as did the construction of the Hotel Tropical, but neither was a significant local employer.

Because fundamental features of Santarém are 'residues' of inexact origin, and because of the fundamentally different orientations of 'land-hungry', immigrant *nordestinos* and sedentary *caboclo* Santarenos, sentiments expressed about the city and locality display contradictions in 'Santareno' self-perception. For the *caboclo* able to cultivate, hunt, fish, gather and produce and sell goods on an extensive scale, 'Santarém' is esteemed. For other Santarenos such as recent agricultural immigrants or entrepreneurs from the South detailed to sell tractors to peasants lacking land titles and credit, the previously cited anatomical metaphor prevails.

From the observer's point of view, the net effect of the 'residual' character of Santarém is the unevenness with which the city presents itself. While Santarém has only one factory in which mass production techniques are employed on a significant scale (jute factory), it contains at least fifty government agencies. The rapid growth of the city in recent years has meant that the portion of the city regarded by long-standing residents as the city proper is very small in relation to the urban sprawl containing squatters and what were previously suburbs on the outskirts. The central area of the city includes not only the more ancient edifices (the main churches, government offices, and trading establishments), but also the newer additions to the city such as automobile salesrooms and cinemas. On the radio, priests rail against backsliders, spiritists and the too-closely married, Eric Clapton covers Bob Marley, and Shirley and Co. follow the Stones. In the cinemas, newsreels document the growth of the plastic surgery industry.

In Table 4.6 are shown the uses to which city land is put. The figures are approximate because of the rate at which settlement on the fringes of the city takes place.

Table 4.6 Land use in Santarém

Use	Area(ha^2)	%	Area/1k inhabitants
Streets	129.3	15.47	4.32
Plazas	3.7	0.44	0.12
Non-usable area, subtotal =	133	15.91	4.43
Residencies with general stores & services	363.5	43.49	12.12
Residencies with specialist stores	5.7	0.68	0.19
Industry	15.5	1.85	0.52
Public and semi-public	34.9	4.18	1.16
Empty lots	280.5	33.57	9.35
Usable area sub-total	702.8	84.09	23.43
TOTAL	836.8	100%	27.86

Source: Water department (1968).

interior (hunting, for example). The term *sítio* once indicated a smallholding, titled or untitled. Increasingly, *sítio* has come to mean rural retreat – for wealthier urbanites, for instance – as well as weekend farm, and one finds very modest family farms now situated next to 'country' homes with swimming pools (fed by streams diverted into wood-lined pits). This area at the base of the plateau effectively marks the edge of the urban sprawl beyond which are Santarém's major *terra firme* satellites.

Political Background

As indicated earlier, political life in Santarém during the period of research was in abeyance. The ascendant political elite consisted of those members of the community for whom federal expansion into Amazonia was of direct financial benefit, and to some degree they constituted a new kind of elite for the municipality. The system of *coronelismo* through which ties of patron–clientage integrated, in segmentary fashion, local, regional and national political structures, had been undercut by the military usurpation of local civilian government. The prefect was an appointee, a member of the offical national ruling party (ARENA) with a 'constituency' long committed to the nominal opposition party (MDB). Given the lack of representation within the local political structure, the prefect was widely regarded (even by those who supported ARENA) as a relatively powerless puppet. City council officials were still elected, but without access to any power they were confined to squabbles of no serious political import.

Political discussions during the period of field research were not open. The Federal Police were treated with considerable 'respect' not least because soldiers performed basic police roles and in many cases were the ultimate arbiters of disputes. In addition, travel between cities required getting permission from the police (mainly a document assuring officials at the other end that one was not wanted for any crimes), and although enforcement was by no means effective, such restrictions indicate the extent of attempts to regiment civilian life. The intrusion of heavy federal controls in the area was not simply a consequence of *Transamazônica* recolonization policies, but was also impelled by a long series of conflicts over succession to the

Prefect's office, disputes which had resulted in shootings of both officials and civilians. In short, political activity in the area was strictly controlled, and had been controlled for a long enough period before fieldwork in such a way that local 'opposition' had not only been suppressed, but in addition, casual discussion of the events leading up to the imposition of military rule presented some danger.

The ability of local bosses to operate within the terms of virtual military occupation varied considerably. The apparently prosperous (under the regime) were a clique of entrepreneurs active as cattle-ranchers, real estate speculators, gold merchants and representatives of enterprises based in the South. Such men as owners of rice mills and large commercial firms (dealing in agricultural tools, for example) continued to sustain networks of patron–clientage articulated within the politico-economic idiom of *aviamento*. Although rural Santarenos speak of a time when they constituted acknowledged political constituencies, high rates of immigration and the generally repressive effects of military rule have fragmented such constituencies. Satellite communities have village councils whose structure matches that of the city, but occupying office in the countryside is an expense which can only be borne by the relatively wealthy, hence the equation of modest political power and modest economic dominance. Political leaders are typically merchants, the expression *chefe* (chief) and *patrão* being virtually interchangeable.

The Church

The Church's position *vis-à-vis* the municipality is comparable to that of the state in terms of its relationship to specifically local aspects of social organization. The Church – like the state – is represented by and large by non-Santarenos. (Historically, Brazil has had difficulty in the internal recruitment of a priesthood.) In Santarém, the Church is mainly represented by members of the Franciscan Order drawn from the mid-Western United States and Canada. The Bishop and 90 per cent of the brothers and priests are non-Brazilian. (German and Italian orders predominated before the Second World War). In addition to their ministerial contributions, members of the Orders run a radio station not wholly devoid of secular content, a medical clinic with a regional reputation and schools.

While the ideological appartus represented in the Church is beyond the scope of this study, a few things should be said by way of relating the Church's local development to that of local society. The Church, unlike any local economic or political institutions, has been a regular feature of local society since the founding of the mission in 1661 (with a brief hiatus in the late seventeenth century). As such, it has a well-established network of metro-satellite relations within the municipality and beyond. The expression used to denote the Church network is the same as that used in describing commercial networks: *matriz:filial* (centre:affiliate).

The Church is maintained only partially through locally extracted tithes, the bulk of its support coming from abroad. By all accounts, the Church's dependency on the local economy has declined in recent years, most notably, say Santarenos, in the degree to which gifts of produce to the Church have been cut back. It is difficult to offer more than a mild speculation concerning this change, but it would appear that two points could be argued: (1) local productivity in the pre-*Transamazônica* period was probably not as low as the 'stagnation' characterization might imply; (2) the expansion of the local market and the increasing commodification of production has taken precedence over the tributary relations previously defined by Church and parishioner. The declining importance of the Church as an apparatus within which were embedded both economic and ideological functions is also indicated by the high incidence of expulsion/attrition within the ranks of novice members of the Orders. Urban Santarenos (post-adolescent/ young adult) who have spent years in the Orders before leaving/being expelled are not rarities, and according to many, this represents a typical religious career path, i.e. indenturehood within the Order, exclusion from advancement within the Order, expulsion/attrition. Some spoke bitterly of the time spent as novices/labourers, manufacturing tiles for example, before realizing that full membership in the Order was unachievable. At least one Santareno was said to have successfully sued the Franciscans for back-pay after his expulsion.

It would not be correct to describe relations between the Church and Santareno society as antagonistic, but it is clear that the Church's view of its position within Santareno society is frequently unacknowledged by many Santarenos. Many Santarenos, for instance, willingly subscribe both to Catholic dogma and *umbanda/macumba* precepts, and resent Church criticism of what they regard as perfectly acceptable co-subscription. Similarly, the Church's condemnation of cousin marriage is, by some, regarded as a presumptuous incursion in secular matters. The issue is further complicated by the Church's presentation of itself as defender of orthodoxy as well as critic of Santarenos' actual behaviour on the grounds of the imputed ignorance of locals. An arena in which this conflict between the Church and its members is particularly fraught is that occupied by the worship of local saints. Many local communities have – in the view of some members of the Church – elevated patron saints to an unwarranted status, performing a pantheistic transformation which justifies – from the Church's point of view – the need for more rigid instruction of the ignorant.

The Church's dominance within the municipality has also been challenged by the increasing number of Protestants and Protestant sects. While hardly a major issue, hostility beween Catholics and Protestants is evident in various common prejudicial stereotypes. More significant is the view held by some Catholic stalwarts that the charismatic movement represents Protestant subversion of the Church. During the period of fieldwork, a Catholic priest, and member of the charismatic movement, who had spent over twenty years in Lower Amazonia was dismissed from his post in one of the Santarém churches having been accused of becoming a holy roller.

In relation to these broad institutional features of Santarém there are two points to be made. The first is that Santareno society has long been 'integrated'. The second is that in the aftermath of *Transamazôica*, Santarém became subject to a pan-Amazonian administrative apparatus (represented by the army, INCRA – the land reform agency – and diverse federal agencies – staffed by generic tecnicos (technicians) and bureaucrats – which not only curtailed local traditional political activities and interests (imposing, for example, a Prefect),[8] but also stifled the growth of organizations amongst the thousands of immigrants who entered the municipality as a result of the failure of *Transamazônica*'s colonist settlement programme. The absorption

8. A report on Santarém (Piazza 1963) noted authorities' fear of the danger posed by local groups promoting 'folklore'.

(rural and urban) or large numbers of migrants too place in a static – if not always overtly repressive – political climate which enhanced the marginality of small-producers in relation to the broad features of 'official' development.[9]

Facing the *O Futuro*

Writing in 1851, the naturalist Henry Bates described houses on the outskirts of Santarém:

> the cabin of the pure-blood indian being distinguished from the mud hovels of the free negroes and mulattoes by its light construction half of it being an open shed where the dusky tenants are seen at all hours of the day lounging in their open-meshed grass hammocks. (1964: 219)

Such a description would not be inadequate today, although the racial stereotypes have changed. Santarém accommodates a mixture of purposes and needs. *Caboclos* in canoes bearing a handful of fish tie up on a quay upon which is perched a bar-restaurant where white-coated *caboclo* waiters serve batidas to *caboclos* in leisure outfits. On the adjacent *praça,* teenagers sip Coca-Cola and spoon. On the river can be seen a cruise-liner with a cargo of tourists.

When Bates was living in Santarém, Amazonia was undergoing a rest period. The conquest of Amerindian societies was virtually complete. The *cabanagem* had come and gone. The rubber industry was still incipient. The conquest of the tropics was in abeyance. A few years later, Santarém would become the refuge of a group of US Confederates (descendants of whom still correspond with kin in Missouri). During the rubber boom, Santarém was overshadowed by Manaus and Belém, but was a not insignificant entrepot for the Tapajós rubber trade (cf. Murphy and Steward 1956; R. Murphy 1960; S. Leacock 1964; Y. and R. Murphy 1974). In the 1920s and 1930s Santarém came to be associated with the efforts of Henry Ford's rubber plantations at Fordlandia and Belterra. Haroldo Veloso's 'coup' briefly put Santarém again in the national picture.

9. The subsequent development – and in the case of fishermen, strengthening – of rural syndicates is represented in LeRoy (1988) and Hine (1991).

The Santarém which Bates described in the nineteenth century had a composite character given a focus during the rubber period and again redefined with the construction of *Transamazônica*. Open construction and reliance on hammocks are enduring features. Many residences double as production (and/or commercial) sites and are – with the exception of the homes of the wealthy – single storey wooden constructions roofed with tile, thatch or corrugated sheet metal. Except in newer, peripheral squatter neighbourhoods, houses (or compounds) are separated from each other by fences. The area of the compounds rarely includes horticultural plots of great size and many houses are without gardens of a dimension larger than that required to situate an outhouse at a reasonable distance. What is different today is that the residual character of Santarém is no longer so obviously Amazonian. Earlier, Santarém exemplified a settler colony within a relatively homogeneous regional economy; today, largely because of the way that roads have dissolved the enclave nature of interior settlements, Santarém exemplifies a process of differentiation within the regional economy in which access to resources comes to be translated into despoliation. On a return visit to Santarém in 1988, what was most striking was that while previously, the urban or settled areas more or less corresponded to the deforested areas, in mature – 'developed' – Santarém, veteran of almost two decades of 'integration' policies was a city in the midst of a levelled forest. The net effect of policies ostensibly intended to relieve an interior peasantry of the burdens of marginality has instead resulted in 'a highly skewed distribution of land ownership, the growth of land-extensive and labor-saving economic activities and a predominantly urban spatial distribution of population' (Wood and Carvalho 1988: 236). They go on to say that: 'For the rural poor the once bright promise of Amazônia has faded as the frontier region increasingly mirrors the inequities that mark the rest of Brazilian society' (Wood and Carvalho 1988: 236).

To this may be added that the 'once bright promise' was actually quite substantial. The period between the collapse of the rubber trade and the mounting of *Transamazônica* has conventionally been characterized as one of stagnation, a period during which Amazonia develoved, awaiting the technocratic assault of *desenvolvimento*. There is something to be said for this thesis in as much as the *Transamazônica* assault not only encountered not a unity of Amazonian peasantries (or Indian societies), but a fragmented social landscape consisting of – to a greater or lesser degree – autonomous regional or local societies linked by a common set of historical antecedents (*aviamento*, the effacement of indigenous societies) – not to mention aspects of the hyleia. On the other hand, however much the stagnation metaphor reflects the change in Amazonia's position nationally (and globally), from the perspective of local societies, the period of decline looks somewhat different. For one thing, it was during this period that the repertoire of petty commodity prodution was extended both in relation to internal markets (cattle ranching), national markets (jute) and international markets (black pepper)[10]. For another thing, there are aspects of local society less transformed by broad economic shifts than are others. Systems of kinship and domestic organization, for example, are hardly susceptible in any serious sense to the metaphors of pathology engaged at the regional level. In the following chapter, the internal organization of local society is examined from the perspective of systems of kinship with particular emphasis on the way in which *caboclo* identity may be expressed through the idiom of kinship. The seeming marginality of *caboclo* society actually disguises a system of kinship which flexibly accommodates the changing fortunes of rural and urban groups subject to, at time, dramatic transformations imposed from outside Amazonia.

10. This is an argument which has greater visibility now that attention has been drawn to *caboclos'* actual and potential contributions to new models of sustainable development.

Chapter 5

Exploring Santareno Identity: Kinship, Domestic Groups and Social Organization

An emphasis on the external, and discontinuous, factors which have constituted Santareno society (such as global demand for rubber and its precipitous end as well as the side-effects of *Transamazônica* colonist schemes) underlines the contingent character of Santareno identity. The effects of these macro-processes are, in any case, hardly specific to Santarém and reflect the fact that *Transamazônica* (and subsequent schemes) paid little attention to differentiation within and among historical peasantries. Thus, such schemes had pan-Amazonian resonances, realized differently from one settlement to another certainly, but the research focus on the mechanisms of 'national integration' (and their manifold inadequacies) has tended to efface real differences among established settlements affected or transformed by the schemes.

The distinctively 'Santareno', therefore, must be approached at another level, and an examination of kinship and domestic organization provides a point of entry. In addition to contradicting widely-held assumptions about the pathology, structurelessness and marginality, such an examination also provides the framework for the discussion of the structure of petty commodity production which is organized largely within parameters set by kinship.

The issues of kinship to which attention is particularly drawn are those associated, respectively, with *caboclo* and *nordestino* groups within Santareno society. In addition, however, there are the important – although minor in terms of extension – examples provided by the Moroccan community (in which parallel cousin marriage features) and the Japanese.

There is a danger of overemphasizing the significance of the 'kinship systems' by making them appear to be the dominant integrative idiom. The relative significance of kinship as an idiom is highly variable. For some sections of Santareno society, the embeddedness of economic and political relations in kinship structures is characteristic, while for other sections kinship provides a quite different metaphorical import. For example, *nordestinos* of recent vintage who regard themselves as extensions of local groups in Ceará, for instance, and who practise kindred endogamy, are quite explicit in defining the nature of their kinship universe. *Caboclo* notions of kindred boundaries, by contrast, are far more flexible and the reclassification of kinship relations is common. There are circumstances in the *caboclo* idiom when Zé's husband is a kinsman, for example, and circumstances when he is not. By the same token, a person introduced one day as a cousin (a term which has strong affective implications) may under other circumstances be regarded as merely 'kin'. Such flexibility in reckoning is also illustrated in the permeability of kingroup membership epitomized in the custom of *filho de criação*,[1] a mechanism of adoption.

A complicating factor in looking at local kinship ideologies is provided by the Church. Although generally speaking there is not a great deal of interest in the 'correctness' of kinship classification, the propagandizing of the Church – the import of which has been heightened by the imminence of 'national integration', a process in which the Church features prominently – has made Santarenos aware that others – Brazilians, foreigners – are preoccupied with certain kinship matters which are, or were, of little consequence locally, and some Santarenos express regret at having been unaware of 'proper' kinship behaviour as propounded by the Church. In this regard, there are two tiers of kinship ideology to which Santarenos subscribe. On one level there are the Church's pronouncements, carried over the radio, for example, as well as being disseminated by priests and

1. *Filho de criação* refers to a child who is reared by someone other than his/her acknowledged parents. The relationship may have aspects of *compadrio* – godparenthood – as well as formal adoption or fostering or master/servant relations. It is widely practised and specifies a kinship relationship rather than indicating a non-kin who lives in the family.

brothers in the course of their daily activities. The notions of proper kinship comportment thus promulgated tend to resemble those of the societies of the padres (Midwestern North America), notions which, however contradicted by fact, derive from assumptions of a nuclear family in which males are the breadwinners and women domestically confined. This model is not matched by the great majority of Santarenos. Indeed, it could be argued that female-centred (typically, a group of land-holding sisters) households represent a contesting norm (see Wyer 1983).

The other level of kinship ideology is that which is associated with actual local practices. The tension generated by the opposition of the two models of proper behaviour is a significant feature of modernizing Santarém. The frequency of cousin marriage among Catholics, for example, is – although hardly unique to Santarém – a significantly public refutation of religious authority.

The Church's authority with regard to 'correct' kinship behaviour is equivocal. On the one hand, a normative Santareno attitude is that the Church's prescriptions are sacred and indisputable. On the other hand, is expressed the view that single men, padres (almost none of whom is Brazilian) – should not presume to tell people what is proper and what is not. For some Santarenos, the explicit claim is that unmarried men are by definition anomolous – whether this is sanctioned by the Church or not – and are, as 'everyone knows', pederasts in any case.

It is important to note the effects of conflict over conceptions of kinship, for the significance of the kinship system in Santarém seems to lie in its potential for being manipulated to serve as an idiom through which other kinds of social relations may be expressed. That is to say that the increasingly nationally-oriented economic activity may be viewed as having revived in some measure the idea of kinship as a system. This position as a reactive system of relations – that is to say, available for use as an idiom for other sorts of relations – gives kinship a central position in many Santareno affairs that is more apparent than actual. The potency of kinship ideology may derive from the fact that the develoment of post-rubber local society has meant an integrated dispersion of the population (as opposed to the production-form specific form of the rubber period). Kinship ties have historically served to maintain connections between dispersed groups both for purposes of cooperation and exploitation as in the case of long-term maintenance of ties between producers and traders who are real or fictive kinsmen.

The kinship system (here read as kinship ideology) defines Santarém society in fundamental respects, but as a pluri-functional system of social relations, the kinship system is both a medium of changing relations in Santarém society and is expressive of those changes as well. Newly emerging class relations, for example, may be articulated through increasingly rigid interpretations of kinship dogma, or those same relations may be rationalized by incipient hierarchization in the kinship system *per se*.

Kindreds

The kinship unit in Santarém is the kindred, individuals locating themselves by reference to a set of male and female consanguines and affines. The circle of kin thus established, the kindred is referred to by the term *a familia* (family) or *parentes* (kin). The term family rarely refers to the unit comprised by parents and siblings or spouse and children even though there is a strong tendency, in following the Church's instructions, to refer obliquely to such a social unit in the vernacular.

The reckoning by individuals of the extent of kinship ties varies in terms of comprehensiveness. An ego-centred or bounded kindred may consist of an extended family of small size, a nuclear family plus one or two affines for example, or it may include hundreds of people the bases of whose affiliations may be obscure, but deducible should the need arise.

Genealogical depth is shallow. Few Santarenos can, without consulting fellow kin, offer much information about kin above parents' ascending generation. Those Santarenos who can trace kinship ties further back than three generations are usually those who claim descent from non-Brazilians. Such ancestors include North Americans (the Confederate Riker family which settled in Santarém after the US Civil War) and Portuguese, as well as Moroccan Jews, Japanese and Lebanese. The eldest kin cited by a Santareno/a is more likely to be male than female.

Contemporary kindreds often are, to use Davenport's phrase (1959: 565), stem kindreds in as much as some idea of perpetuity is asserted, and this idea is often expressed with patrilateral bias. Criteria other than biological/genealogical ones, however, affect this notion of perpetuity. Ethnic considerations are commonly influential as in the cases of non-Brazilian ancestry noted above. They may also enter into the tracing of non-foreign links of some depth. A small kindred, for example, might have relatively great genealogical depth – implying a notion of corporateness and perpetuity – on the basis of an ego's claim of descent from, for example, 'a beautiful white woman'. In other words, in addition to Davenport's example of the basis of a stem kindred, that is the possibility of inheritance of land establishing kindred perpetuity, in Santarém, stem kindreds may be based on value-added ethnic criteria as well. In the context of increasing awareness of the terms of 'national integration', extra-regional (and national) and ethnic components of kinship identity play a prominent role (e.g. 'my father's father's brother was a *Sulista*').

The Range of the Kindred and Kinship Ideology

The ways in which the term kindred is used in the literature are numerous and often confused (cf. Mitchell 1963). A brief review of some of the literature should establish the reasons for my use of a broadly defined term.

What is stressed in my discussion of the kindred is the multiplicity of contexts according to which the kindred has differential significance. For my purposes, then, it is the flexibility of kin relations which is of greatest interest, and as a corollary it is the most inclusive definition of kindred which has greatest utility.

Sahlins' (1962) use of the term kindred to refer to any collectivity of kin is useful in as much as it compresses the anthropological model and the native model. This general notion of kindred is suitable for discussion of Santareno kinship because one of the salient feature of Santareno society is that given the relative absence of other enduring institutions, kinship has provided some continuity. It makes good sense to use such a broad definition in Santarém given the high permeability of Santareno society: membership in Santareno society is easy to achieve, mere residence being adequate. In these circumstances, it is not surprising that the question of identity not be restricted by a rigid notion of fundamental and essentialist Santareno-ness.

Distinctions have been made between personal kindreds as define by Goodenough (1970: 47), Mitchell (1963) and Freeman

(1961) among others, and the notion of bounded or residential kindreds as put forward by Pehrson (1964: 200) and Davenport (1963: 565) among others. It is not my interest to enter into the debate over whether these definitions are compatible. What I am concerned to do is describe and analyse Santareno kinship behaviour, and to do this a variety of trajectories is required. The reasons for the variety are that kinship organization has relevance for a number of different aspects of social organization which are not wholly expressed through the idiom of kinship, but which cannot be adequately explained without reference to it. In brief, I shall move from discussing the range of an individual's ties to discussing the range of behaviour of kinship groups, bounded kindreds.

Kaplan (1973: 556) has argued that a conceptual dependence on models of descent as the starting point for kinship analysis has tended to push analysis of cognatic systems outside the realm of 'proper' kinship studies. Her response to this tendency has been to show that the alleged incompatibility of positive marriage rules and an absence of a descent rule is a consequence of certain formal styles of kinship analysis specifically revealed in the lumping together (e.g. by Lévi-Strauss 1969: 45–51) of different phenomena under the label 'endogamy'.

One indication of the rigidity of this conceptual dependence which has followed on the centrality of 'descent' as an issue is the hesitancy with which its critics, Davenport (1959), for example, have argued. Davenport's 'stem kindred' straddles an argument: while seeming to argue against the notion that only a descent principle permits the analyst to speak of group continuity, he tries to draw an analogy between the kindred's corporateness and a descent group. We can state more strongly their structural similarities.

My own interest in these matters of kinship – while I concur with Kaplan in her criticism of the narrow focus of certain kinship arguments – does not lie in considering the 'kinship system' as a structure which can be dealt with in isolation. There are two reasons for this: (1) complex or degenerate systems (in the sense of 'ambiguous') tend to be defined outside of the field of anthropology; they appear not to have 'classic' features, and are thereby, and quite unreasonably, held to be inappropriate objects of anthropological scrutiny; (2) there is a practical issue in the case of Santarém: there is no particularly well-defined congruence between 'kinship' system and 'social' system. Kinship in Santarém is highly negotiable, and the operation of the 'kinship system' is contingent on determinant features of social relations which prevail from outside the local system. Santarém is in many crucial respects a society of immigrants, thus its fundamental character is a synthetic realization of various kinship (and other) systems.

This is not just a matter of there being a number of coexisting systems; it is also a matter of non-dysfunctional discrepancies within the sub-systems, e.g. the prohibition on cousin marriage among Catholics is broken frequently in Santarém. These contraventions of the 'rules' do not suggest to me that this is evidence of a system accommodating itself to conditions which the kinship system is unprepared to account for, rather I see it as evidence of contradictory demands being placed on fractions of Santarenos who are disunited in terms of kinship behaviour, but who are united in terms of their participating in an economic system which has redefined the terms of embeddedness of kinship and economic relations. Recent economic shifts have led to the breakdown of rural-based domestic kin groups, but the shift has not led to alternative forms of labour absorption. The result has been, in the city especially, the formation of household organization in which different members or fractions of kindreds express different, incipient class relations: an urban household may contain wage-labourers (in primary, secondary and tertiary sectors), petty commodity producers, traders, unpaid domestic labourers and a variety of dependent-producers (e.g. senior women herbalists, juvenile shoe-shiners, and so on). Households, therefore, which have an obvious 'kinship' base, are increasingly unstable both in terms of the economic conditions of different members and in terms of the durability of kinship links over time as economic differentiation is registered within the domestic unit. In this light, the kinship system makes its most forceful appearance in terms of sloughing off and accreting members, yet the conditions which precipitate these processes are not of the kinship system *per se*, but are the result of structural features of Santareno society in which kinship is expressive, not determinant. In analysing kinship in Santarém there are multiple sets of 'rules' which emerge appropriate to context.

Kin Groups

The category 'kin' as it applies to the notion 'family' is roughly synonymous with 'household', and as it applies to 'relations' (*parentes*) includes both residential groups and dispersed individuals. A frequently used term which seems to cut across both senses is *gente*, people who because they interact on a daily, familiar basis, or because they recognize a class identity, are virtually 'family'.

Primary kin are parents, parents' parents, siblings, children, parents' siblings (frequently) and spouse. Siblings' spouses, cousins, nephews and nieces, spouse's parents, children's spouses may or may not be considered primary kin. There is a term (*primo/a irmo/a*) which explicitly denotes cousins as primary kin.

Beyond the circle of primary kin there is a lack of specificity in terms of degree of relatedness. The kindred beyond these limits consists of kin referred to generally by the term parentes. In practice, if one of these vaguely positioned (in genealogical terms) members of the kindred is in continual contact with ego or a segment of ego's kindred, such a person may be given the generic title *primo/a*. For example, members of an urban household may, in a conversation, refer to some kin who live in the interior and in talking about these kin and their activities there may be no effort to specify the genealogical relationship. If these kin should happen to be travelling to the city and stay there a while, they would no longer be merely *parentes*, that is 'distant'; it would be insulting to introduce such a person as merely 'related'. The specificity of the term supplied is effectively not much greater than *primo*, but the point is that right of residence (as a visitor in the urban household) is a prerogative which is contextually variable. A parallel condition would apply if, for instance, a distant kinsman were known to be contemplating a business transaction with a close kinsman of ego. In such circumstances the ambiguity of ego's relationship to the distant kinsman might be abrogated by the conditions of propinquity implied by the imminent business transaction.

The more exact the kin term use, the closer the relationship implied between individuals. The insistence, for example, that 'Zé is my cousin, our fathers are brothers' indicates the high degree of importance placed on particular relationship, i.e. the relationship is bolstered by reference to exact genealogical links. It does not indicate that any ego will refer to his relationship with a cousin as being one which is directly read from the kinship model.

In the examples mentioned above, proximity of residence, economic calculation and biological kinship reckoning are all shown to be variables which affect estimates of kinship relatedness, but these are by no means the only variables.Other factors which influence ego's *estimatino* of what constitutes his kindred include various sorts of status variables such as social prestige, ethnic and biological conventions. Biologically related kin may be ignored because of their poverty. An example of this is offered by a relatively well-off woman who lives in a compound which includes an unmarried mother's brother. If the man (MB) were married and were he not impoverished, his kin status would be indisputable, but as it is, his kinship connection is played down. He is never referred to by the conventional term for uncle (*tio*), and is introduced to others (whether they know better or not) as merely a family retainer. The fact that he is a bachelor no doubt contributes to his being defined outside of the kindred in many circumstances.

The occasionally high prestige or defect attached to physical features such as skin and hair colour is manipulated within the terms of kinship ideology as well. Darker-skinned children may be ranked lower than their lighter-skinned siblings. More distant kin may be ranked similarly and in some cases aspersions are placed on the honour of the mother of such kin by claiming that only adultery could account for deviations of physical type.

From the discussion so far it should be clear that the vagueness in specifying the limits of the personal kindred is not dysfunctional for Santarenos; on the contrary, the changing boundary of a personal kindred may be conceived of as a system of negotiation in which kinship ideology – traditionally fairly fluid – is exploited in the confirmation of other categories of social distinction. There is nothing unusual in this, but given the common characterization of lumpenness of such 'marginal peasantries' as that represented by Santarém, it is important to draw attention to the structured aspects of local society. It is also worth noting that the Church's attempts to define the notion of family is actually an attempt to redefine the notion.

Personal Kindreds

A personal kindred is defined primarily by biological relatedness. The terms used are the standard Western kin terms, mother, father, sister, brother, and so on. The boundaries of the personal kindred become vague in the use of two categories of kin: cousins and in-laws. For example, there is no agreement on the genealogical status of siblings of an in-law; a person standing in that relationship to ego may be as close as the in-law and the spouse (i.e. either affine or consanguine) or may be regarded as outside the kindred.

Within the realm of peripheral kinsmen there are no conventions for ranking kin. There are not, for instance, terms for elder or younger cousins; there are no rules for determining relatedness of distant kinsmen who marry, although in the case of some *nordestinos* practising kindred endogamy it is a moot point.

The question of biological relatedness has obvious bearing on notions of genealogical relatedness. The positions of Davenport (1959: 501), Mitchell (1963: 350), and Goodenough (1970: 47) all permit a limited idea of descent within the kindred, although clearly this is in the context of bounded, not personal kindreds. In the manner of nodal kindreds, as described by Goodenough for the Lakalai (1970: 49–50), the overlapping of Santareno kindreds results in people's being able to establish ties to people not usually included in peronal kindreds. This is done through citing persons shared by two personal kindreds. In such a case, egos A and B, who would not recognize each other as being kinsmen, might do so under certain conditions, establishing a trading relationship for example, and the basis of the kin tie would be some mututally recognized member of both of their personal kindreds. Such a relationship might well continue for A and B progeny, who would be, in effect, cousins.

Filiation is not sufficient on its own to establish recognized kin ties. By the same token, genealogical ties may be effectively repudiated. In Figure 5.4 (p. 165) the male head of household is the father of a number of children in the adjacent household. His legitimate children regard their half-siblings as affines. Biological relatedness is ambiguous, in sum, in its position in kinship reckoning. Blood metaphors are used in discussing relations among individuals, but blood-relatedness is never metaphorically extended to a whole kindred. A man (and his brothers or sons) may be said to have certain characteristics implying heritability, but such qualities are not attributed to kin groups *per se* except as these are viewed as sub-sets of ethnic categories (e.g. '*nordestinos* are known to be like that').

Other Conditioning Factors

The ethnic homogeneity of a kindred is problematic. For Cearanese (and other *nordestino* groups) it often goes without saying that a personal kindred consists of ethnically uniform Santarenos, but for the majority of Santarenos, ethnicity is a manipulable attribute of kinship itself. Ethnicity compares best in its ambiguity with affinity: it is useful in the sorts of relationships that, if desired for other reasons (e.g. economic advantage), may be reified ('he is one of us, he's short and squat') or denied ('we're all just people'). In short, ethnicity may be used to refute kinship ties established on other grounds, or it may be used to enhance ties.

Kindreds are generally geographically extensive in terms of reference. For the purposes of daily, practical interaction, occupational considerations determine the geographical limits. For example, a trader is likely to have a personal kindred of greater scope than is a house-bound Santareno. With the opening of the *Transamazônica*, the high rate of immigration, and the self-conscious attitude towards participation in national affairs, the geographical extensivenss of kindreds is increasing. The possibilities for emigrating to areas of high employment may be just one impetus to an expansion of the kindred scale since the opening of the Highway. For some Cearaense merchants, trade networks are coterminous with kindreds stretching from Northeast metropoles, through Santarém, and into interior Amazonia (see Figure 5.1, p.156).

In terms of status and class, personal kindreds are most interesting not only in the way they flexibly define the limits of kin group interaction, although this is clearly of relevance, but also in the way in which kin are ranked, and this point has bearing on the kind of perpetuity represented within kindreds. When genealogical proximity and status or class ranking do not coincide, when, for example, the sort of respect due a father is mitigated by his poverty, the corporatenes of the kindred may be emphasized with other senior members being treated as the focal members of the group.

Corporateness is also enhanced by parallel social organizations, football and social clubs for example, as well as by Church-based organizations. Such membership enhances corporateness as illustrated, for example, by the way in which a guest at such a formal gathering (e.g. at the local yacht club) is clearly a guest of *'a familia'* rather than the actual host/hostess who tendered the invitation. In the same way, domestic labourers attending such gatherings are freely exploited by non-employer kin.

Bounded Kindreds

Bounded kindreds are established in Santarém according to a number of criteria among which residence is predominant. Only the very smallest kindreds are contained within a single household. Most kindreds are constituted by a number of households among which there are varying degrees of interaction such as regular exchanges of assistance and communal gatherings (e.g. birthday parties).

Most kindreds are centred on the eldest economically active males or females. These may be sets of siblings, but more often the acknowledged centre of a kindred is a couple with children and attached relatives in more or less permanent co-occupation of a house or compound. Even if, as is often the case, the husband is absent regularly, such husband/wife couples are still identified as the kindred centre. Non-labouring elders who no longer direct the activities of younger kin are placed in one of two positions. If the kindred to which they belong can afford it, they are put in houses of their own and are looked after by grandchildren or other juniors. Sometimes the houses of these inactive kin are within the compounds of kindred households, but they may be located elsewhere. The alternative to such set-ups is to establish inactive elders as transient members of several kindred households. In this case, and one which most often applies to elderly widows, such senior members stay in one household acting as domestics, looking after and being looked after by children until such time as there is pressure to move on. The pressure may take the form of exhaustion of hospitality offered by the hosts, the feeling on the part of the elder that he or she is being a exploited, or the desire of other households to offer a place to the elder, whether for reasons of charity or exploitation.

As in the case of personal kindreds, the criteria for membership are varied, but the absence of strict rules does not mean that kindred organization is not structured (see Pehrson 1964: 199–200). The structure of kinship relations, rather, simply does not lie within the province of either local or anthropological models of kinship.

One of the most important sets of non-kin relations which have bearing on the composition of the kindred is the set of integative economic relations through which rural and urban Santarenos depend on each other for goods and services. Such relations may consist of exchanges of labour, during harvest, for instance, and hospitality, allowing rural children a place in the city while they study, and, as noted above, provision for senior members. Pehrson (1964: 200) has indicated some of the features of a kindred which are emphasized in terminology, such things as complete symmetry of consanguineal terms, rigid differentiation into generations, and the equivalence of siblings expressed in classifying cousins with siblings and expressed through extending such classificatory status to affinal kin. Similar features apply to Santareno kindreds.

Brothers and sisters are addressed and referred to by the terms *irmão* and *irma* respectively, or by their proper names. There are no terms which distinguish beween junior and senior siblings. Terms which denote age, such as *rapaz* (youth), *menino* (little child) or *molequi* (small child, brat), may be used as kin terms in circumstances where the kin relationship is understood.

Terms of address and reference used among brothers and sisters vary according to siblings' membership in vaguely defined age-sets or activity groups. Before puberty, male and female children play with and look after each other. Young girls, four or five years old for example, may be responsible (individually or collectively) for looking after infants. Even before puberty, children are often required to contribute to the family's income by street-selling, and such activities remove them from the age-set. In general, however, there are no rigid guidelines for the composition of these groups. A child moving out of such a group – due, for instance, to work patterns – may be conceived of as becoming more 'cousin-like'.

The distances in familial relations among siblings is greatest when there is a large age difference, but other factors account for differential acknowledgement of sibling bonds. Among the common practices which account for the variety of degrees of siblingness are: the giving up of children for adoption (*filhos de criação*), the seasonal shifts in residence incumbent on changes in agricultural practice, the assigning of children to different sectors of the domestic economy.

The greatest sibling group identity is found among those kinfolk whose economic circumstance have not forced them to become, as it were, disenfranchised segments of a kindred. That is to say there is no kinship structure which itself maintains the kin group if certain complementary conditions, economic for example, are not met. A group of siblings from a relatively wealthy family, for example, would be rather more obviously grouped around their parents and parents' siblings, the apparent corporateness of this group being a feature of class position rather than something isolatable within kinship structure. A group of siblings from a poor family would be forced out of the kindred at a relatively early age, and reference to that kindred core would take the form of ego's referring to his parents; that is the fundamental relationship would not be conceived of as siblings:parents, but of son/daughter:parents.

Until such age as junior members of a residential kindred are obliged to take up residence elsewhere, through the exigencies of labour in most cases, there are no great differences in terms of perceived relatedness among male and female siblings, older or younger.

Sibling solidarity is intimately related to the siblings' socio-economic position. Economic inactivity is a corollary of sibling group disintegration. This is illustrated to some degree by the treatment of the elderly. In many respects, elders' social identities collapse as their ability to participate fully in kindred matters declines. Grandparents, as representatives of a generation, are more often referred to as parents' parents, rarely as a generational group. Most often they are simply referred to as 'old ones' (*os velhos*).

The emphasis on sibling solidarity, which is in this sense euphemistically kindred solidarity, is shown in the treatment of uncles and aunts (*tios/tias*). Unlike other kinsmen, aunt and uncle are often addresed with the appropriate (e.g. '*Tia Emelda*'). The degree to which a mother's or father's siblings are seen to be more closely related to ego is largely a function of residential proximity and if a father, for example, has many brothers living close by, there is an acknowledged pre-eminence of strong affective ties between father's brother(s) and ego and his/her siblings. The same holds for a mother's siblings and their relations to nephews and nieces (*sobrinhos/as*).

The same sorts of conditions that lead to a high degree of generational solidarity in the kindred with regard to siblings applies to solidarity between aunts/uncles and nephews/nieces. That is, if socio-economic conditions permit residential proximity and the integration of the household economy with the level of socialization of labour in Santarém, then there are strong bonds between members of ego's generation and that of ego's parents. For example, adjacent houses of brothers may contain wholesalers and retailers of the same sort of produce, hence there be a correspondence between kindred division of labour and the more general urban division of labour.

Cousins, *primos/as,* are referred to and addressed by their proper names as well as by the term (less frequent). The position of cousins in the kindred is among the more complex of all kinship relations in terms of the possibilities for defining the limits of the kindred and the criteria for membership. A cousin whose closeness is to be emphasized may be referred to by the term for 'brother'. At the other extreme, the genealogical proximity may be denied, the person in question being simply referred to as 'kin' (*parente*). Different circumstances permit the same actor to be treated in either extreme manner by another kinsman. Wishing to emphasize, for example, the marriage of a male cousin to a woman from a high-status family, a man might stress the brotherly quality of the cousin's relationship to him.

Authority in the Kindred: Male and Female

The stated pre-eminence of male authority in Santarém is a notable feature of domestic relations, and the ideology of patriarchy is quite consistently displayed. The actual position of women, however, is not uniformly subordinate and the out-migration of males (to the gold fields near Itaituba, for example) has led to a devolution of authority.

The head male in a household is granted respect that follows on his being a father. Single males – e.g. unattached brothers of a head of household – by contrast, are in an equivocal position, contributing neither to the reproduction of kindred personnel nor to the apparatus of belief defining 'proper' gender roles in Santarém. Continued attachment to a household/kindred group in such a position of dependency, and failure to perform in acceptably male fashion results in being designated 'weak/feeble' (*fraco*). The reference is to both physical and moral deficiency. A neighbour, for example, who at the age of thirty-five had still not married (and thereby established a separate household within the kindred compound) was dismissed by parents and siblings as someone merely content 'to live with his ducks and chickens'.

The rigidity of forms for proper male comportment within the household is matched by equally rigid but less clearly stated prescriptions for women. A woman is the ruler of the house, a role granted the title *dona de casa*. She allocates tasks and has considerable control over the disposition of labour within the residential kindred. The respect shown the *dona de casa* takes the form of following injunctions to perform tasks crucial for the functioning of the household. Male authority, by contrast, is extraordinary in the sense that it pertains to the behaviour of individuals *vis-à-vis* extra-household contexts; women control matters within.

The identification of male authority with society at large and female with intra-household matters is not exact, but the application of domestic claims outside the domestic context (in hauling a recalcitrant spouse out of a drinking session at a *taberna*, for example) are so fraught as to reveal the extreme unconventionality of such moves.

There is an important sense in which kinship relations are confirmed by co-residency, and in the absence of co-residency, such relations are not seen to be durable. There is more to this than simply the assertion of some kind of complementarity. Rather, there is also the implication that kinship relations are so dependent on non-kinship social relations, that it is impossible to speak of an autonomous 'kinship system.

The average size of households in Santarém according to 1970 census figures (IBGE: 1973) is six, a number confirmed by Wyer's survey (1983). What is disguised in such a reckoning, however, is the change in household size over the course of a year, change which is in large part due to movements of people from the flooded *várzeas* during winter months and other shifts associated with changes in the agricultural cycle.

Another factor which affects assessment of household size is the contingent nature of many urban households, i.e. their being extensions of rural domestic groups, virtual satellites of kindreds whose focal groups are basically tied to non-urban lands. Generalizations about household size are not very useful unless account is taken of the many reasons for Santarenos' moving from place to place, and unless account is taken of the flexibility of the definition of kindred boundaries. For most Santarenos the possibilities for occupancy of a wide range of households are numerous. Kinship operates as belief, in the sense of providing sanction for mobility, and also organizes behaviour within the actual kindred households.

The complexities of embeddedness of function of kinship, economic, political and religious relations are considerable. One feature of this embeddedness which is of particular interest is that concerning adoption, a common practice in Santarém. The matter of adoption illustrates several of the levels at which the 'kinship system' operates as both ideology and practice. As note earlier, *filho/a de criação* is a term whose connotations move across a range of relations between ego and parent, e.g. child, adopted child, fostered child, godchild, domestic servant, and may also complement other formal kin relationships as in the case, for example, of an aunt's rearing her niece. It is also a concept which usefully marks out the ways in which the idiom of kinship is used to legitimate other kinds of status categories. For instance, the most frequently cited reason for giving away a child is financial exigency and the relationship between child-giver and child-receiver is really an additional kind of kinship relation rather than a substitute one. In the case of poverty-motivated fostering, for example, there may well be continuity of contact between natal parent and child, yet articulated through the patron–client relation which obtains between givers and receivers (e.g. the natal mother may live in the patron's house as a domestic). It may also be the case that a *filho/a de criação*, having achieved the social and economic status of his/her adoptive parents, then maintains (in maturity) a patron status with regard to his/her natal parent (in most cases I am familiar with, single parenthood is strongly associated with establishing *filho/a de criação* relations).

Put slightly differently, *filho/a de criação* relations may be viewed as a way of using the kinship idiom for legitimating other kinds of relations (e.g. exploitative economic ones, most obviously). This is not to say that *filho/a de criação* relations are automatically exploitative for there is an important rationale from the point of view of the client or donor parent(s): in the absence of a viable kin network (epitomized in the stereotypical social outcast Zé Ninguem – Joe Nobody, the man-without-a-family), a *filho/a de criação* relationship is a mechanism through which one may be reconstituted within a kin network. The significance of 'network' should be underlined: *filho/a de criação* relations do not merely obtain between patron and client parents, but invest the *filho/a de criação* with kindred identity such that, for example, a *filho/a de criação* may circulate among several kindred households (much as might other members of the kindred) and in the course of an individual's developmental cycle occupy different positions within the kindred division of labour, living as an infant/child, for example, as a companion to senior kin and when of labouring age, shifting to another household to work in agriculture or petty trading.

The phenomenon (or mechanism) of *filho/a de criação* is an interesting limiting case of kindred composition for it demonstrates well the malleability of the kinship idiom in accommodating displaced people, acquiring new labourers in an economy in which direct control of labour via kinship ties is vital for the maintenance of dispersed and diverse production forms (e.g. seasonal moves to different resource bases), and enhancing the personal followings of the more economically powerful kindred segments.

There are few studies of *caboclo* kinship,[2] but it may be speculated that some of the particular features of kindred organization reflect two constraints which are broadly characteristic in Amazonia: peasant dependence on the use of public lands right of control of which is legitimated through continuous occupation, not official title, and the dominance of labour processes in which mechanical substitution is problematic. The low organic composition of capital, coupled with the need to justify control of land through demonstrated use means that kindreds not only pursue their own developmental cycles, but are also the main vehicles through which economic livelihood is secured. Thus if one views

2. See Ayres 1992 for one of the few thorough case studies.

kindreds in generational terms, at any given moment the dynamic of the group is shaped by episodic (seasonal, market-driven, ecological) demands which result in, at times, radically different kin group configurations. The urban household composed of aged kin and a few youthful companions may, during the winter flood (*enchente*) for example, transform into the focal point for a range of petty commodity activities and *terra firme* agricultural, pastoral and extractive ones. Similarly, in the mid-1970s there were many households whose nominal male heads were chronically absent (working in the goldfields upstream on the Tapajós).[3] The point is that through the idiom of kinship, the strategies necessary for social reproduction can be continually rearticulated to accommodate changes in livelihood.

Case Studies of Kindreds

In the following section, several examples of typical kindreds are presented. In discussing these kindreds I wish to show certain features of household composition, intra-kindred division of labour, the sorts of information about kindreds deemed relevant by members of those kindreds, and the nature of movement among kindred households. There is no term in Santarém which defines the kindred object I am describing. The terms *parentes* (kin) may actually correspond to the effective kindred, but the term for house (*casa*) may perform the same function. These accounts of kindreds represent personal kindreds of male egos except in the case of No. 4, which is the kindred of a household group. In this case, the head male of household 1 (H1) is designated 'ego' for purposes of exposition. Kindred members who are co-resident are boxed and their households marked (e.g. H1) (see Figure 5.1).

The first example shows a minimal kin group, one which because it is poor and urban, is relatively isolated within Santareno society. The second example shows a kin group with fairly stable rural and urban bases. The occasionally diminishing fortunes of this group has led to withdrawal to a rural base when necessary, an extension of agricultural and extractive

3. See Wyer (1983), esp. chapter 12, for discussion of female-headed households and female sibling sets.

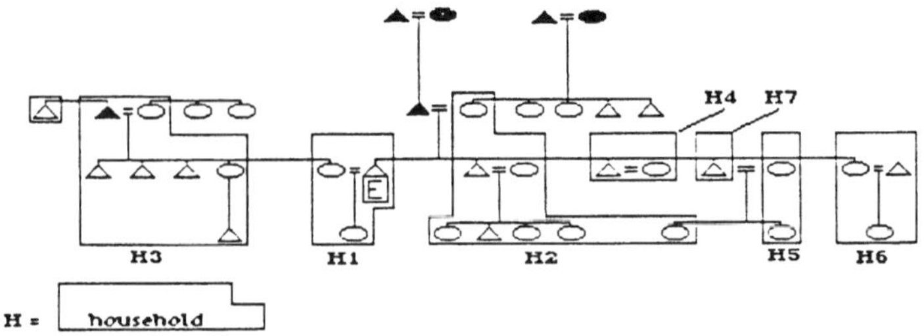

Figure 5.1 Tatu's kindred

activities into the interior for example, an option that the first example did not possess. In the third example, a representative Cearaense immigrant group is shown not only to have a varied economic base typical of many long-settled immigrants, but also a corporate character which is by and large a typical for the region, a corporate character which indicates the assimilation of local productive possibilities within a kinship idiom recognized locally as being foreign. The ability of such a group to maintain such rigid boundaries undoubtedly reflects on the expansion of the local mercantile economy, an expansion which favours those who can depend on credit's being forthcoming from within the extended (in this case, as far as Ceará) kin group. The fourth example illustrates the impact of changing class structue on the composition of a kindred, an example in which the focal household is less dependent on maintaining relations with rural kin and more concerned with redefining kins relations in terms of a fixed economic hierarchy.

Kindred No. 1: Tatu's Kindred

The major feature of No. 1 is its instability over time. When households have aggregated, they have generally done so through reoccupying ego's mother's house. The kindred in this figure is fairly simple by Santareno standards, although it represents considerable geographical diversity in as much as H6 is located in North America, H7 in Rio de Janeiro, and H5 in Manaus, while the remainder of the households are in Santarém or the immediate environs.

Tatu's father was an immigrant from Ceará; his mother is the daughter of immigrants from Ceará. She is the doyennne of a household which is continually used by migratory/peripatetic sons when they are in need of a roof. During a year-long period, for example, three of her four sons (all mature, married and nominally established in own homes) at one time or another were temporarily settled in her house, and a child of the other son, usually found in H2, was occasionally there as well. The only child of hers who did not stay in the house was the daughter, an emigrant to the United States.

Tatu's mother supports herself through remittances from H6 and through a small state pension (her deceased husband having been disabled while employed as a roadbuilder). These remittances permit her to support herself as well as the son's family more or less permanently residing in a household – H2 – within her own compound.

Tatu and his brothers see each other regularly. Tatu, a former novice in the Franciscan Order, is not regularly employed and depends on his brother in H4 – a builder – to find him work. He and his brothers in H2 and H4 have made two major attempts at establishing themselves on agricultural sites in the interior, neither of which was remotely successful.

The fragmentation of this kindred may be attributed to the impoverishment of H2. Tatu's mother is unwilling (unable) to permit her house to be a place of retreat for her children, because the remaining son – in H2 – is a struggling woodworker whose financial demands on his mother are already excessive. Tatu, who moved from H2 during the course of fieldwork, cannot depend on help from H3 because his wife's mother is Protestant, and staying there would entail church attendance, something Tatu is unwilling to permit his wife. He would prefer to join his sister, H1, in the United States. Both Tatu and his sister are former members of religious orders. His sister, in fact, is married to a former Franciscan brother, a US citizen who spent several years in Santarém.

The nominal head of H7, who lives in Manaus, is separated from his wife. Their elder daugher has been sent to live in the H2 household, another cause of the financial strain experienced there, and a contributing factor in the gradual expulsion of Tatu and his siblings from the natal compound.

This kindred is notable for the lack of rural kin. None of Tatu's primary kin is a cultivator in the area of Santarém, and this is a significant financial liability. His wife's family, however, is primarily rural, and his increasing reliance on his wife's father's brother is in direct response to his exclusion from his mother's household. Tatu's wife's natal household, H3, is largely dependent on petty trade in agricultural products brought from her father's brother's small holding (*sítio*) on the plateau. During the course of fieldwork, which began at about the same time that Tatu married, he redefined the specificity of his relations to his wife's father's brothers. These were initially referred to as *parentes* (kin), but as Tatu came to spend more time 'visiting', a euphemism for agricultural labour, he began referring to them by the term his wife used, i.e. *tio* (uncle).

Tatu's relations with his wife's group, then, are complex. On the one hand, religious differences prevent a great deal contact with the urban-dwelling wife's mother and sisters. On the other hand, however, wife's rural uncles provide crucial support. In addition, Tatu occasionally pimps for one of his wife's sisters.

His having been incorporated into his wife's kindred, and seeming distance from his natal group, is in large part due to his natal kindred's small size. His father's death (when Tatu was ten) left his immigrant mother as an urban resident without agriculturally-based relations in the region. Tatu's childhood consisted of such activities as gathering firewood for sale in the city, and his mother's poverty eventually led to his being sent to a Franciscan monastary.[4]

Kindred No. 2: Zé's Kindred

This kindred is similar to No. 1 in terms of its tendency towards atomization. The major difference between the two is that No. 2 has a firm rural base as well as an urban one: Zé's parents and certain of his siblings are almost continuously moving from town to country and back again, participating in agricultural activities as well as those specifically urban such as secondary schooling.

Zé's father is a labourer at the federal government installation at Belterra, the former rubber plantation founded by Henry Ford. Zé's grandfather emigrated from Ceará to Belterra in the late 1920s when this rubber scheme was first conceived. Like many others of his generation, Zé's father has carried on living in Belterra in one of the original workers' houses in spite of the virtual abandonment of the plantation.

4. This may also be an instance of/variation on the *filho de criação* relationship.

One of the ways in which members of this kindred are able to support themselves in the city – where Zé, for example, attends the city's best school as well as working as a clerk in a national firm – is through relying on foodstuffs produced on the *sítio* maintained by the father in Belterra. Zé's mother is employed as a nurse's helper/midwife in Belterra, spending, on a weekly basis, equal time in Belterra and Santarém. This dual-residency basis has continued for over twenty years.

This kindred includes no members of Zé's parents' generation other than the parents themselves. Those ascending kin noted in Figure 5.2 had rarely been seen by Zé, but although father's and mother's kin are equally distant, there is more emphasis placed on relations with the former because of their being Paraense rather than immigrant Cearaense. Hence, even though Zé does not do much more than acknowledge the existence of these people as kin, he knows more about his mother's side, and uses the weight of these small details to assert claims about his ethnic origins. He is often openly abusive of *nordestino* immigrants, mocking their accents (nasal), pencil-line moustaches, and hats (typical features of ridicule) even though by many Santarenos' standards he himself is 'obviously *nordestino*'.

His sisters are, with one exception, unmarried and live in Santarém in order to attend school. During those periods when the mother is in Belterra, Zé is master of the house; he is waited on by his younger sisters, and even prevails over his married sister and her husband (in spite of their seniority). His authority is largely based on his clearly marked trajectory of upward mobility: as a good student in a good school and as an employee of a national firm he has clear promise as the focus of the kindred. When his mother is present in the Santarém house, however, he becomes just another sibling. (A postcard from him some years later indicated a path not foretold during the field period: he had joined the merchant marine and lived in Rio where he had acquired a dog, a flat and a girlfriend, listed in that order.)

As in the case of kindred No. 1, the dependence of married children on the central household(s) of the kindred is desirable from the point of view of all members in as much as this sort of kindred solidarity is socially valued, but this dependence is too expensive to maintain in the city alone (as shown in No. 1); cohesion is achieved by a dual-residence arrangement, the primary advantage being the household's self-provision in terms

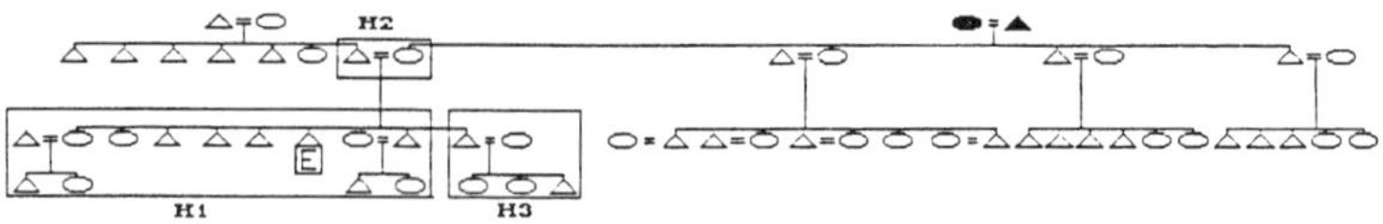

Figure 5.2 Zé's kindred

of basic foodstuffs. The movement of kin within such an arrangement is not only short-cycle – as in the case of Zé's mother – but also longer-cycle as in the case of his brother-in-law's seasonal work on the *sítio*. Such movements are usually described in terms of 'visiting' whether or not the terms of visiting represent exploitation of labour or impositions on hospitality.

Kindred No. 3: Joaquim's Kindred

The kindred represented in Figure 5.3 epitomizes at least one local form of Cearaense kindred solidarity. This kindred is complex both locally and in terms of enduring bonds with geographically remote (Ceará and Maranhão) kin.

The kindred is too complex to permit representing patterns of residency in Figure 5.3. Not only are there frequent changes of rural and urban locations on a weekly basis, for example, but also cousins of Joaquím may move from one house to another in various domestic capacities, as child-minders for instance, or as workers in an uncle's *taberna,* on a daily basis. This fluidity of movement within the kindred contrasts sharply with kindred members' relations with non-kin in that extreme corporateness is emphasised.

Joaquím knows the names, addresses and occupations of all kin of his own, his parents, and his parents' parents' generation as well as many of the names of children of his numerous cousins. Beyond this range, which essentially means non-Santareno kin, there is uncertainty, and the term for cousin is used indiscriminately in relation to penumbral kin, the validity of this term being guaranteed by virtual kindred endogamy.

His primary kin are distinguished from others according to residence, the former being a *casa* (the house) and the rest a *familia* or mere *parentes.* With one exception, every marriage in his

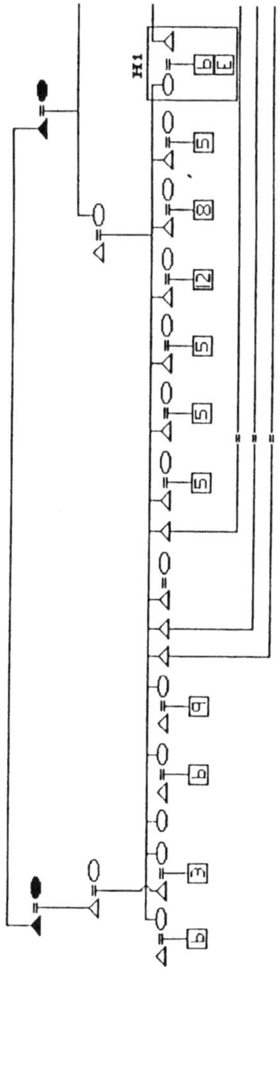

Figure 5.3a Joaquim's kindred

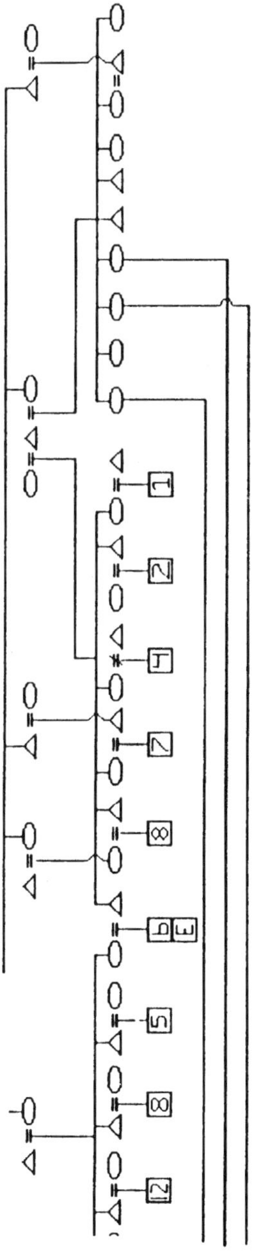

Figure 5.3b

kindred is between kin, the exception being a woman whose marriage with an outsider ended in his attacking her with a cleaver thus confirming the correctness of the proscription on exogamous marriages. This frequently cited example of the dangers of extra-kindred marriages underlines the variable – but commonly considerable – hostility of relations between *caboclo* and *nordestino* Santarenos. Joaquím, however, hopes that he (and his age-mates) will be able to marry out. He trivializes the reasons (all his cousins are 'too ugly'), but a more significant reason is a desire to escape the authority of his father and uncles whose control over his work is considerable: he is on call for members of his parents' generation to perform whatever tasks they set him.

Each of the brothers in Joaquím's parents' generation occupies a separate residence, but living within each household at any time there will be children who are nephews and nieces. Joaquim, for example, lives with his parents along with several siblings and cousins. The reasons for the latter group's presence are various: overcrowding, fighting (a girl is courting a man of whom her father does not approve), performing domestic chores such as cooking and child-minding. This sharing of children-as-labourers occurs outside the domestic setting as well. Joaquím, for example, has worked for uncles as a door-to-door salesman (*ambulante*) in the urban periphery (and beyond), carrying goods strapped to the back of a bicycle, and is on call to help load goods into the *tabernas* and warehouses.

The business operations of this kindred are complex and I am ignorant of all but the gross features. Certainly none of Joaquím's uncles (or his father) was willing to divulge anything about their various enterprises. Local activities consist mainly of trading operations at both the small retail level (*tabernas*) and wholesale level, and involving both locally produced agricultural and extractive produce and imported domestic manufactured goods (e.g. cheap kitchen utensils). While much of the trading is strictly in consumer goods, some of it involves the marketing of produce derived from within the kindred, e.g. beans and *farinha* acquired from *planalto* relations. Manufactured goods are imported via kin in Ceará. The family is also involved in organizing cockfighting.

Joaquím, the eldest in his residential age-set, is responsible for looking after one of his father's stalls (*banco*) in the city's main market area. His efforts to attend school have been thwarted by his father (himself illiterate and, before settling in Santarém, a barber and gold-panner in Jacareacanga, upstream on the Tapajós).

During the period of fieldwork, his father decided that Joaquím was old enough to be set up in his own business. His father paid six months' rent on a stall, and goods were advanced from various uncles (sheath knives, risqué personal effects, e.g. hand mirrors backed with pneumatic bathing beauties, and so on). Joaquím, in other words, was placed at the end of a chain of commercial operations, a position comparable to that occupied by his father. By contrast, his cousins, sons of father's brother who is wholesale merchant, were given positions commensurate with their father's standing within the kindred.

The hierarchy of commercial enterprises within the kindred finds expression in the characterisation of different households within the kindred. Joaquím's household, for example, is retail in character and its function embodies more generalized features of the kindred division of labour. At one point, for example, one of his father's wholesaling brothers befriended a vagabond who had just disembarked from a Manaus-bound boat, and the man was given a job as an ambulatory hammock salesman. Even though the man had been introduced via the wholesaler, he was housed in Joaquím's home, a location appropriate to his retailing role within the kindred, in spite of the fact that his presence was deeply resented by ego and his parents.

Despite the strongly corporate character of the kindred, there is obviously a division of labour within it, and this division seems mainly derived from the pre-Santarém activities of its members. Joaquím's uncles migrated as travelling salesmen, extending a network which now joins geographically dispersed kin, while ego's father's service and petty trade activities forestalled the creation of such a network (except as it is expressed through others in the kindred), and his occupation as petty retailer in Santarém is complemented by petty production of chickens and black pepper.

There is also a division of labour expressed in terms of Joaquím's matriline versus the patriline. Mother's brothers are concentrated in rural commerce (as well as production), their enterprises serving to provide agricultural products for urban wholesalers. Much of their activity consists of forwarding credit to rural producers in exchange for crops, the prices of which are relatively high status placed on Paraense ethnicity. In example No. 3, the great grandparents of ego represent major ethnic/geographical reference points: it was from their homestead in Ceará that the contemporary Santareno kin group set out (staggered over a period of fifteen years).

I preface my remarks on kindred No. 4 with this discussion of ancestors because this kindred embodies a contradiction which is important in terms of the positions of ancestors and senior members within kinship ideology: ancestors and senior members are acknowledged in many ways as prominent members of the kindred in terms of kinship ideology (respect of elders, and so on), but in practice, because of their low socio-economic status, these same members are ignored and, not infrequently, denied status as kin.

These contrary criteria of kin group members' importance – that is, seniority versus class position – increase the flexibility of kindred boundaries, the criteria for inclusion or exclusion varying according to many changing circumstances. In the discussion of this kin group, I use the expression 'core members' in lieu of 'ego'. There are two reasons for introducing this term. One is that in this context, an ego's personal kindred assumes – at times, radically – different forms. The second is that within this group, there is a core household occupied by core kin. Unlike the other examples in which kinship is decentred and, with respect to residence, for example, accommodates the variable circumstances of its members, in this case kinship ideology and residence are coextensive: there is a kin group cynosure which rigidly regulates membership. The core members in this case correspond to the houshold which I treat as central to this kindred. By using the notion of a kindred-as-houshold I hope to show the contradictory features of kinship ideology when confronted with a class structure which denies the importance of the traditional kinship idiom.

A further reason for using the notion core-household-member is to illustrate the way in which the kin group to which H1 is central is redefined as expediency demands. Other constituent households of the kin group, for example, acknowledge kin which H1 does not, although they may interact regularly and in ostensibly kin group settings (e.g. birthday parties). There are also certain ancestors unacknowledged by H1, but treated as such by other households in the kindred. These include

Santarenos descended from US Civil War refugees and segments of a Moroccan Jewish lineage. While the core-members of H1 do not acknowledge these last mentioned as kin, some primary kin of the members of H1 do.

The core household's central position (H1 in Figure 5.4) in defining the overall character of the kindred is based primarily on the economic status of the household head. He is the owner of an accountancy business which includes a notary service (*cartorio*) used by illiterates requiring help with official/bureaucratic correspondence and real estate interests.

H1 consists of an accountant (age 26), his wife (age 24), and two young children (2 and 1 years old). Their house is the central building in a fenced compound which includes H2 and H3. H2 is occupied by wife's mother and sisters and brothers. H3 is occupied by wife's mother's brother. Across the road lives wife's mother's half-sister and her children (her husband spends most of the year near Itaituba as a gold-miner). Another half-sister of wife's mother lives within half a mile of the central compound.

These three half-sisters and another who lives in a distant neighbourhood were, before the marriage of the accountant and his wife, the core members of this kin group. They are first-generation Santarenos, their parents having emigrated from Ceará. In Santareno terms they represent a long-established pattern of *caboclo* development having settled in – and continuing to maintain networks in – both the *várzeas* and *planalto* niches as well as the town/city. This network of connections throughout the region contrasts with that characteristic of the groups described in cases 1–3.

The half-sisters are all owners of the land on which and houses in which they live, and H4 also owns several *sítios*. Within the kin group, the houses/households are always referred to as the houses of the women except for H1, which is acknowledged as jointly owned by the accountant and his wife (in spite of the fact that it is actually owned by the wife's mother).

This female focus is an important feature of the first ascending generation, and it is a focus which has endured (and is indeed characteristic of Santarém as a whole even though H1 is now the kin group cynosure. The husband in H5, for example, has a socio-economic status (bank clerk) almost commensurate with that of the accountant in H1, but his status as householder is subordinate to that of his wife, a member of this land-owning sibling set. This is also the case with the husband in H4. The men in these cases are notably marginal in terms of conferring kinship group identity.

The important role of women in defining the character of the kin group is congruent with part of the kinship ideology, the modified corporate character. It is the women – especially in relation to the half-sibling set – who are active in maintaining connections with dispersed rural kin, and they acknowledge Cearaense antecedents unlike the core-members of H1 for whom the kind of corporateness implied by this Cearaense connection is archaic. The notion of solidarity present among the half-sibling set is extended to include numerous *filhos de criação* within the group. The half-sibling set itself is comprised of illegitimate children and *filhas de criação*: the mother of the women in households H2, H4, H5, and H6 (i.e. the half-sibling set) was never married to either of the two men by whom she had children, nor was the daughter in H2 married. For these women the taint of 'illegitimacy' is of no great consequence. For the core couple in H1, however, this illegitimacy is incommensurate with their (H1's) social position, and geneaological links are casually deniable even in the presence of such kin (e.g. visiting relatives from the *várzeas*).

The contradiction between the ideology kin group solidarity and the attainment and maintenance of new social status (e.g. membership of the Yacht Club) incumbent on an emerging class structure is illustrated well by this kindred. In the marriage between the core members of H1, the husband virtually separated himself from his primary kin group. Aside from his parents – who, when visiting in town, are treated as remote family retainers – members of his pre-marriage personal kindred are unacknowledged. While his assimilation within the urban economy resulted in the sloughing off of kin, his marriage resulted in the congealing of his wife's kindred. Until the time of marriage, his wife's family had occupied a tenuous position in town, most of the half-sibling set surviving as menials and seamstresses. The core wife, in fact, had been given away as a *filha de criação* (to a remotely related Moroccan family), a matter of considerable embarrassment to the girl who now has a socio-economic status equivalent to that of the adoptive family.

Now established as the core household, the accountant and his wife pursue divergent aspects of kinship ideology: sloughing off kin (mainly those of the husband) and reifying the positions of certain kin (the half-sister sibling set). The treatment meted out by the core couple to their kin is necessarily complicated and inconsistent. While the husband's kin are sloughed off as social inferiors, the wife's kin – because they are living close by – are more difficult to reject, even though some are clearly regarded as rustics and menials. Her mother, for example, works as a cleaner, cook, childminder and seamstress both for her daughter and for other households. Her two brothers are similarly engaged in low-status occupations. This subordinate position of close (genealogically and residentially) kin makes it possible for some of the husband's kin to find a place within the urban kindred – for example, a cousin works as a domestic in the household of one of the half-sisters – a position parallel to that cited in example No. 3 when the itinerant hammock salesman was lodged not with his host, but in the kindred household whose status most nearly matched his own.

These varying relationships between inferior and superior kin illustrate the competing pressures of kinship ideology and class/status as urban development presents possibilities for a shift away from the embeddedness of kinship and diffuse economic roles. Just as kindred structure accommodated the demands of pre-*Transamazônica* livelihoods, so is it accessible for changes in class structure incumbent upon the emergence of '*desenvolvimento*'. What is pronounced is the tendency for the overall character of the kindred to be defined in relation to the core household. Even the residential compound which embraces H1, H2, H3 and, to some extent, H4 may be described in relatively unadorned terms as an extended family of some complexity, it is clear that some of the priorities of kinship reckoning – the importance of seniority, for example – are suppressed in favour of a different set of exigencies, in this case recognition of a socio-economic status which prescribes how and when kinship relations *per se* will be important and when they will not be. The core-members of H1 in effect employ most of their kin as servants (or maintain them as retainers. On occasions when kinship ideology is to be emphatically demonstrated – birthday parties, for example – not only are generally neglected kin conscripted as spear carriers, but they are granted the kind of respect due them according to the nominal features of kinship ideology, proper terms of address are employed, senior women are waited on and so on; when, by contrast, the core-members are entertaining a *compadre*, a fictive kinsman of superior or equivalent social status, the same women are treated as domestics. This behaviour is most dramatically presented in high-status public gatherings, at the Yacht Club, for example, when the aspirant members of the urban elite compete with their social superiors (who invariably have numerous domestic retainers in tow) by conscripting kin for the task.

In examples 1–3, the breadth of kin groups (when maintainable) reflects in general form the exigencies of economic life in the *município*: for most urban Santarenos the maintenace of kin networks that extend into the countryside is important for subsidizing life in the city. The possibilities for urban employment are limited, and the fierce competition among petty commodity producers tends, as Kahn (1980) has illustrated in different setting, to produce a lack of differentiation among such producers, comparative advantage being conferred on those whose auto-subsistence possibilities are greater. Thus, for most Santarenos who have migrated to the city, migration is not an end in itself, but represents a strategy that only makes sense when combined with complementary efforts to ensure a wide basis for survival in both country and city. The group described in example 4 departs from this model in that the core household is more or less fully absorbed in a formal sector, thus the functional rationale of the extended kin network has been transformed: the network is useful to the degree that prestige may be derived from it. While there are clear strategic features in this kind of manipulation of kinship links, they are of a different sort from those apparent in the other examples. For most Santarenos kinship networks confer residential possibilities, which themselves imply economic possibilities. For the group decribed in example 4, it is the core household itself which, if it were to be available as coextensive residential and economic possibility, would be overwhelmed, as it were, by kinship.

The suggestion put forward is not that simple economic considerations lead automatically to the sloughing off of kin. On the contrary, the emphasis is placed on the problems engendered by the lack of congruence between domestic group organization and aspects of kinship ideology. In pre-expansion Santarém (i.e. pre-1970), class structure was defined in terms of a relatively small, urban, mercantile fraction and a large rural sector for which kinship ideology matched the varying requirements of a fluid peasantry which relied on a broad definition of effective kinship links. In terms of this 'traditional' class structure, the position of H1 is dysfunctional. According to kinship ideology, H1 should include (or be capable and willing to do so) a wide range of kin, but the terms under which – in traditional circumstances – a household absorbed kin according to seasonal (and other) shifts in the locus of production were based on an equivalence of class position of members of the kin group. With the differentiation of the local economy, this rough equivalence no longer exists because the demands placed on kindred organization are now derived less from shifts within local society than they are responses to a reordering of the position of Amazonia on a national and global scale.[5]

Kindred Composition and the Transformation of 'Traditional' Society

In this chapter I have tried to show that kinship relations, while they may, not unexpectedly, be said to have embedded in them other sorts of social relations, are also transformed by the effects of extra-Amazonian influences. In particular, kinship ideology is not merely responsive to changes in the composition of kindreds (or kin groups more generally), but nor is kinship ideology merely a product of kinship practice. It serves as well to mediate changes initially wrought at other levels, embodying conflicts engendered by changes in the productive base. As the local economy is transformed from without, the local rationale of kinship organization – which, as I have argued, is best seen in terms of establishing a broad base for a range of petty commodity forms – is undercut. Where before a loose notion of kin group, *parentes, a familia, meus primos, o gente,* reflected the diverse bases of peasant production, recent economic transformations – the increasing commoditization of local production in the most general sense – undercuts the tenability

5. The accountant, for example, is now an agent for a multinational mining firm.

of such a notion. In its place appears a more strictly defined notion of the kinship universe, one which, however, seems unlikely to supersede in straightforward manner the older one. The reason for this is analogous to that offered in explanations for the unlikelihood of the disappearance of the peasantry in Lower Amazonia: just as the new forms of productive activity in Amzonia displace peasant forms without absorbing the labour thus dispossessed, leading rather to further migration, the proliferation of small-scale peasant, and petty commodity units of production, so is the nucleated kin group likely to be confined to those niches within the enclave economy where it is supportable.

Figure 5.5 shows the distribution of households in one of the older neighbourhoods in Santarém. Without too much qualification it could be said to represent a typical neighbourhood the activities of whose members reflect the diversity of urban livelihoods as well as dynamic links with co-respondent rural households (members of which are frequently to be found in the city).

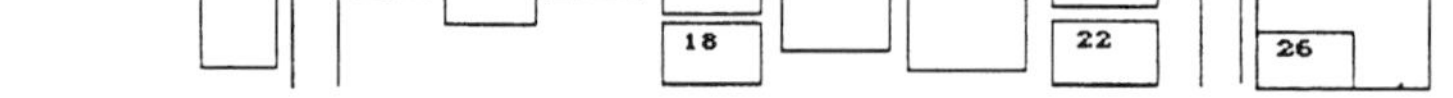

Figure 5.5 Neighbourhood distribution of petty commodity producers

1. A household nominally headed by a woman who identifies herself as Paraense. Her parents were immigrants from Ceará. She has three children (1–8 years of age). Her husband is construction worker at a remote site (Curua-Una) and he visits twice a month. Also living in the house is a single woman – a *filha de criação*, who serves as a domestic – and her child. Also living in the house occasionally is a child of the construction worker by another woman (who lives

close by, but not in one of the households depicted). This child often looks after her half-siblings. In the garden, pigs are raised for household consumption. In addition to her husband's wages, the woman has an income from dress-making and giving injections.

2. A single male, brother of the headwoman in 1. He raises ducks and chickens in his quintal and does odd jobs for 4.
3. Half-sister of headwoman in 1 [same mother]. She works as a dress-maker and has two sons, one a clerk, the other a schoolboy. The latter does odd-jobs/domestic chores for 4. Her daughter is married to the household head of 4.
4. Head of household is a Paraense businessman born in a *várzea* settlement where his parents still live. His elder brother is a *várzea* agriculturalist who also has a small *taberna* in this neighbourhood where he trades in *várzea* produce. The household head's sister lives in 4 while attending night school, but otherwise lives on the *várzeas*. During the day, she stays in the house working as domestic (cooking, cleaning, and looking after her brother's two small children).
5. A single woman with three young children. She works as a cook in a humble hotel/pension.

6–8. All three houses are occupied by young couples with children.

9. An old man whose wife has abandoned him and moved to the countryside. *Quintal* larger than most and has room for horses and goats. Intermittent visitors include two grown sons (*várzeas*). The house is the most rustic in the neighbourhood, made of wattle and daub and with a thatched roof. No electricity.
10. Nothing known. Occupied by ± five persons.
11. This building is an abandoned schoolhouse, usually occupied by three or four families of squatters few of which stay more than a couple of months.
12. A household headed by an old woman and occupied by several of her married sons and daughters. She is a laundress.
13. A house occupied by an old couple and their grandchildren. They sell ice.
14. A large household headed by a middle-aged woman who gives manicures. Two married daughters and their

husbands – both of whom are taxi drivers – and small children live there as well.

15. A *taberna* owned by Cearaense family (father, mother, mature son, two young daughters) who live in another neighbourhood; children work in the *taberna* which is affiliated with another family-owned *taberna* in the *Centro*.
16. Cearaense-owned *taberna* run by non-resident.
17. Warehouse of stationers in *Centro*.
18. Foreign couple.
19. Household of couple from Santa Caterina who came to city as part of labour force of army battallion of engineers; head male is a truck mechanic as is one of the sons; the other son and daughter are secondary school students.
20. Funeral parlour/casket maker; non-resident.
21. A house occupied by a group of secondary school students from distant *várzea* communities; their mothers take it in turn to live in the house as chaperones/domestics.
22. Paraense household consisting of husband, wife, two teen-aged sons, two young daughters, and floating population of *várzea* kin. Live on sales of petty produce: charcoal, shoats, fruit juices, animals (pets), bananas, ducks, chickens, herbs.
23. Pensioned male (work-related accident), his wife and three children. Like 22, sellers of diverse petty produce.
24. Widowed middle-aged woman, four young children. Small garden plot, chickens.
25. Single woman, two small daughters.
26. Non-resident refigerator repairman/ice seller.
27. Large Paraense *taberna*, resident owners (man, wife, four school-age children and infant). Numerous short-term visiting kin from *várzeas*.
28. Aged couple and domestic (with a son). They are supported by non-resident businessman son.
29. *Taberna*; only occasionally open.
30. A woman from the neighbourhood who sells *tacaca* most afternoons.

What these notes may convey is the contingency of 'urban' households. While the composition of some (multi-generation, diverse livelihoods, combination of residential/production space) may fit certain stereotypes of 'peasants in cities', in fact the urban household may be better viewed as a subset of a larger residential and spatially non-contiguous residential structure. The demographic composition of urban households fluctuates most dramatically following the *enchente* and at times of *várzea* and *terra firme* harvest and with increasing competition for *várzea* (*vis-à-vis* large-scale cattle breeders in search of good seasonal pasture) and *terra firme* land (swidden agriculture) urban residences have a fixity threatened in the countryside. While economic expansion in the city has created certain opportunities, these tend to be located in the informal sector and urban residential groups' composition reflects the contingent character of urban employment.

The pressure on land is a direct result of *Transamazônica* (increased in-migration of colonists whose needs were not met by official settlement programmes) and the cattle-ranching incentives which followed. While it would be hard to romanticize rural modes of livelihood in the pre-*Transamazônica* period, it is equally difficult to celebrate the consequences of gross forest conversion for cattle ranches or the effects of *várzea* cattle grazing on *caboclo* livelihoods and the city becomes a collection point for the residual effects of a process of social change in which the second wave of 'original inhabitants' is not so much developed as displaced. Thus the differentiation resulting from the impact of *Transamazônica* is both articulated through the idiom of kinship and serves to dissolve it, for some Santarenos, at the same time.

Chapter 6

Petty Commodity Production and Formal Subsumption: *Caboclo* Peasants

The metaphor of stagnation which has come to be widely employed in characterizing Amazonian peasant economy obscures the fact that peasant societies in Amazonia, while no doubt less than dynamic, have endured. If they are in fact 'stagnant', then this is true only in relation to conventional economic indicators which are not relevant in the local context. Much recent work on petty commodity production, for example, draws attention to the ways in which the structure of the non-valorized spheres of peasant production are both crucial for commodity production and yet are disguised when emphasis is placed on the ways in which peasant production generally is articulated with the larger market economy (cf. Kahn 1980).

While much debate has focused on characterizing peasant versus petty commodity production (see for example Bernstein 1977; Ennew, Hirst and Tribe 1977; Friedmann 1980; *Labour. Capital and Society* 19:1, April 1986; Reinhardt 1988 for review), a debate growing out of a disenchantment with 'a reigning teleology [which] suggested the transitory nature of small enterprises, of household or family organization of work, and of the combination of property and labour in a single person or domestic group' (Friedmann 1986: 117), has, according to Friedmann (1986: 125–6), resulted in two complementary lines of inquiry in relation to petty commodity production, one concerned with the increasing subordination of peasant/petty commodity producers (macro-level), the other concerned with the internal structure of petty commodity households/domestic units (micro-level).

In looking at petty commodity production, then, it is necessary to distinguish between the nature of commodity relations as they mediate the 'peasant economy' and the larger economic sphere, and the impact of commodity relations as they shape and are shaped by features of domestic/household units.

In Kahn's analysis, to take one of the most thorough accounts of a 'petty commodity economy', the dynamic features of petty commodity producers' articulation with the larger economy are based on three sets of constraints: the variable degree of self-exploitation (or self-subsidy) in terms of rice cultivation ('subsistence' production); the variable nature of external market demand for commodities; and the competition among petty commodity producers themselves, competition which, among other things, tends to depress prices. In his account, the structure of petty commodity production exhibits a fundamental contradiction: the greater the output of petty commodity producers (the more they appear to become 'capitalist') the more dependent they become on non-capitalist forms (peasant production of rice), and as a consequence, the more value their non-food commodities embody, value lost through unequal exchange in the market. Although Kahn has drawn attention to the way in which the structure of Minangkabau society has been transformed by the particular features of Dutch colonialism, it would appear that rice cultivation on ancestral lands constitutes an enduring feature of Minangkabau, a direct connection with the pre-capitalist form. I mention this only to highlight the contrast with the Santareno peasantry, for while I wish to elaborate an argument which depends on the examination of the relationship between petty commodity production and non-valorized economic structures, the character of Santareno society as a neo-colonial social formation differs markedly from that described by Kahn for Minangkabau, and this difference has important implications for characterizing the relationship between local society and the larger system within which it is implicated.

As noted earlier, the emergence of peasantries in Lower Amazonia did not depend on a forced transformation of indigenous societies (unlike, for example, in the Andes where tributary relations between local units and the state survived, in some significant measure, the usurpation of central powers by European conquerors). The Santareno peasantry emerged from the wreckage of colonial efforts to extract wealth from the region; the peasantry was, in short, constituted by default. The major implication of this in terms of a discussion of the genesis and transformation of petty commodity production is that the relationship between a subsistence sector and a petty commodity sector has no correlates in terms of 'indigenous versus colonial'. The 'indigenous' no longer exists. The indigene has been swept aside, and in its place, European colonialism has provided not only a graphic record of carnage, but has also provided an image of itself which disguises the rapacity with which the New World was assaulted. It is in this sense that Geoffrey Kay (1975) has argued that capitalism underdeveloped not only through the extraction of surplus, but also through failing to exploit the periphery sufficiently.

In short, what is required in the analysis of the Santareno peasantry (and, I would think, for Amazonian peasantries generally) is a shift of emphasis in the discussion of petty commodity production: the preconditions for petty commodity production in Amazonia did not lie in pre-capitalist forms, rather they lay in transformations effected in Amazonia by capitalist penetration itself. By this reading, petty commodity production is less a transitional form that it is a suspended form, the relic of a particular moment of capitalist transformation.

In what follows, I concentrate on three quite distinct petty commodity complexes, what I shall call the 'traditional' *caboclo*, the 'immigrant' *nordestino* and the 'urban' Japanese. Despite the fact that each complex is identified as an 'ethnic' type, ethnicity is not really at issue, indeed most *caboclos* are descendants of earlier *nordestino* immigrants. Similarly, distinctively 'Japanese' practices (market gardening, for example) have been both widely adopted by (and adapted from, in some ways) *caboclos* and *nordestinos*. The ethnic glosses are used locally and although such usage may have significance in some kinds of local discourse – when, for example, some *caboclos* use the terms 'Protestant' and 'Cearaense' interchangeably – for my purposes the terms are merely a shorthand for three quite different tendencies among the smallholder peasantry.

My purpose is not so much to provide an ethnographic account of the three types than it is to identify those distinctive features which are relevant for a discussion of the possibilities for the social reproduction of a generalized peasantry in the context of Amazonian modernization. While admitting that this effort requires a degree of idealization, the point is less to provide a documentary account of three different peasant modes – for which an adequate if hardly exhaustive literature exists – than it is to illustrate some of what has been lost in the cyncial 'conquest of the tropics'. Thus, the discussion of these petty commodity complexes lies midway between two well-established lines of research on Amazonian peasantries: the community-based case study (Wagley, Moran, Gentil, Staniford) and regional overviews (Hecht and Cockburn, Bunker, Branford and Glock).

In very short form, the *caboclo* complex represents an extensive form of resource use embracing agriculture, terrestrial and riverine extraction, small-scale mercantile activities, wage labour and the production of goods and services in the urban setting (e.g. dressmaking, charcoal manufacture). The *nordestino* complex is less extensive and is focused on *terra firme* agriculture. The Japanese complex is focused on urban vegetable gardens.

The *Caboclo* Complex

From the point of view of Santarenos whose residence pre-dates the building of the *Transamazônica* road network, the concentration of agriculture on the plateau – the major focus of post-*Transamaôznica* peasants – represents a distortion of the complex of traditional rural production. For *caboclos, terra firme* agriculture is merely part of a repertoire, thus it is important to establish at the outset that *caboclo* production represents a far more elaborate conception of 'peasant' production. Land may well be a significant object of labour for *caboclos*, but it is not central. Rather, *caboclo* production is characterized by a systematic shifting among various sites of labour and entails widely different forms of the social mobilization of labour, from collective kin-based to individual sale of labour-power.

The decline of the Santareno economy in the decades following the collapse of the rubber industry – the opening phase of the period of so-called 'stagnation' – was not as precipitous as that of Manaus. In part this is explained by Santarém's having been overshadowed in commercial terms by

Manaus and by its never having become more than a relatively minor entrepot for a region (the margins of the Tapajós River) which, while exploited for rubber, was not particularly outstanding. It is from the period of rubber decline that what I shall refer to as the *caboclo* complex emerges. Central to the *caboclo* complex are the flood plains (*várzeas*), although the cultivation of *terra firme* is an important seasonal feature of the *caboclo* cycle. The important vrzeas are mainly those on the margins of the Amazon River itself, the margins of the Tapajós being relatively infertile. The *várzea* population is highly dispersed by virtue of the fact that cultivation and habitation are possible only on relatively narrow margins of the river's canals.

Várzea communities vary in terms of size and complexity, but they are similar in terms of their dependence on seasonally variable resources, most notably soils replenished by deposits following the annual flood of the river and fish whose dispersal in times of flood results in much lower yields. While the replenishment of *várzea* occurs annually and results in significantly higher levels of agricultural output than can be obtained on *terra firme* swiddens (see Eden 1989; Barrow 1990 for recent reviews of increased *várzea* fertility), the flooding is unpredictable both in terms of onset and retreat and in terms of height. This unpredictability is an important constraint on sedentary agricultural production (as well as continuous human habitation).

Land actually accessible for cultivation is limited to built-up sections adjacent to main channels. Interior land, frequently *igapó* or swampland, is insufficiently drained to permit exensive agricultural use. The speed of the water's rise means that too extensively cultivated a given piece of land may not be harvestable given the simultaneous high demands on labour for all producers in the same area. Beyond that, for those cultivating jute, it is preferable that the jute be harvested after a period of submersion (which improves the quality of the fibre). Such harvesting is hard work and dangerous owing to the threat of collapsing river banks (*terra caida*) and various aquatic predators.

Thus, the flood (*enchente*) is a mixed blessing. While it permits sedentary cultivation (within limits to be discussed below), it is not susceptible to significant technical control. It presents a strict ceiling on production, but a ceiling which changes from year to year based on climatological factors outside the immediate environment.

While *várzea* land presents technical problems which have yet to be overcome (although various water control measures and experiments are frequently alluded to in the literature), the *várzeas* also present a major obstacle to agricultural development policies: given that the contours of river channels change – often significantly – with each flood, *várzea* land represents a form of unfixed property, thus its value as collateral for bank loans, for instance, is dubious. The valorization of land which has been one of the most important features of post-*Transamazônica* development thereby has a special meaning for *várzea* agriculturalists: they require relatively little land to achieve a reasonable standard of living, yet the only way they can ensure the viability of their 'family farms' is to have access, in principle, to far more than they actually need at any given time. Commercial cattle-breeders, by contrast, operate on a scale which can accommodate annual changes in topography, and in addition, cattle/buffalo can exploit *várzea* pastures which are unsuitable for agriculturalists. Thus, *ribeirinho*s can tolerate environmental constraints only if they can use the *várzeas* in concert with other forms of land use and petty commodity production.

Várzea production, then, is something of a misnomer. While certain large-scale forms of production – pastoralism, for instance – are tolerated, for most *ribeirinhos*, the *várzeas* are only one site within an annual production cycle. Ideally, a *várzea* household will also have access to terra firme where extraction of forest-products, cultivation of perennials and cultivation of non-*várzea* foodcrops can be pursued, as well as access to an urban household where, for example, children can live while attending school and where women and elders can retreat during the height of the flood.

The comparative advantage of *várzea* production from the point of view of high-yield, sedentary agriculture entails high mobility (viewed over an annual production cycle), and also requires the inclusion of many other forms of petty commodity production. Significant among these are cattle-breeding (for milk and beef), craft manufacture (baskets, canoes) and fishing. There are varying degrees of marketability of these products and a noteworthy feature of many *várzea* communities/settlements is the central role of *tabernas* operating on *aviamento* terms, that is as providers of credit and goods in exchange for guaranteed delivery of particular crops. Despite the frequently central role of petty traders (whose standards of living are hardly greater than those of their clients), there is a great variety of ways in which *ribeirinhos* are integrated in regional markets. These range from individuals' carrying goods to urban beach markets in canoes to complex family-based networks which include fractions of kin continuously occupying *várzea*, urban and *terra firme* sites. There is regular boat traffic linking *várzea* settlements with Santarém and other long-standing trading centres.

There are a number of issues pertaining to the *caboclo* complex which have special relevance in the context of current debates about Amazonian development. The first of these is that the *caboclo* complex represents not merely a crude accommodation to rigid environmental features, but represents a dynamic system which accommodates not only environmental features, but the wreckage of a colonial system abandoned after the collapse of the rubber boom. In the post-rubber period, *caboclo* society expanded its repertoire of forms, shifting from monocultural export extractivism to broad-based production which included a variety of food and non-food crops as well as various forms of petty extractivism. The development of a highly adapted pastoralism (e.g. involving the use of corral islands during the flood, *marombas*) and the addition of new crops (e.g. jute) are but two ways in which the 'stagnancy' depiction is contradicted. Significantly, these forms of *caboclo* expansion were achieved without significant deforestation or other forms of environmental degradation familiar in the recent period of 'planned development'.

Second, this expansion of the *caboclo* repertoire represents a model of resource-use based on public access to public land, i.e. it is a significant precursor to models of extractive reserves which are at the forefront of current attempts to legitimate forest and river peoples' claims to public resources, and as such, the *caboclo* complex deserves closer attention as a well-established system for achieving an environmentally suitable mode of human appropriation of Amazonian natural resources. It is, in short, a *de facto ejidoisation*[1] long preceding the *de jure*

1. A neologism referring to the agrarian reform programme initiated after the Mexican revolution. *Ejidos* are grants of (in principle) non-partible communal property. Extractive reserves in Amazonia bear a similarity (as do their immediate antecedents, Indian reserves), but the permeability of the latters' boundaries is a salutary reminder of the Brazilian government's notorious failure to enforce statutes (cf. the case of the Yanomami).

ejidoisation now on the formal political agenda (e.g. extractive reserves).

Petty Commodity Production: The 'Immigrant' *Nordestino* Complex

From the point of view of recent *nordestino* immigrants, *terra firme* agriculture is the focal activity. For many *nordestinos* in Santarem, riverine activities (*várzea* agriculture, fishing) are 'typically' backward – *caboclo* – and *terra firme* agriculture not only represents 'proper' smallholder activity, but is also viewed as a first step into expanded forms of *terra firme* use with a cattle ranch or large estate of perennials such as black pepper as the ultimate goal.

Until the construction of the *Transamazônica* highway network, significant Santareno penetration of *terra firme* forest was limited. There were numerous small *sítios* or *roças* for the cultivation of foodstuffs and as collection sites for extractive activities, but they were mainly confined to the margins of the plateau, immediately above the city and along the eastern bank of the Tapajós towards Alter do Chão.

The most important of the plateau communities is Mojui dos Campos, since the late 1950s known as a 'Cearaense' town. Effectively isolated from Santarém by poor transport, Mojui became the focus of smallholder *nordestino* immigration once the plateau was made accessible by BR-164 and the road connecting Santarém to the hydroelectric project at Curua-Una. What is distinctive about Mojui dos Campos – for present purposes an archetypal *terra firme* community – is its near-total dependence on agriculture. Adjacent areas below the escarpment rim, Diamantino for example, have long been sites of *caboclo roças* which also functioned as collection sites for extractive activities, but on the plateau, the rate at which forest has been felled for swiddens has meant that the extractivist resource base has been severely reduced. The road margins have *capoeira* cover and one must walk many hours into the interior to find climax forest. Because of the relatively long period of smallholder colonization, succession forest represents various stages of maturity, but the landscape is, generally speaking, denuded. While gross conversion of forest was, in the late 1970s, largely the result of attempts to lay claim to land through 'improving' it, by the late 1980s, numerous sawmills had encouraged the rate of predation.

The change in the status of the forest (from extractive resource to agricultural land) has been very poorly documented. Since Santarém was not a major area directly affected by *Transamazônica* settler recolonization schemes, the provisions for rationalization of land claims (which, even in the target areas, were inadequate) failed to do much more than confuse Santareno claimants. Many recent plateau colonists were in possession of receipts for their land claims (and many mistakenly believed that such receipts conferred title), but given that the influx of *Transamazônica* drop-outs and spontaneous colonists found themselves moving into an already established community, their relationship to land was most often expressed in share-tenant terms.

In 1940 there were only 24 families (114 people) in Mojui. In 1950 the population had grown by only 12. In a brief description of the town published in a Church document, cotton was noted as the settlement's main crop. This was supplanted in the late 1920s by rice, presumably in response to demand from the Belterra rubber plantation. In the mid-1970s, food crops prevailed (rice, beans, maize, manioc) although *malva* was an important non-food crop.

Generally speaking, plateau agriculture may be characterized as predatory: with the exhaustion of swiddens, new land has to be brought into production by felling intact forest or recultivating *capoeira*. With the influx of large numbers of post-*Transamazônica* settlers, the rate at which new land was brought into cultivation had increased rapidly and given both the exhaustion of soils and higher population density, the distance from town to field had increased dramatically. Many cultivators had to walk an hour or more to get to their *roças*. The marginality of such producers was marked, and on a return visit in 1988, I met few people whom I had known a decade before.

This marginality is not only the result of predation, but also due to the fact that in the early 1950s, Mojui had been 'settled' by several large Cearaense families ('the clans') who recruited new settlers from within kin networks in Ceará. Such recruits/kinsfolk worked land on share-cropper/tenant arrangements and constituted a resilient land-controlling group firmly in place when post-*Transamazônica* settlers began to arrive in the early 1970s. The possibilities for establishing oneself as an independent smallholder were thus severely curtailed. While longer established residents controlled land adjacent to the main settlement and newcomers were forced to the margins, the latter depended heavily on the mercantile facilities provided by the former. Two examples of outcome of the encounter between these two waves of immigrants are provided by the *taberna* system and the *casa de farinha*.

For second wave, marginal producers, the costs of transport of crops to the Santareno market are prohibitive and there exist in Mojui a number of *tabernas* which purchase crops and sell goods on credit. Such *tabernas* supply wholesalers and retailers in the city – not infrequently kinfolk – and provide direct producers with overpriced consumer goods. There is nothing unusual in this, but what is of importance is the striking contrast provided by *caboclo* producers: while *terra firme* producers sell (or consume directly) what they produce, and buy what they need through the same medium they use for selling (*tabernas*), *caboclos* do not; rather *caboclos* depend not only a wider range of use-values for direct consumption, but they also have wider access to the market by virtue of the fact that they (may) produce a wider variety of exchange-values.

The role of the *casa de farinha* shows a similar restriction on *terra firme* smallholders' freedom of movement. *Farinha* is a major (if not the major) food item in Mojui, a reflection on the relative poverty of the population. Because much of the cultivation of residential manioc plots and the bulk of processing is undertaken by women and children, male cultivation of other crops is to a significant degree subsidized within the narrowly defined domestic sphere. Much of this labour, in addition, is collective, with women working in groups peeling, soaking and shredding tubers. While many *caboclos* process manioc themselves (using either a *tipití* or press and home oven), in Mojui, the processing of manioc usually benefits from some mechanization and apparatus capable of dealing with relatively large quantities at one time, and the cost of using such facilities is high. The main *casa de farinha* in Mojui consists of a fenced and roofed enclosure adjacent to the stream (for easy access for soaking the tubers). The facilities include a petrol-engine driven shredder, a large press and two large (1.5 m diameter) griddles. Although there is a supervisor, almost all the work is done by the direct producers.

After the tubers have soaked for three days or so the mass is wrapped in burlap and leaves and put into the press. With the prussic acid removed, the mass is shredded and then filtered through a fibre mesh to remove and break up large lumps. Finally, the mass is thrown onto the heated griddles and stirred with paddles until transformed into dry meal. Payment takes place at the end of the cycle and consists of payment in kind of 4 litres per *lata* (18 litres), i.e. 22 per cent. Such a *casa* may process as much as 300 kg/day. The important points here are that *farinha* is central to the diet; it is mainly processed by women and children; the volume required for normal consumption entails the use of facilities of scale which must be hired; the entrepreneur extracts a significant, marketable surplus.

What is suggested by these examples is the highly restricted terms according to which *terra firme* smallholders gain access to the market. An analogy is suggested by developments in the latter stages of the rubber period: during the height of the boom, direct producers – like contemporary *terra firme* agriculturalists in Mojui – were reproduced via exchanges administered through a single agency – the rubber trader who purchased *borracha* in exchange for credit realized as direct consumables. As the rubber trade declined, however, tappers could no longer be reproduced through the market because the price of rubber was no longer high enough to sustain the credit levels required to supply tappers with basic consumables. The solution put forward, although impossible to act upon, was that tappers be encouraged to divert some of their labour-time to agriculture and non-rubber extraction, i.e. that they be forced to reproduce themselves partially outside the rubber market.

This is, of course, precisely what the *caboclo* complex represents: a proliferation of petty commodity forms to compensate for the collapse of the monocultural market. Contemporary *terra firme* colonists are in a position structurally similar to that of rubber-tappers before the collapse (with the important difference that they are supplying a soft market).

Formal Subsumption in the Absence of Real Subsumption

The *caboclo* and *nordestino* complexes may be said to represent two different examples of formal subsumption. While much discussion of contemporary peasantries/petty commodity producers has made use of Marx's distinction between formal and real subsumption (1954 I: 478),[2] the major effort has been to understand exactly what is the nature of the transition from formal to real subsumption and how one might set about characterizing what seems to be a prevalent phenomenon: the suspension of the transition. Stoler (1986), for example (among others), has drawn attention to the fact that much as formal subsumption may be 'functional' to capitalism in as much as it reduces costs of labour, the forms of economic independence implied in the forms of petty commodity production formally subsumed may 'be grounded in popular resistance to capitalism itself' (1986: 559). In Stoler's discussion – and in most of the corroborative literature she refers to – the circumstances in which formal subsumption is considered include proximate examples of real subsumption, e.g. the ethnographic domain of Northern Sumatra provides estate production articulated with petty commodity, formally subsumed forms of production. What is lacking in Amazonia, for comparative purposes, is precisely this historically realized possibility for transition. Amazonian petty commodity producers are not formally subsumed rather than being really subsumed: the latter possibility is not a realistic alternative to formal subsumption. Thus, we are presented not with a condition of formal subsumption which can be assessed in relationship to a 'real' alternative, but with a condition of formal subsumption which is relatively autonomous. If there is a strong analogue for real subsumption, it is represented – as in the case of *terra firme* agriculturalists – in the mercantile network, hardly a strong candidate for real subsumption given that it represents accumulation of absolute rather than relative surplus value.

What is proposed here is that the various forms of formal subsumption presented in Amazonia (of which the *caboclo* and *nordestino* complexes are two) fit well with Stoler's depiction of formal subsumption as embodying the contradictory character of capitalist development, but they represent responses to

2. Real subsumption refers to circumstances in which labour exchanges directly with capital (purchase of labour-power in exchange for a wage) while formal subsumption refers to circumstances in which the rationale of production is to create exchange-values (commodities), but outside of the direct supervision of the purchaser of such values. There are numerous euphemisms for formal subsumption: informal sector, petty commodity production, casual labour, etc.

different moments of capital penetration: the *caboclo* complex represents a relatively mature distancing of direct producers from the control of capital, a distancing achieved in the aftermath of the rubber period when, for all practical purposes, capital was engaged elsewhere, and a distancing which has achieved a degree of political force as exemplified in the Forest Peoples' Alliance and the forcing of extractive reserves onto the regional and national political agendas. The *nordestino* complex's formal subsumption, by contrast, represents a different moment of capital penetration of the region, that associated with *Transamazônica*. In this case, formal subsumption is the indirect effect of a set of policies in which the goals of development are not representative of mature capital – i.e. accumulation via relative surplus value – but speculative and mercantile capital. In brief, the goals of contemporary Amazonian development are the valorization of land and the extraction of raw materials. It is perhaps incautious to include extraction/extractivism within the terms of mercantile capitalism, but I think a strong argument can be made: despite the impressive scale of investment in 'Amazonian development', most of this investment is not in production *per se*, i.e. capital exchanged against labour, but in apparatus which ensures that extractive produce can be bought cheap and sold dear. Recent Amazonian investment has been notoriously unabsorptive of labour despite its 'hi-tech, industrial' appearance.

These circumstances, then, require a modification of the concept of formal subsumption, and the *caboclo* and *nordestino* complexes require separate treatment because they represent two quite different historical examples. The *caboclo* complex is formally subsumed not in relation to real subsumption, but in relation to the dominant form of capital penetration in Amazonia: mercantile capital. During the rubber epoch, the most potent predecessor of the *caboclo* complex, Amazonian commodity production was a classic example of petty commodity production dominated by merchant capital: the function of merchant capital was to buy cheap and sell dear. It was agnostic with regard to the relations of production under which commodities (rubber) were produced, and as the historical record shows these included a diverse set of servile forms. What has perhaps prevented wider recognition of the distinctive relationship between merchant capital and petty commodity production in Amazonia is the fact that the monopoly which traders had on rubber did not require the kind of political/military apparatus required elsewhere when European empires attempted to maintain control over tropical preciosities (cf. Indonesia), although there is no shortage of examples of non-economic forms of coercion (cf. Taussig 1987). Rather, monopoly conditions were given naturally: *hevea brasiliensis* did not grow anywhere else in abundance. Thus, unlike conflicts focused around sugar, *cacao* and coffee, for instance, in other colonial/Imperial domains, the rubber monopoly could be ensured by what seemed to be merely 'economic' means. Put another way, merchant capital's control over Amazonia during the period of the rubber boom appears severely 'underdetermined'. In addition, and contributing to the economistic gloss of merchant capital in Amazonia, is the fact that little could be done technically to improve output or productivity, thus merchant capital was not challenged by its successor capital, industrial. For a number of environmental reasons, Amazonian rubber production could not be (and continues to resist being) rationalized on rubber estates. (See Dean (1987) for extensive discussion.) Hence, the only way to increase output was to increase the number of tappers, i.e. to encourage the proliferation of petty commodity production.

Under what, then, is the *caboclo* complex formally subsumed? It is formally subsumed under 'pre-capitalism', i.e. merchant capital. This subsumption is both a strength and a weakness. As Stoler has argued for a different set of circumstances (i.e. where formal subsumption occurs alongside real subsumption), petty commodity production has the potential for realizing an autonomy from the discipline of capital because its maintenance as a cost-reducing mechanism implies the development of strategies of resistance. What is clearly different about Amazonia is the absence of the 'supervision' of capital in the period from the First World War until the inception of *Transamzônica* development, and during this period, I would argue, one saw the maturing of the *caboclo* complex, a maturing threatened, if not brought to a close, by subsequent 'development' in Amazonia.

One of the reasons for the failure to recognize the *caboclo* complex as a significant development is precisely that its genesis lay not only in Amazonia (i.e. constrained by ecosystemic features), but in the particular way in which Amazonia was drawn into the world economy: aboriginal social systems were eradicated and replaced by forms of commodity production organized under and eventually abandoned by merchant capital. Thus, Amazonian *caboclo* societies are, to employ Mintz's phrase, reconstituted societies. Their particular dynamics can not be appraised simply in terms of local factors (e.g. 'Amazonian ecology'), but must be addressed in terms of rationale underlying their creation, a rationale which was, indeed, 'the conquest of the tropics'.

The *nordestino* complex is formally subsumed in a different manner and one which, I would argue, has less to do with Amazonia *per se* than it has to do with Brazilian agrarian structure. Among the spurs to the implementation of the Programme of National Integration under which *Transamazônica* became the most visible centrepiece was an agrarian crisis which threatened the stability of the military government. On one hand, the plight of the landless, especially in the Northeast, had to be addressed, but on the other hand, reform of existing agrarian structure was (and continues to be) political unfeasible. As a number of authors have argued (cf. Velho 1972; Foweraker 1981), the designation of Amazonia as a 'new frontier' provided a pragmatic if unrealistic solution to the crisis. The state-directed colonization of Amazonia provided 'land' to the landless and, not inconsequentially, deflected demand for increased food production away from land committed to export agriculture (Velho 1972). It also provided a safe investment landscape/business environment to extra-Amazonian investors. Through schemes of generous tax incentives, investors were encouraged to capitalize on the valorization of non-productive Amazonian land.

Terra firme agricultural immigrants were the rank and file of this frontier occupation. Their enthusiasm in part legitimated the government's near-universally condemned 'plans' and provided concrete proof of the national will to 'develop' the region. In terms of subsumption, colonists functioned not only in the manner outlined early by Velho as providers of cheap foodstuffs for urban markets, but also as agents of land valorization. Given that public land is valorized by improving it (i.e. clearing the forest), smallholder immigrants performed the most important and expensive improvements which could later be realized by speculators who either purchased the land from them or, frequently, forcibly excluded them.

This is a different kind of formal subsumption from that outlined for the *caboclo* complex, for, on one hand, it has little at all to do with production, and on the other hand, it has little to do with Amazonia, but much to do with national political and economic machinations. In the comprehensive treatments of Amazonian development policy in relation to the state provided, for example, by Hecht and Cockburn (1989), Hall (1989), Treece (1987), Goodman and Hall (1990) and Bunker (1980), one of the major themes – sometimes implicit, but frequently explicit – is the irrelevance, except in a pathological sense, of state-directed Amazonian development policy for smallholder agricultural immigrants. In this sense, formal subsumption has more than an economically-focused aspect, rather it includes a range of subsumption connotations not least of which is the fact that the political marginality of Amazonia *vis-à-vis* the state meant that economic actors – the immigrant colonists – were relocated in a political vacuum. Thus, formal subsumption for the *colonos* meant submission to a frontier rationale in which by which real subsumption (integration within the national economy) was substituted by mere gesture.

The 'Japanese Complex'

Implicit in the discussion of formal and real subsumption has been the notion that the transition involves, in gross form, peasants' becoming proletarians (cf. Roseberry 1978; Foweraker 1981; Goodman and Redclift 1981; Roseberry 1983). The fact that large-scale commercialization of agriculture has not occurred in Amazonia has tended to obscure the fact that while Amazonian agriculture is not, generally speaking, of the plantation variety, it is still far from being subsistence agriculture. To the contrary, Amazonian producers are commercial producers, albeit representing a heterogeneous set of petty commodity forms. A striking exception to this is presented by Japanese immigrant communities in Amazonia which, while operating on a small scale, display the structural features of highly commercialized agriculture.

The marginality of Amazonia and Amazonians is a major theme addressed by both developmentalists and critics of developmentalism, and within both camps prescriptions have in recent years been focused on the notion of sustainability. While there are many strands to the sustainability debate, two themes are common: ecological constraint and the desirability of commodification of agricultural production. From various positions within the debate there is a consensus that the prospects for agrarian development are being restrained by intrinsic inadequacies of Amazonia to support permanent cultivations of the sort which could ensure the long-term viability of an agricultural sector. The consensus prevails despite evidence that pre-colonial social formations overcame these 'natural' obstacles by exploiting arable *várzea* land and despite the fact that immigrant Japanese commercial farmers have succeeded in maintaining permanent cultivations on *terra firme* soils.

What is here designated the 'Japanese complex', then, represents an anomaly: it has provided a strong model for sustainability, has been present in Amazonia for many decades, yet is generally treated as an exotic footnote. In short form, the 'Japanese complex' already provides a strong example of what some in the sustainability caucus claim to be *terra incognita*.

Discussion of the 'Japanese complex' in Amazonia is usually focused on the town of Tomé-Açu, in Eastern Pará, despite the fact that comparable – if not so obviously important – examples of Japanese colonisation are found elsewhere in Amazonia. Staniford's *Pioneers in the Tropics* (1973) is the only full-length study of Tomé-Açu, but Subler and Uhl's recent work (1990) provides a concise update cast in terms of current Amazonianist preoccupation with sustainability.

The 'Japanese complex' differs most markedly from both the '*caboclo* and *nordestino* complexes' in being highly commodified. This is hardly to discount the important role of non-valorized labour and other features of 'peasant' production, but the 'Japanese complex' is overtly market-oriented, requires high levels of commoditized inputs (especially fertilizers) as well as mechanization (tractors), and involves a significant level of wage-labour. In the case of Tomé-Açu, according to Subler and Uhl (1990), the success of the 'Japanese complex' has taken place despite such 'natural' obstacles as declining soil fertility and environmental degradation widely assumed to place a short ceiling on sedentary agriculture.

It is worth reviewing some of the main points of Subler and Uhl's analysis of Tomé-Açu for two reasons. First, the analysis deals cogently with what is entailed in maintaining commercial agriculture in circumstances long regarded as problematic if not impossible. Second, despite the strength of the 'Japanese complex', Subler and Uhl's conclusions reflect a pessimism which implicitly subverts the main thrust of their argument, that is they attribute a provisionality to the success of Tomé-Açu, a provisionality which reflects views about Amazonian agriculture in general.

Within thirty years of its founding (1929), Tomé-Açu was the first significant source of black pepper in the western hemisphere, responsible for more than 5 per cent of total world production (Subler and Uhl 1990: 155). While black pepper continues to be the main crop, accounting for almost 80 per cent of income, it is complemented by a number of other cultigens. The average cultivated area per farm is about 20 ha, well within the range of 'peasant' farms throughout Amazonia, although the average family holdings are 100–50 hectares (the remainder consisting of regenerated/fallow *capoeira* and intact forest). The Japanese employ a form of succession management achieved through trial and error and the combination of inter-cropping and high levels of fertilizer input have meant that some plots of land have been under continuous cultivation for up to 15 years (Subler and Uhl 1990: 162). As they note, this durability has been achieved through intensive management, intensive labour input and intensive capital input, the average farm employing five full-time labourers and spending US $1,000 per ha/year, i.e. the equivalent of almost twice the minimum annual salary (1988) for a wage-worker in Brazil (1990: 163).

The success of Tomé-Açu is highly suggestive with regard to the prospects for the expansion of commercial agriculture in Amazonia, but Tomé-Açu's viability is in part due to a number of factors which are not necessarily transferable elsewhere in Amazonia. For one thing, the residents of Tomé-Açu have secure title to their land, thus they have access to agricultural credit denied the mass of Amazonian peasants (1990: 163). Without security of tenure, the risk of large capital investment required of this kind of intensive agriculture is not transferable. Other advantages which Tomé-Açu has – proximity to the Belém market – however, are replicable in Amazonia.

It is the matter of land tenure which shifts the issue of 'the Japanese complex' from one of technical mastery of an untoward environment to one of political uncertainty. The 'Japanese complex' is an enclave whose historical preconditions are hard to replicate elsewhere, and as Subler and Uhl note (1990: 163), those non-Japanese Amazonians who have managed to pursue the intensive agricultural path are 'middle-class', southern immigrants who have brought with them technical expertise and capital sufficient to evade being pulled into the mode of predatory, expansionist agriculture.

The 'Japanese complex' as exemplified in Tomé-Açu represents a highly developed and – to the degree that world commodity prices have some stability – sustainable form of commercial agriculture in Amazonia, but there are examples of intermediate forms, as is the case in Santarém.

The 'Japanese complex' in Santarém is not located in a Japanese community, but within a setting dominated by the *caboclo* complex and, much more recently, complemented by the *nordestino* complex. The initial Japanese presence in Santarém was prompted by speculation that the *várzeas* presented a promising setting for the cultivation of jute. Employing local labourers, Japanese entrepreneurs attempted to mount jute plantations, the produce of which was processed in a factory (Tece-Juta) and destined for markets in the South (coffee). The plantation programme was short-lived as plantation workers deserted to become petty producers of jute on their own holdings, a situation which prevails today. (See Gentil (1989) for an extensive discussion of contemporary jute-growing.)

While in relation to the plantation ambitions of the first cultivators jute production has become atomized – and fits comfortably within the disputed characterization of the 'stagnant' and *ad hoc caboclo* economy – from the point of view of *caboclo* petty commodity producers, jute has been a significant addition to their repertoire of petty forms. The continued Japanese presence in Santarém is also atomized. The 'Japanese complex' I shall discuss is represented by single family farms carrying out intensive agriculture in an urban setting. Unlike Tomé-Açu farmers, Santareno Japanese are not primarily pepper farmers, but are market gardeners producing for local consumption. Although pepper has been taken up in recent years, it is not the focus of the 'Japanese complex'. In addition, and unlike the immigrants to Tomé-Açu, Santareno Japanese arrived as members of loose networks and display little of the co-operative character of the Tomé-Açu community.

In broad terms, a Santareno Japanese approach is similar to that of Tomé-Açu: capital-intensive, employing wage-labour, multi-cropped and highly integrated with the market. It is highly commodified production and although employing non-valorized labour to a significant degree, the auto-subsistence component is insubstantial.

It differs, however, in being strongly shaped by the particular demands of the direct consumers and by virtue of the fact that producers are also direct sellers. In relation to the former, for example, farmers grow 'heads of lettuce', although they do not sell 'heads of lettuce': they sell a few leaves tied as a bundle, in accord with the demands of a market in which consumers shop daily for their immediate needs; similarly, herbs (*cheiro verde*), okra and scallions used in 'regional' cooking (in *caldeira de peixe*, for instance) are not sold as individual products by weight or unit, but are packaged in a combined form suitable for immediate consumption and according to the demands of local cuisine. In relation to the latter, because the farmer is also the retailer, there is great sensitivity to changes in demand. There are many products which do not follow this pattern of commercialization (cucumbers, for example, and tomatoes and eggs), but generally speaking, uncertainties of marketing are minimized by adjusting production to meet immediate changes in demand. For example, a Japanese market garden includes a number of raised beds (*canteiras*) which contain crops (lettuce, say) at all stages of maturity. Depending on daily changes in demand (and anticipated changes, when, for example, the daily provision of a vegetable is exhausted early in the marketing day), not fully mature specimens can be marketed early, subsitutes can be incorporated, or different sized bundles of greens made up.

The Santareno model is a small-scale version of Tomé-Açu: instead of producing bulk produce for regional, national and international markets, Santareno production is ordered by the needs of direct consumers, and this highly localized orientation contributes to the invisibility of such production. Although it is a form of production which is significantly commercialized (and indeed has led to a standard of living far higher than that of adjacent, non-Japanese farmers), it evades 'official' notice except in so far as municipal tax authorities in the central market appreciate its significance. It evades official statistical recognition both because it deals with crops which fall outside the official categories (e.g. cucumbers, radishes, runner beans, aubergines, okra, coriander, parsley, watercress), but also because although these crops go through the market, they do so under the control of the direct producers.[3]

There is another contrast to be made vis-à-vis the 'model' of Tomé-Açu as a workable programme of commercial agriculture, and this is that the Santareno complex operates at the scale of petty commodity production even if its commercial consequences are hardly 'petty'. Put another way, Tomé-Açu has significance as an alternative to the bulk of agricultural production (peasant, extensive, mobile) and is properly regarded as a strong candidate for a re-evaluation of commercial agriculture's role in Amazonian development; the Santareno model is integral in terms of a set of competing peasant strategies. It is very different from both *caboclo* and *nordestino* forms, but is not an alternative form of petty commodity production in an antagonistic sense, but in the sense of being additional. Indeed, and unlike the observations of Subler and Uhl to the effect that mimicry of Japanese in Tomé-Açu occurs among southern immigrants with capital and technical expertise, in Santarém, the effect of the Japanese complex has been to encourage *caboclo* petty commodity producers to adopt Japanese practices in order to enhance existing ones. Thus, for example, one finds widespread use of *canteiras* for the production of marketable perishable vegetables (the Japanese area of expertise) by *caboclo* petty commodity producers.

The three idealized petty commodity complexes are subject to different environmental and social constraints. The *caboclo* complex (repertoire of diverse forms pursued in different resource domains) is the outcome of a long process of haphazard colonial expansion the most significant episode of which was the rubber boom. Within the terms of the commercial framework established by the rubber trade, petty producers have functioned as marginal producers within a highly fragmented market. While not reproducing themselves entirely through the market, the existence of a market

3. One important consequence of this is that the effects of unequal exchange are mollified: there is no cut for the middleman. Furthermore, such products are used for barter. One family I know typically paid for their petrol with eggs.

(regional for foodstuffs; external for preciosities/extractivist materials) is a precondition for the complex, and the gradual incorporation of new products within the repertoire of petty forms attests to some degree to their sensitivity to the market.

Nordestino terra firme producers represent a recent, and by and large doomed, strategy. By concentrating on the swidden production of foodstuffs they rapidly exceed the carrying capacity of unsuitable soils and must regularly bring new land under cultivation. This predatory expansion results in a valorization of cleared land which they are not, generally speaking, in a position to profit from both because of the lack of institutional and technical support, and because they are in competition with non-productive land speculators. In a literal sense, they consume resources absolutely while at the same time failing to reproduce themselves.

The status of the 'Japanese model' is perplexing because of the lack of attention it has drawn. It refutes two of the most frequently cited observations about the possibilities for a durable smallholder peasantry – a not inconsequential achievement – yet appears to be regarded as an unreplicable anomoly: Japanese colonists do not follow *caboclos'* strategy of seeking out the comparative advantage of the *várzeas*, nor do they encounter the same insuperable obstacles said to explain *nordestino* failure to sustain terra firme agriculture.

The profound differences among the three models attests to the importance of situating contemporary peasantries in terms rather more complex and historical than has tended to be the case. It is noteworthy that if one looks for anthropological (or closely allied) examples of the three models in order to establish a comparative and historical framework which can accommodate both pan-Amazonian perspectives as well as particularities, the list is short. The *'caboclo'* characterization established almost forty years by Wagley (1953) still prevails (cf. Praker (1985a). Staniford's *Pioneers of the Tropics* (1973) is the prime case study of Tomé-Açu (and its main focus is internal political organization rather than aspects of Amazonian peasanthood); Moran's *Developing the Amazon* (1981) emphasized the differences between *nordestino* and *caboclo* adaptive strategies; and Santos' *Historia Econômica da Amazonia* (1980) provided an overview of the crucial period during which the broad features of modern *caboclo* society were formed.

The recent rediscovery of the virtues of 'traditional' knowledge (i.e. non-Indian), prompted not only by scholarly concerns, but more contentiously by commercial ones, threatens to efface what little understanding of the historical roots of contemporary Amazonia has managed to emerge through the apparatus of a mythic naturalism. In this chapter and in what follows the case is presented that the differentiation which exists within the Amazonian peasantry results not from the pursuit of diverse 'adaptive strategies', but from a set of preconditions which are the legacy of a penetration of capital, and which served both to transform and conserve Amazonian peasantries – transform in the sense that merchant capital encouraged the production of exchange values (and made possible access to a market), but conserve in the sense that merchant capital did not enter directly into production, rather it accommodated whatever relations of production were available. In part, then, the invisibility attributed to *caboclo* society is a product of its origin within the structure of merchant capital, a structure of accumulation (absolute surplus value) superseded by industrial capital (relative surplus value), but one still instrumental in the accumulative process.

Chapter 7

Merchant Capital, Social Reproduction and Blockage

> For the modern reader in the West, the respectability of the merchant class is self-evident. The word has become commonplace, and we use it automatically without considering the system of laws which over the centuries has put these people in the center of economic activity (Tigar and Levy 1977: 3–4).

Filho de criação may serve as a metaphor for Santarém's being both a child of colonial penetration and also a child periodically abandoned by its ambitious parents. It also serves as a metaphor which expresses the ambiguous role of merchant capital, that form of capital which is both transformative – encouraging the production of commodities – but also deeply conservative in as much as it commits its surplus to the purchase of more commodities, not altering the relations of production under which such commodities are produced:

> [m]erchant capital could not itself cause this transformation [of labour-power into a commodity] ... [r]ather it contributed to organizing economic space and exchange in a way that permitted the eventual emergence of a fully developed capitalist system. (Genovese and Fox-Genovese 1983: 36)[1]

1. Merchant capital refers to capital which profits through buying commodities cheap and selling them dear, unlike mature (industrial) capital which purchases a particular kind of commodity – labour-power – and sells the resulting exchange values for a price which exceeds the wage. Although discussion of merchant capital has had only modest prominence in the development/underdevelopment literature and is by now regarded as doubly passé (historically archaic; theoretically undeveloped) it served as the focus of one of the most illuminating works to emerge in the literature, Geoffrey Kay's *Development and Underdevelopment: a Marxist Analysis* (1975), rarely cited, but regularly reprinted. As insightful as Kay, although pre-dating the underdevelopment literature, was Sidney Coontz whose *Productive Labour and Effective Demand* (1965) depicted well the way in which merchant capital – initially synonymous with capital – was with the rise of relative accumulation of surplus forced into an auxiliary role in the service of industrial capital. William Roseberry is one of the few who has invoked merchant capital in the South American anthropology (see also Taussig 1980 for a more 'culturalist' account).

Santareno society (and generic *caboclo* society) is thus multiply orphaned: its Amazonian parentage is equivocal (*Tapajônica* civilization died not during the birth of Santarém, but before); it matured under the supervision of merchant capital, a parasitic form (in retrospect) which merely shifts values and hence is rootless, serving to link commodity producers to the world market, but maintaining them as subservient.

Following this line of argument, the metaphors of pathology and stagnation seem at first sight apposite, and further analysis would consist only in confirming empirically the subsequent devolution of ersatz *caboclo* society (see G. Kay 1975). From the ground – in Santarém, for instance – the degenerative effects of merchant capital's dominance have a different significance: mechant capital, whatever its intrinsic faults, sets limits on the possibilities of social reproduction and however grim the prospects, Santarenos persist. The strategies pursued were outlined in the previous chapter, strategies that are heterogeneous to a degree disguised by the bald claims of pathology. *Caboclo* petty commodity producers – historical peasantries – have built up commodity production within the limits set by the mercantile network and the regional market. In the expanded form, *caboclo* petty commodity production includes agricultural production on *várzea* and *terra firme* (including foodstuffs as well as non-comestibles such as jute and malva); extractivism; pastoralism; craft manufacture. Recent frontier colonists, *nordestino* farmers and *Transamazônica* land settlers, have pursued a smallholder predatory strategy seeking to use an agricultural base to launch commercialized agricultural/pastoral projects. Japanese colonists have pursued a strategy of specialized commodity production for both local and global markets. Each of these strategies represents a different accommodation to the stultification imposed by the dominance of merchant capital and collectively they suggest that merchant capital's dominance has implications which are ill-served by the assumption that the metaphors of pathology and stagnation fairly reflect the lives so dominated.

The distinctiveness of the Santareno social formation is derived from its contingent position within a larger system. Historically, local society has been most clearly bounded when it has been less implicated in the larger system and it has appeared most amorphous when more clearly integrated within the larger system. The viability of the local system is inversely proportional to the degree to which it is incorporated.

From the time of conquest until the early/mid-nineteenth century the colonization of Amazonia was fragmentary in character from the point of view of bringing it into line either with Brazilian national development or the global economy. Beginning in the early decades of the nineteenth century and continuing until the early decades of the twentieth century, Amazonia became a regional economy (based on rubber extraction) clearly integrated in the global economy (if not the Brazilian). Until the 1960s (and more realistically, 1970), Amazonia dropped out of the global economy to return with the construction of *Transamazônica* and a dramatic elevation of foreign investment.

In terms of these periods, definitions of the limits of Santareno society vary according to the degree to which the terms of social reproduction are locally or externally determined. In addition however, during periods of intensification of external relations (during the rubber boom, for instance, and currently), external interest in Amazonian surplus has little to do with surplus produced within the terms of peasant systems. Thus, to speak of such periods as ones characterized by integration is to misrepresent the rationale for capital penetration: periods of integration of Amazonian social systems and the global economy are periods in which there is competition for Amazonian resources, not incorporation of Amazonian forms of production within larger economic systems except to the degree that non-valorized labour forms in Amazonia serve to subsidize commercial extraction (as in, for example, charcoal production). During the rubber boom, Amazonian peasantries *per se* were not incorporated, rather Amazonian workers were absorbed into a large-scale extractive sector. Peasant production, as a consequence, became less cohesive as a system. During the current phase of capital investment, peasant production is, once again, more or less peripheralized. Capitalism competes not directly with peasant production, but indirectly through dominating in the extraction of resources which in themselves are not sought by peasant producers, but which as parts of a repertoire of resources are necessary for local social reproduction to take place. For example, the large-scale felling of forests is not destructive of the peasantry because such activities preclude peasant felling of forest (although this is a factor), but because it restricts peasants' access to resources whose seasonal – not absolute – availability is crucial for social reproduction.

Contradicting the received wisdom about the stagnation of Amazonian peasant production, I would argue that what emerged in the aftermath of the rubber boom was – in Santarém, for instance – an expanding system of peasant production. The elements of this system are derived from a number of ostensibly incompatible structures: the system of petty commodity production is capitalist in that production is for the market, but it is based on familial kinds of self-exploitation and non-separation of worker from means of production; although marginal capitalism, this system is different from other kinds of petty commodity systems in that it emerged after the period of greatest capitalist penetration, i.e. after the rubber boom. The emergence of this system constitutes a particular kind of capitalist transformation, and although in certain respects the stagnation metaphor may be apposite, it is only so in relation to the possibilities for surplus accumulation of the sort encountered when there is separation of producers from control over means of production. In suggesting that Santareno peasant economy might be reconsidered without the mediating influence of the metaphors of pathology and stagnation which usually typify characterization of Amazonian peasantries is not to argue for a hitherto unrecognized utopia. It is, however, to argue for a kind of social formation which is integral in a sense not easily recognized when the dominant relations are defined by the demands of merchant capital, but subsequently relegated to an auxiliary position *vis-à-vis* industrial capital. Santareno peasant economy is the offspring of merchant capitalism and as such displays the contradictory features of a transitional system: production directed towards the market, but prevailing relations of production which are not straightforwardly capitalist.

Social Reproduction and the Petty Commodity Repertoire

Contemporary peasant forms of production represent an accommodation to the failure of development during the period of the rubber boom. With the withdrawal of the apparatus of the rubber industry, tendencies toward centralization – typified in the hierarchical trading mechanisms – were undercut, yet the lower reaches of the mercantile network remained intact. In terms of the possibilities for expanded peasant production, the trading network embracing direct producers and small-scale traders (*tabernas* and *regatões*) maintained both local markets and links with external ones (e.g. for tropical preciosities). The separation of direct producers and merchants, however, did not represent an unambiguous differentiation and there is considerable overlap, small-scale traders, for example, frequently being producers themselves as well as functioning as merchants. The living standards of such traders are in many respects equivalent to those of their debtors.

As shown in chapter 6, it is possible to distinguish among three broad types of peasant economy in Santarém: the *caboclo* complex, the post-*Transamazônica nordestino*, and the Japanese urban market gardening sectors. The *caboclo* complex represents the peasant formation around which the distinctive features of Santareno society are based. It is also the peasant form whose expanded reproduction is most directly blocked by the effects of *Transamazônica* development policies. In examining the structure of the *caboclo* complex, particular attention is drawn to the way in which this complex became elaborated in the period between the collapse of the rubber boom and the instigation of *Transamazônica* development.

Recent investigations of peasant and petty commodity production have, in spite of improved theoretical rigour, reasserted the classic distinction between subsistence production and commodity production. While some writers have tried to map the distinction between peasants and petty commodity producers directly onto the subsistence versus commoditized-factors-of-production contrast (Friedmann 1980), and others have argued for the mutual dependence of subsistence production and petty commodity production (Kahn 1980: 126, viz. the contributions of the French structural-Marxists), such attempts at maintaining the distinction beg several crucial questions. In the first place, if the distinction is to be kept, then it follows that two kinds of economic rationality must be maintained simultaneously, one bearing on the way in which the logic of capital is seen to structure commodity production, and the other bearing on the way in which the logic of non-capitalist or pre-capitalist relations of production maintain a degree of autonomy from the strictures of capitalist production. Many of the interesting questions raised in economic anthropology over the last twenty years have centred precisely on this issue of transformability or non-transformability of capitalist and non-capitalist relations of production (see, for example, *Social Analysis* 19: 1986, especially the article by Terry Turner). The empirical materials around which such arguments have been developed have, for the most part, included enough in the way of elements of pre-capitalist social formations for arguments to be phrased in the following way: what is it about the relations of production of X social formation that make capitalist exploitation possible. Within this argument, one of the functions of the concept of subsistence is to designate the domain of non-capitalism, and although the notion of 'natural economy' is rarely made explicit (but see Bradby 1975), it does seem to be inherent in the notion of subsistence. Looking at Santareno peasant formations, however, it is difficult to know where to locate 'subsistence'. It cannot be derived from a primordial social formation of which peasant Santarém is the modern, multiply transformed version, for there is no reasonable link between pre-colonial Santarém and the later versions of colonial and neo-colonial social formations. There is no significant peasant production in Santarém which does not have its genesis in the colonial transformation of the region. However tenuous the links between local production complexes and the capitalist world economy might appear, it is through the latter that there is peasant production in the first place. The concept of 'subsistence', then, really does not serve to mark off a realm of alternative economic rationality: the conditions of existence necessary to maintain 'subsistence' production derive from capitalism.

The problem with this formulation, however, and the source of ambiguity, is that it is not the actual production which is capitalist, but the general conditions within which such production takes place. In the anthropological literature concerned with this point, convincing arguments have been advanced to the effect that capitalism, in the neo-colonial context for instance, reproduces such 'subsistence' production as a means of lowering wages through displacing the costs of social reproduction and/or through maintaining a reserve army of labour.

The Santareno situation is somewhat different in that the relationship between capitalist and non-capitalist relations of production is not representable in terms of a pre-capitalist social formation articulated with capitalism. The pre-capitalist elements are aspects of the particular way in which colonial power came to dominate in the region, thus what is at issue in the questions raised about 'subsistence' production is not the character of the dominated form of local society, but the character of the kind of capitalism which prevailed, merchant capitalism. The argument put forward here is that from the point of view of merchant capital's dynamic, all production is in principle commodity production. The structure of the local social formation (in which peasant = subsistence = petty commodity production) is derived from merchant capital's agnosticism *vis-à-vis* relations of production. Merchant capital represents the conditions of existence for the maintenance of local forms of production, but does not enter directly into production. What has emerged – and is best represented in the *caboclo* complex – is a repertoire of production forms which is (1) compatible with the demands of merchant capital and (2) capable of expansion even in the absence of significant flows of capital. In terms of the former, Santareno commodity production is heterogeneous and includes a variety of agricultural (food as well as non-food) and extractive goods which are locally consumable as well as exportable. In terms of the latter, there is a sufficient (although not marked) degree of specialization and differentiation such that there exists a local market. In other words, the character of social reproduction, although derived from the historically interrupted interventions of merchant capital, maintains (or did, until the post-*Transamazônica* phase) a significant degree of autonomy. That the possible importance of this autonomy has been for the most part unacknowledged is indicated by the widely-held view that Amazonian peasant economy following the collapse of the rubber boom is reasonably describable as 'stagnant'. If such a pejorative term is appropriate in the Amazonian setting, however, it might be more reasonably attached to a form of development whose primary aim was – and continues to be, albeit with much vaunted technocratic expertise – the extraction of natural resources from a region whose human occupants have been regarded as hardly worthy of the programmes set by the captains of commerce.

The origins of this pathological state of affairs may be sought in the encounter of fragmentary social formations and the colonial apparatus charged with bringing 'progress', but such an effort would depend on a number of problematic assumptions. In the first place, while there were certain generalized effects according to which it is reasonable to speak of the 'colonial process', the effects of this process were not the same for all Amazonian societies thus embroiled. In the second place, peasantries in Amazonia originate as much (if not more) in failed colonial schemes as they do in the colonial absorption of Amerindian societies. To put this briefly, the generalized effects pertinent to a study of Amazonian peasantries are to be sought in the structure of colonial penetration and transformation, not in an adding up of these effects as they were realized by the different victims. What is particularly pertinent is the enduring effect of merchant capital's service as both conduit of extractive surplus and as the structural basis for the proliferation of commodity production. This is to say that merchant capital – without entering directly into production – nevertheless provided the conditions of existence necessary for the establishment and proliferation of petty commodity production which itself has provided the basis for the social reproduction of such peasantries as that represented in Santarém.

In at least one recent treatment of a Latin American peasantry (Roseberry 1983) the role of merchant capital as agent-of-capitalism has been prominent, yet in this work and critiques of it (see C. Smith 1985), attention has been focused on the sorts of questions raised earlier in this chapter, i.e. are these people peasants or are they petty commodity producers; is this capitalism, or is it disguised capitalism? Here, the concern is somewhat different. I am less concerned with the question of characterization than I am with the way in which the conditions of existence of a set of production forms shifts from local control to external control. This is not to relegate the characterization debate; it is to make a more general point: characterization depends on a number of factors not directly derivable from an examination of production forms. The particular combination of production forms in Amazonia is structured not just by the apparant comparative advantage of extraction (see Bunker 1985 for discussion of an alleged 'extractive mode of production'), but also, and more importantly, by the way in which colonial incorporation of the region resulted first in the eradication of indigenous social formations, and then the reconstitution of a peasantry on the basis of export demand. The character of the production forms is therefore as much a reflection of the specific kinds of linkage created between local producers and external markets as it is an intrinsic feature of a reified 'Amazonia'.

In chapter 6 material was presented which illustrated the ways in which different production forms were combined by different sectors of the Santareno peasantry. The possibilities for social reproduction, it was argued, depend heavily on continued access to non-valorized land and other resources. In addition, however, there is conflict between an exclusively agricultural peasantry (represented by recent *nordestino* immigrants) and the *caboclo* peasantry whose extension of production forms to include a wide variety of terrestrial and riverine extractive resources represents a more flexible accommodation (and greater possibility for exploitation) of Amazonian ecosystems. The conflict between these two kinds of appropriation (setting aside for the moment the unique trajectory of Japanese colonists) is central to much contemporary analyses of the change in Amazonian agrarian structure (cf. Branford and Glock 1985; Anderson 1990), but underlying the questions of contemporary transformations must be the question of why this conflict should be emerging at such a late stage.

This question is present in almost all discussions of Amazonian peasantries, although in most cases it is rapidly disposed of. A set of positions roughly glossed as 'ecological' has argued that the profitable exploitation of the tropical forest ecosystem is constrained by the inherent poverty of Amazonian land in terms of large-scale, capitalist agriculture. Another common claim is that the demographic vacuum in Amazonia has stunted economic development because of the high cost of acquiring local labour. A further claim is that the sheer size of Amazonia – and the restrictions on overland access – have meant that imperial and colonial powers could not afford to maintain the kind of territorial control which could ensure a stable environment for profitable development. While each of these arguments is tenable in part, each depends for its explanatory power on bringing to the fore certain distinctive features of Amazonia which are not, in fact, all that distinctive. Examples of both developed and underdeveloped regions can be cited which also include such 'distinctive' features. The alternative is to suggest that the reasons for Amazonia's apparant backwardness have as much to do with the terms of its incorporation[2] in the world economy as they have to do with regionally specific – primarily ecological – factors.

Amazonian societies were virtually destroyed in the course of colonization rather than being incorporated while coastal societies were colonized and then replaced. The primary consequence of these differences was that imperial and colonial penetration of Amazonia created a bowdlerized 'natural economy'. After conquest, the extraction of surplus from Amazonia depended not on the maintenance of an externally dominated tributary system – as in Spanish America for example – but on the enterprise of private colonial agents themselves with (on a limited scale in Amazonia) a labour force composed of African slaves and subject Amerindian populations. In considering the preconditions for the social reproduction of contemporary Santareno peasantries, the most prominent feature in the social landscape, and that which embodies the central contradiction, is not composed of the encounter between Amerindian social formations and European imperialism, but is rather located in the structure of economic relations imposed by the colonists.

Let me summarize a few points before moving to a discussion of merchant capital and the implications which its dominance has had for the emerging peasantries of Santarém. The stagnation thesis – the conventional wisdom – goes something like this: pre-colonial Amazonia was sparsely populated by a variety of tribes characterized by their mobility, low level of technology, low absolute and relative populations, and general subservience to the demands of an inflexible environment; their replacement by colonials resulted in a virtual duplication of simple modes of subsistence, in some respects linked to external markets, but for the most part marginalized from the general developments of Brazil. The subtext (although frequently made explicit) of this argument is that intrinsic features of the Amazonian environment have restricted not only the social

2. Moulder's (1977) comparison of the trajectories of Japan and China in relation to the emerging capitalist world economy suggests one concrete way of approaching the anachronisms of Amazonia. In her analysis, there is an inverse relation between degree of capital penetration and subsequent capitalist development.

evolution of indigenous peoples, but colonials as well, and this argument is highlighted in contemporary modernizationist claims about the prospects for Amazonian development: in such an unfavourable natural setting, hi-tech extractive development is all that can be expected.

An alternative argument is that the apparent stasis of Amazonian development is attributable to the way in which Amazonia was inserted into the world economy. The contradictory tendencies of merchant capital in an environmental setting of admittedly limited flexibility created the conditions of stasis. With the eradication of Amerindian social formations as the dominant local modes of economic and social organization, merchant capital operated within a European-created 'natural economy', one in which merchant capital became the organizational framework for the proliferation of a variety of forms of petty commodity production, forms which when combined – as they are in Santarém – appear as coherent local systems. The contradiction which lies at the base of Amazonian peasant stagnation is not simply read off the conflict between social demand and environmental possibility, but is the unresolved tension within merchant capital's adaptability to a variety of forms of production and its subservient position in relation to the demands of fully developed capitalist production. In this context, it is possible to see why the non-valorized character of land and resources in Amazonia has been maintained so long: if it is the case that merchant capital has structured the basic features of Santareno peasant production, the absence of commodification of land and resources would be expected. Merchant capital's agnosticism *vis-à-vis* the relations of production within which commodities are produced made possible a set of conditions within which nascent capitalist development was constrained by the circumstances which it had created itself: commodity production oriented towards export, yet relations of production which bore no particular connection to those of the the ultimate users of such commodities. The link between the cayman-killer and the recipient of the purse is achieved by a set of exchanges which, because there is an apparently obvious common feature in the beast's skin, obscures the fact that the value to the direct producer is different in kind from that of the consumer. What links these two kinds of value is merchant capital interested in purchasing the skin and selling it. The value of the cayman-skin from the point of view of the producer is provided by the merchant. As a local use-value it has virtually no existence. As a commodity in the purse-consuming community, the value of the cayman-skin is a result of a radically different set of criteria of use and exchange-value.

Locating Merchant Capital

Two extensive discussions of merchant capital have drawn particular attention to the relevance of the concept for the analysis of contemporary aspects of underdevelopment (Kay 1975; da Silva 1982) and an earlier work (Coontz 1965) emphasizes the ambiguity which surrounds the categories productive and unproductive labour in the context of the shift from merchant capital accumulation's being capitalist accumulation proper to its becoming an agent in capital accumulation under the domination of industrial capital. The ambiguity of merchant capital raises issues germane to the analysis of forms of peasant production such as those in Santarém for which capitalism is a necessary, but insufficient basis for social reproduction. In reviewing some arguments concerning merchant capital, the main purpose is to argue that it is the contradictory tendencies of merchant capital itself which constrain the possibilites for social reproduction among the Santareno peasantry. The opposition between peasant and non-peasant production is embodied in the structure of merchant capital itself.

Merchant Capital, Social Reproduction and Use-values, Export of Surplus Value

Merchant capital, it has been argued, is unproductive capital, confined to circulation. Within this conceptualization, pre-capitalist production is frequently depicted as being articulated to capitalist production via the transparent medium, the circuit of merchant capital. Merchant capital makes surplus realization possible although in itself it is incapable of adding value to commodities. One of the problems with this conceptualization is that it is assumed that productivity has some intrinsic link with use-value, yet as Kay argues:

> In fact, the irrationality of capitalist production is complete and the production of use-values is nothing more than an inevitable but incidential constraint upon accumulation. Hence the practical definition of productive labour in capitalist society is not that labour which produces use-values, but that which produces surplus value. The usefulness of a product does not count here; or even the fact that it is necessary and indispensible for social reproduction: the preoccupation of capital with its own self-expansion is so complete that everything else is incidental. Only that labour which produces surplus value is productive, the rest is unproductive. (Kay 1975: 132)

And:

> The definition of productive labour as only that labour which produces surplus value is not a theoretical definition made for the purposes of studying capitalism, but a practical definition made by capitalism in its modus operandi. (Kay 1975: 133)

And:

> all production is subject to the control of capital and contained within the circuit M ... P ... M′. The ideal form of this circuit, which states its only possible raison d'être, is M – M′, where production is dispensed with altogether. Since this is impossible, capital is forced to accept the inevitability of material production, but only on condition that it becomes a process for producing surplus value. (Kay 1975: 133)

Kay's views on these matters are among the most clearly stated, and draw particular attention to the fact that the rationality of production from the point of view, say, of the peasant is not merely an expression of the larger system of generalized commodity production of which peasant production is a part. Rather, the logic of generalized commodity exchange does not entail the transformation of peasant production into capitalist production: since capital accumulation is based on the appropriation of surplus value, peasant production is not systematically subordinated to capitalist production except to the degree that peasant production includes the production of an appropriable surplus. The main components of Santareno peasant production, regardless of how dependent such production is on commodified inputs, are not directly appropriable by capital (and hence, not too surprisingly, such a peasant form, if we take the Santareno peasantry to be archetypally 'Amazonian', is derided as stagnant/backward/etc.). For one thing, most production takes place in circumstances in which questions of property ownership (of land, for example, or riverine resources) do not arise. The fact that commodities traverse the peasant/capitalist divide does not mean that one can read back from the character of exchange value and deduce that peasant production is a sub-set of capitalist production. While the literature is full of examples showing a functional relationship between peasant production and capital accumulation, this functionality merely illustrates the heterogeneity of possible articulations between ideal-typical 'capitalism' and subordinate systems of production. That there is something common to peasant production and capitalism is assured by the dominance of one over the other.

In Marx's discussion of the special features of merchant capital what is most emphasized is its suspended, transitional character. Merchant capital precedes capitalism proper (appropriation of relative surplus value), yet persists under the dominance of industrial capital by virtue of its mediative capacity *vis-à-vis* pre-capitalist (or non-capitalist) forms of production and the capitalist mode. What is also stressed in discussing merchant capital's relationship with pre-capitalist modes is its active role in bringing about dissolution, and 'whither this process of dissolution will lead, in other words, what new mode of production will replace the old, does not depend on commerce, but on the character of the old mode of production itself' (Marx 1959: III: 332).

Kay has pursued this line of inquiry, drawing attention to two aspects in particular. One of these is the paradox of capitalist development under merchant capital: (1) its encouraging of commodity production (echoing Marx's comments: 'merchant capital gives rise everywhere to the tendency towards production of exchange-values, increases its volume, multiplies it, makes it cosmopolitan' Marx 1959: III: 331), (2) yet its failure to revolutionize production, its capacity to profit through unequal exchange without entering directly into production.

The second aspect is one not particularly foreseen in the work of Marx, namely that merchant capital's continued dominance in the periphery – long after the ascendency of industrial capital accumulation through appropriation of relative surplus value – would result in such carnage among societies enduringly under the influence of merchant capital that the subsequent development of industrial capitalism would be seriously impeded. For Kay, the prospects of 'normal' capitalist development in the periphery are blocked by merchant capital's enhancing of forms of production which are capitalist to the degree that they are producing exchange-values, but non-capitalist to the degree that the dominant relations of production do not necessarily entail the crucial separation of direct producers from means of production. The reproduction of this state of affairs – an array of atomized, uncapitalist production units – makes possible the periodic integration of petty commodity producers into the global market, but does not entail permanence.

Thus, while for Marx, under the domination of merchant capital, 'this system [petty commodity production] presents everywhere an obstacle to the real capitalist mode of production and goes under with its development' (Marx 1959: III: 334), for Kay, the 'going under' is by no means a certainty. In both accounts, however, the implications of the term 'dissolution' are not spelled out. There is, in fact, a convergence on this term by a variety of writers, one which is suggestive but undeveloped. Bettelheim (1972), for example, uses the expression 'conservation-dissolution' to describe the suspended state of transformation from pre-capitalist to capitalist relations of production, and some of the French structural-Marxists employ a similar notion in accounting for the maintenance of pre-capitalist relations of production within tribal social formations whose capacity for surplus creation is seen to be functional for capital accumulation within colonial social formations which assert political control over the terms of social reproduction (see Foster-Carter 1978; Kahn and Llobera 1981 for discussion). In all of these cases, however, the object of attention – aspects of which, varying from case to case, are conserved and/or dissolved – is a social formation which, albeit hardly pristine, is a recognizable version of a pre-capitalist form, whether this be a highly transformed one, e.g. Kahn's Sumatrans whose 'traditional' subsistence rice-lands are relics of the Dutch implementation of the 'Culture System', or more apparently antediluvian, e.g. the 'lineage mode of production' as revealed in

West Africa. In the case of Santarém (and Amazonia generally), what is conserved is not a version of a primordial social formation, but a mode of peasant organization created by merchant capital itself, thus focusing on the question of 'conservation/dissolution' refers us back not directly to the character of peasant organization (the stagnation thesis), but to the preconditons of this, namely the kind of social reproduction required for merchant capital's continued circulation.

To summarize, for Marx, the eventual relegation of merchant capital by industrial capital was accompanied by the proletarianization of peasants/independent producers (Europe) and petty commodity production became obsolete as independent producers were uncompetitive under conditions of increasing capital investment. For Kay, in the periphery, the continued dominance by merchant capital resulted in a bowdlerized capitalist development, one in which surplus value is extracted via unequal exchange, and one which, albeit capitalist in the sense that it is value which is realized (after processing in core) through relative surplus value appropriation, for the direct producer does not result in the transformation of relations of production; over time the reproduction of such marginal forms of capitalist development destructures the social organization of direct producers in such a way as to obviate the possibility for subsequent capitalist development. For Marx, what was dissolved was the pre-capitalist nexus of production; for Kay, dissolution refers to the base upon which capitalist production might develop.

The pertinent question for Santarém is: what happens after dissolution? There is the stagnation thesis, but there are several objections to it. First, it is quite obvious that the 'stagnant' peasantries of Amazonia have continued in spite of the predictions of imminent demise implicit in the thesis, neither devolving into ciphers of 'natural economies' nor becoming proletarianized. Second, the 'stagnation' characterization is self-serving of developmentalist interests and acts as a pretext for the kinds of intervention which, as a number of recent publications have demonstrated, have resulted in widespread conflict, conflict which in itself contradicts the premises of the 'stagnation' thesis: if Amazonian social formations were as degraded as the developmentalists would have it, why is there any effective resistance to the new interventions? Third, the thesis is an easily recognized version of the imperial claims long used to justify interference in other peoples' affairs. While in previous epochs – when, for example, the cross led the sword – the barbarity of the conquered was offered as grounds for the imperial assumption of responsibility for the pagans' well-being, the contemporary justification is masked by the ideology of management science.

An alternative approach to the question of 'dissolution' must begin by querying what is being dissolved. It is obviously not an indigenous, pre-capitalist social formation. It is equally obvious that what is being dissolved is not something 'opposed' to capitalism, but something which is a product of capitalism, namely a social formation cast up by merchant capital which at the time of the local system's emergence was the dominant form of surplus accumulation, but which is now an auxiliary form. What is being 'dissolved', then, is a system of commodity production generated by capitalism itself, but one which is incapable of effecting the transformation itself. Merchant capital, in a word, created an 'unnatural economy' which because of both its tangential relationship with development in Brazil as a whole and because of Brazil's unique semi-peripheral position within the world economy (characterized by Bill Warren-like repudiation of crude dependency as well as backward agrarian structure with regard to the internal market),[3] maintained a position of dominance within the local systems of the regional economy.

One of the implications of a 'conservation/dissolution' thesis is that the development of the local system is constrained by external features. Typically, for example, the backwardness of capitalist agriculture in Amazonia is explained by reference to the comparative advantage of coastal plantation development, one of the consequences being the diversion of capital away from Amazonia (cf. Wagley 1953). While this is no doubt true, it does not account for the kind of development which does take place – or has taken place, as it were, by default. By regarding local development as merely a manifestation of retarded, not to say degenerative accommodation to untoward circumstances, the local formation is portrayed as an anti-system, an *ad hoc*

3. Warren is notorious for his critique of the cruder assertions of early versions of dependency theory noting, among other things, that despite the satellite-metropilis flows of surplus, industrial development takes place on the periphery. For recent discussion see Ramirez-Faria (1991: 265–70).

collection of features attesting to the failure of development. Wagley writes, for example, that:

> Out of the historical background of Itá and of the entire region emerge the basic reasons for its relative backwardness. A culture is above all a product of history – of the man-made sequence of events and influences which combine through time to create the present way of life in any area. The aboriginal cultures of the Amazon forest were well adapted to the tropical environment, but their technological adaptation was of such simple form that it offered only survival or bare subsistence to the European newcomer. (1976: 61)

Paraphrasing: what is wrong with Amazonian society is the lack of fit between European expectations and local possibilities. The implication here is that development has not yet taken place, but that once the techno-social fit can be achieved, development will be possible. Against this, one might note that regardless of which labels one uses to describe post-colonial Amazonian societies, the characterization must be presented in at least two parts: (1) as it relates to the colonial/imperial system which transformed local social formations; and (2) as it relates to more or less cohesive, and perhaps somewhat autonomous, local systems. The 'anti-system' or 'stagnant' characterization comes through concentrating on the latter. Amazonian peasantries, to the limited degree they have been studied, are not all that striking, but the tendency has been, as in the case of Wagley's *Amazon Town*, to emphasize what they are not. Rather than prompting an inquiry into the causes of their lack of definition and their awkward profiles, the difficulties in fitting them into available categories have resulted in a characterization by default.

This characteristic of boundary vagueness – depicted by Wagley as the lack of fit between European expectation and the local system's ability to deliver – and resulting consignment of Amazonian peasantries to a taxonomical penumbra (part of the syncretic universe outlined by Freyre) need not be that problematic if attention is paid to the fact that what has been conserved/dissolved in Amazonia is not an archaic and unsuccessfully transformed antediluvian social formation (or set of), but rather a colonial system whose mediative properties (effecting the transfer of goods between direct producers and global markets) are redundant (plantations are more dependable) yet ineradicably embossed on a social landscape in which the possibility of a marginal existence in the interior has been a perhaps grim but nonetheless viable alternative to *minifundium* penury elsewhere (especially in the northeast) in Brazil.

The conditions of existence required for merchant capital's circulation do not entail the transformation of production within Amazonian peasant forms, but are broadly compatible with such developments and when transformations do occur – as, for example, in the extension of the repertoire of petty commodity forms, adding, for instance, jute, black pepper, garden vegetables – these take place in spite of merchant capital not because of it. Merchant capital's interest is in exportable tropical preciosities whose value can be realized in the external market. The local production of other commodities – foodstuffs by and large – is not directly structured by the circuit of merchant capital, but it is an elaboration of the possibilities posed by merchant capital's encouragement of petty commodity production in a general sense. This coexistence of merchant capital and indirectly related forms of petty commodity production may be characterized as production by default: merchant capital is interested in commodity production only to the degree that something is being produced which may be purchased and sold elsewhere. The exclusive production of commodities which interest merchant capital, however, precludes the possibility of local social reproduction, these commodities embodying little use-value in local terms, and their production (mainly extractive) entailing the dispersal of social groups and an undermining of stable social organization. To the degree that merchant capital's interest has been discontinuous, rising and falling with changes in global demand for such tropical goods as rubber, skins, spices, nuts, tropical fish and so on, and because merchant capital's lack of direct investment excludes it from directly structuring emerging forms of commodity production, local peasantries' expansion of production forms constitutes a system-within-a-system.

Merchant Capital and Subordination

Da Silva sums up a standard view of the place of merchant capital as mediator between precapitalist and capitalist production: 'I shall conceptualize the phenomenon of underdevelopment in terms of the persistence of precapitalist structures in the periphery, based on the independent existence of merchant capital and its predominance over industrial capital' (1982: 417). Although in the core, industrial capital comes to be able to finance itself through its own liquid assets and credit from non-mercantile financial sources, merchant capital continues to function as a mediator between peripheral producers of raw materials and the apparatus of industrial transformation in the core. In Marx's account:

> Within capitalist production merchant's capital is reduced from its former independent existence to a special phase in the investment of capital ... The special social conditions that take shape with the development of merchant's capital, are here no longer paramount. On the contrary, wherever merchant's capital still predominates we find backward conditions ... The independent development of merchant's capital, therefore, stands in inverse proportion to the general economic development of society. (1959 III: 327–8)

Contemporary interest in merchant capital has largely focused on the way in which merchant capital's subordination to industrial capital is partially offset by its continued utility as a colonial conduit, that is its functional role within capital accumulation has become the specialized one of conveying surplus from the non-capitalist nexus to the capitalist. In a sense it is merchant capital's being itself an 'undeveloped' form of capital accumulation which enhances its mediative capacity as a structural link between different kinds of social formations, but the capital-logic emphasis in this kind of analysis has led some to argue that this account is burdened by its Eurocentric or Western focus. Wolf (1982), for example, cautions against assuming that the logic of capital accumulation obliterates the significance of the heterogeneity of social formations dominated by capital, and in a similar vein, Trimberger (1977) criticizes the approach of Wallerstein which, she says, by giving 'primary emphasis to the impact of external capitalist relations in determining the path of development in the third world' (1977: 96) perhaps fails to consider the the impact of differential subordination within the capitalist world economy. She notes that:

> The course of development of non-Western societies has not been determined only by the impact of external capital, but as much by the social relations in pre-capitalist social formations and how these

relations both helped structure the imperialist challenge and were themselves altered by it. (ibid.)

Her discussion of Japanese 'feudalism', Moulder's discussion of Japan and China (1977) as well as Wolf's more wide-ranging analysis, represent a convergence around a set of arguments raised earlier in chapter 6, namely those concerned with the way in which alternative economic rationalities may be compared and with the way in which the transformation from pre-capitalist to capitalist relations of production is not a linear process.

This convergence represents, in part, the outcome of a non-debate between modernizationists and critics of modernization theory. On the one hand, debates about underdevelopment, its causes and possible solutions have mainly been located on the Left. The details of these internecine arguments are well documented, and there is certainly not space here to attempt even a cursory summary. (But see Ramirez-Faria (1991) for an interesting commentary.) In the place of counter-arguments from the modernizationist camp and its apologists has been the promulgation of policies of direct and indirect intervention in the internal affairs of the former colonial and imperial territories, much of the focus of which has been on the construction of the National Security State (see Chomsky and Herman 1979; Herman 1982). While critiques of development/underdevelopment have produced a body of literature in which a number of explanatory accounts have been put forward, at the same time, practitioners of developmentalism/modernization have carried on with the implementation of a set of policies (many of which are neatly summarized in the stated goals of the Alliance for Progress (see Gordon 1963), World Bank statements of purpose, and so on) which are by and large totally unaffected by criticism of the manifest failure of modernization to achieve anything more than further immiseration and increasing dependence of its 'target groups'.

In this context, it is interesting to consider how critiques of modernization theory have converged in spite of considerable disagreements within the group of critics (cf. Frank versus Laclau polemic; Warren versus *dependistas*; Wolf versus Wallerstein): one anodyne point (although not in the view of modernizationists) is that the study of development/underdevelopment must take account of historical perspectives:

such categories as 'the West' and 'the tribal economy' are historical artefacts, not given analytic categories. A second point, and again unremarkable, except that it is so banal as to be consistently disregarded, is that in spite of the globalist perspective which provides a common ground for many discussions (after all, both Rostow's and Wallerstein's theories are about 'world systems'), the structure of that global system is decidely hierarchical. The concept of 'global community' or 'global village' is a mystifying metaphor. The fact that Amazonian peasants might wear Yves St Laurent 'designer' sunglasses and listen to the Beatles on a Phillips cassette machine is a trivialization of the concept of community. Similarly, the concept of 'integration' (according to which, for example, in an earlier epoch, North American Indians became part of the 'melting pot' of American society) is an abused notion.

At a more specific level, there is a consensus concerning the way in which the anthropological object of analysis has been reformulated, a consensus represented in traditions as diverse as those of the French structural-Marxists, British structural-Marxists and the American tradition represented by Wolf. The basis of this consensus is formulated around a contradiction which has characterized anthropological work since the discipline was professionalized: on the one hand, there are detailed empirical studies, and on the other hand, the scientific legitimacy of such studies derives from the degree to which general anthropological, sociological or historical principles can be applied cross-culturally and trans-historically; at what point is the distinctiveness of a society, culture, social formation generalizable? The consensus referred to above is not an allusion to a 'solution' to this problem. The consensus concerns the nature of the theoretical object: it is one which is in history; it is one which transforms as the result of the kind of intellectual activity brought to bear on it, and it is one which offers a better explanation than those proferred from other quarters.

One gloss provided for this consensus is the notion of 'social reproduction'. In spite of its biologistic implications (unfortunately enhanced in the important and influential work of Meillassoux), the term refers not the reproduction of things but to the reproduction of social relations. In the British tradition, where resistance to the ideas of Lévi-Strauss – not to mention Marx – has been represented as a principled rejection of 'unnecessary' abstraction, and where the term 'social relations' has a strongly empiricist valence, the concept of social reproduction has not been viewed as having any particular utility: among other things, anthropologists study social relations, and in as much as a certain consistency of social relations over time is observable, the expression social reproduction will do as well as any other for describing this process. In a different sense, however, social reproduction refers not just to the process according to which particular social relations endure, but to the conditions necessary to maintain that endurance. For example, it is one thing to say that a set of marriage patterns is congruent with a domestic division of labour within which wife-givers obtain control of the husband's output for a period of time, and quite another to specify what conditions, at a more general level, are necessary to maintain that congruence. The last mentioned notion of social reproduction entails, therefore, not just taking account of the way in which ostensibly different kinds of social relations are coordinated (kinship, politics, economics, cosmology) and are seen to be compatible, but also, and more crucially in the context of peripheral and semi-peripheral social formations, taking acount of the way in which subordinated social formations are simultaneously structured by a logic internal to the particular set of social relations according to which such a social formation is distinctive (bounded in some way) and the logic according to which this subordination is reproduced.

Central to the development of the concept of 'social reproduction' has been a feminist critique which, according to N. Redclift (1985: 95), 'has undermined the unitary nature of conventional concepts and has suggested that women's relationship to these processes must be seen as specific and distinctive'. This critique, more than many others, highlights the character of the convergence on the questions of subordination, articulation, and subsumption, but does so in a way which implies that the complications in analysing the relationship between non-capitalist relations (in this case particularly those that define the domestic sphere) and capitalist ones have to do primarily with the heterogeneity (and hence difficulty of generalizing) of non-formal labour under capitalism. In this argument, however, the logic of capitalism is attributed a unity which is derived from its dominant position in relation to the subordinated forms (e.g. domestic or non-formal relations). Redclift writes that

> [S]uch labour cannot be located outside the circuit of capital, yet as Bernstein (1979) points out it exists 'in conditions less determinate than those of the proletariat'. It is 'not subject to complete expropriation nor to the particular modes of regulation and discipline of labour exercised within the capitalist production process'. Thus it is subsumed, yet it obeys a different 'logic'. Such formulations remain ambiguous. (Redclift 1985: 95)

The question is, might this ambiguity not derive from the illogical aspects of capital rather than its imputed 'logic'?

This is the point at which merchant capital might be reintroduced as the possible source of ambiguity, for the maintenance of merchant capital – the social reproduction of merchant capital – requires exactly the kind of conditions in which, in Bernstein's words, labour exists 'in conditions less determinate than those of the proletariat'. In the periphery, Santarém, for example, merchant capital is not simply an agent of industrial capital. It is not merely 'subordinated capital', the used-car (or Trabant) of the nineteenth century. Rather, it sets limiting conditions on production generally, conditions which effectively defy capitalist logic, but conditions which are adequate for local social reproduction. The emphasis on subsumption which has characterized much of the debate about the endurance of pre-/non-capitalist 'modes' is in part based on the assumption that the logic of capital constitutes a clearly defined domain against which the not-quite-capitalist forms may be contrasted. While there are obvious heuristic reasons for this assumption, it is equally clear that the term 'logic' has euphemistic connotations of rationality and unity which do not bear up under examination. The term 'logic' is a gloss for the dominance of capitalist relations over non-capitalist. The crisis of capital accumulation is part and parcel of the 'logic' of capital.

Banaji has drawn attention to Marx's characterization of peasant production under capitalism as 'the whole of capitalist production without its advantages' (citing *Theories of Surplus Value* 3: 165):

> That is the labour-process, still being a process specific to the form of smallscale parcellized peasant production, allowed no scope for a production of relative surplus-value or for the technical renovations presupposed therein. It follows also that dominaton by capital ... would force [it] outwards in its drive to self-expand, force capital to extend the sphere of its domination laterally, to draw into its network an ever-growing mass of peasant households. (1977: 36)

Banaji's discussion, like that of da Silva and indeed most others who, in the debates about underdevelopment, draw particular attention to the suspended character of capitalist transformation of the peasantry, alludes to a kind of peasantry widely taken to be normative, but which is not immediately germane in the Amazonian context, namely a peasantry directly confronted by capitalist production (as in plantations, mines or forced deliveries). Bernstein, for example, in his critique of Kay (1975) refers to 'peasants [who] were commonly directed what to grow and in what quantities' and 'as the peasantry became more involved in commodity relations ... the coercion to produce certain crops became increasingly economic, that is, more items of consumption for their own reproduction had to be purchased with cash which could only be obtained through the production of commodities or wage-labour (e.g. plantations)' (1976: 58). Now, however apposite this characterizaton of peasant possibilities may be in some circumstances, it is by no means generalizable (cf. 'peasants in cities'), but the fact that it is so widely accepted makes possible the apparently reasonable inference that the lumpen label borne by the peasantry can only be removed once the peasantry can be precisely defined in relation to the imputed future possibility of aborption in a formal sector (at which point the peasant problem disappears because they will have become members of the proletariat).

In Amazonia, plantation agriculture appeared only sporadically and was never established in such a way that proletarianization was a realiable alternative to smallholder petty commodity production. In other words, the suspension of capitalist transformation was a structural feature in Amazonia. The consequence of this suspension (lumpenness in one discourse, stagnation in another) is what is at issue in Bernstein's critique of Kay, for Bernstein argues that merchant capital cannot have both of the characteristics attributed to it by Kay, namely retention of its pre-capitalist character and a new status as agent of modern capitalism (1976: 60). The reason for this, according to Bernstein, is that 'the analysis of merchant capital (as a unitary category) cannot explain the changes in the conditions and relations of production in the Third World' (1976: 60). According to Bernstein, Kay is employing a model in which capital imposes itself on pre-capitalist forms rather than 'penetrating' those forms. Were it the case that peasant agriculture in Amazonia was basically plantation in form, Bernstein's critique would be more telling, but given the failure of modern capitalism to transform the production process from an independent peasant form to one dominated by the wage-form (as in plantations), the imposition model fits the facts somewhat better. The question is not really one of locating the structures of domination (if not 'purely' capitalist, they certainly are not pre-capitalist), but rather concerns the structure of reproduction, and in this respect the ambiguity of merchant capital's position as mediator is crucial for the precisely the reasons which Bernstein rejects, in particular Kay's claim that industrial capital's grasp on Third World development was (is) made difficult by virtue of the social incoherence created by merchant capital's depredations in an earlier epoch (Kay 1975: 99; Bernstein 1976: 61). Against this view Bernstein offers the articulation argument as a preferable explanation, one which constitutes 'theoretically the specificity of different social formations according to their pre-capitalist nature, the forms of capitalist penetration, their rhythm and degree, and the resulting articulation' (1976: 61).

The problem here, however, is that the character of the pre-capitalist social formation – in Santarém, for instance – is, at the very least, extremely obscure, and the term articulation hardly does justice to what is known about the transition from dominance by pre-capitalist forms to dominance by 'capitalism'.

While it is true that studies of articulation of the sort referred to by Bernstein have provided considerable insight into the way in which certain African tribal formations are drawn into the nexus of capitalist production, it is not true that this articulation model is generally adequate in analysing pre-capitalist to capitalist transitions elsewhere. In Bernstein's account, the term peasant is the concrete realization of articulation:

> Again, the articulation approach poses the question of such alliances in more rigorous terms of production – the economic and political

> mechanism of control (including 'traditional' modes of tribute and labour-service exacted by pre-capitalist ruling groups and usually intensified or even invented under colonialism) to bring peasant production in line with the needs of capital, supplying the latter with commodities and labour for plantations, mines, transport, etc. As has been stressed, this could be accomplished with few changes in the forms of the labour process or instruments of labour of the peasant household. (1976: 61)

While this may hold for a number of ethnographic cases (as elaborated by Meillassoux (1975) and Wolpe (1972), for example), it is an idealization which does not necessarily travel well. What, for instance, is the relevance of the concept of articulation when, as Kay argues, and as illustrated by the case of Amazonian peasantries, the pre-capitalist social formation is characterized not by its susceptibility to subordination in the idealized form documented for many African examples, but is characterized by 'social incoherence'? In the latter case, the structures of social organization directly germane to questions of social reproduction do not represent an asymmetrical alliance between the pre-capitalist and capitalist formations, but are structures arising from the wholesale destruction of the dominated form. Peasants are, in this case, not the realization of a process of articulation, but are structurally identifiable only in relation to the dominating system.

Bernstein presents the peasant as a survival of pre-capitalism. In summarizing his critique of Kay he says that:

> the maintenance of 'non-capitalist' forms of production is emphasised and attributed to the intrinsic qualities of merchant capital in general, irrespective of the historical epoch in which it is operating. This fails to pose the question of how the conditions and functions of production were radically changed although its forms (such as the peasant household) were retained. (1976: 64)

If, as I am arguing here, the peasant-as-transitional-category is not the result of articulation, but is a synthetic, then Kay's arguments for the privileged analytic status of merchant capital is retained, for the question raised in such circumstances is not how does social formation A come to be dominated by B, but rather, when A is obliterated in the course of being dominanted by B, what are the conditions of existence necessary for the continued reproduction of the resulting, synthetic social form, the constituted or reconstituted peasantry? The key to this seems to lie in the structure of merchant capital which requires of the local peasantry exchange values, but not proletarianization. What Bernstein sees as an equivocating ambiguity (merchant capital as imperfect capital) is from the point of the view of the local peasant formation not ambiguous at all, but rather a structure which specifies form but not content, that is it requires commodity production in general, but not commodity production in particular (that is to say via the wage-form).

Against an unstated but implicit notion of the unilineal development of capitalism, Wolf (1982) has persuasively argued that merchant capitalism is not capitalism, or if it is capitalism, then the distinction between capitalism and pre-capitalism loses meaning. His critique is largely directed towards a version of world systems theory which, according to its critics, mistakenly takes the rise of a capitalist world economy in the sixteenth century to be equivalent to the global dominance of capitalist relations of production, relations defined merely as production for the market. Among Wolf's objections to the notion that merchant capital is capitalist is the fact that the labour process under merchant capital does not entail separation of labourer from means of production. The heterogeneity of relations of production compatible with the dominance the merchant capital dispels, empirically, the unity of merchant capital and capital proper. While agreeing, it is also necessary to point out that merchant capital sits no more easily within a pre-capitalist category than it does within a capitalist one. As a heuristic, though, the concept of merchant capital can help account for a category of anthropological object which lies between two broad sets of anthropological concerns. One of these is the study of the bounded social formation; the other is the study of social change. In spite of a notable shift away from the study of conventional 'anthropological' societies to a study of the nature of transition and integration into larger units, anthropological discussions are usually situated within some notion of 'traditional society'. The work of the French structural-Marxists, work which more than any other has drawn attention to fundamental processes of social change, depends for much of its force on the idea that there is a base-line according to which to assess change and transformation, and the base-line is the 'traditional' community. In Kahn's work as well, another case in which the implications of his arguments concerning change and transformation go well beyond the immediate details of Minangkabau society, there is a unity to the concept of 'traditional' society (even if aspects of the 'traditionalism' of Minangkabau society are clearly marked by Dutch colonial intervention). As repeatedly stressed, for Santarém society, the pre-capitalist past finds few resonances in the present-day social formation. The base-line for a discussion of social change of the sort taking place over the past twenty years is the colonial wreckage of an unrealized European effort to create a society in its own image, yet for the period between the demise of the pre-colonial/pre-capitalist social formation and the emergence of post-*Transamazônica* society some characterization must be possible which does not have to resort to the marginalist categories reserved for those social formations outside what are perceived to be the main currents of modern development. It is difficult to perceive the structure of such societies once they have been consigned to the margins because they are known by terms which rarely implicate a notion of the social: there are spatial metaphors (marginal), biologistic ones (pathological), environmentalist (stagnant), as well as the respectable social science terms peasant and lumpen. These terms reflect more on the inadequacy of a discipline to include within its terms of reference those societies not conveniently defined as tribalist, post-tribalist or ethnic community. More important than this, however, is the fact of a resolute commitment to a notion of anthropological object which is bounded in space and time. The durability of this commitment is evident in the way in which structural-Marxist arguments were grafted onto earlier structure-functionalist conceptions: instead of the concept of mode of production's being taken as dissolving the notion of 'society' as conventionally studied by anthropologists, the term mode of production was simply widely used as a synonym for 'society' and there was, not surprisingly, a proliferation of modes of production where before there had been only 'societies' or 'cultures'.

The Allocthanous Origins of Amazonian Peasantries

If the interest lies in documenting and analysing the social organization of the other, then it matters little whether the other is described as a society, culture or people. If interest also lies in trying to account for the continued existence of the other, that is the nature of social reproduction, then it is crucial that mode of production (or social formation) is not a term equivalent to 'society'. There are two main reasons for this. One is that attention to the level of production (and by implication, following Meillassoux, reproduction) obviously involves dynamic processes (and hence systems) which are unstable. In this reading, the study of social systems is the study of social change. The other reason is that the notion of a bounded social system is now less a heuristic than a fiction which impedes the discovery of adequate sociological generalizations about social systems.

What happens after merchant capital's domination is broken? The classic assumption has been that merchant capital anticipates the emergence of capitalist relations of production, and historically, in the core, this sequence has occurred. On the periphery, however, the transition has been prolonged. In part this is because the integration of core and periphery in the early colonial period was of a different sort. The periphery provided raw materials which were transformed in the core, but the market for these manufactured goods was overdeveloped in the core in relation to what happened on the periphery. At the same time, the concentration and centralization of capitalist production in the core rendered the periphery less integrated than had previously been the case, and one find, as in the case of Brazil, differentiation of rich and poor which exceeds that in the core. With the internationalization of capital – particularly in the form of MNCs/TNCs – the way in which core and periphery were articulated came to depend less on the relations between the political units representing core and periphery and was achievable through particularistic relations such that the kinds of backward linkages associated with capitalist development in the core were not created in the periphery. In the periphery, commodity production under the aegis of core capital was specialist production more oriented towards core structure than local socio-economic structures. Merchant capital's role in all this is, then, doubly ambiguous: (1) it serves to link local commodity production with industrial manufacture in the core thereby appearing to discipline local production without yet entering directly into production; (2) in relation to the production of certain local commodities it is the major economic framework, yet in relation to parallel local economic activities it provides a general context of production without providing a specific mediating function *vis-à-vis* global trade. It becomes necessary but insufficient for specifying the general character of local economic development. It is an extension of industrial capital, but it is also an expression of local social totalities.

Merchant capital, to the limited degree that it has been a topic of interest in the underdevelopment literature, has been used to account for the unevenness of development on the periphery. For Banaji and da Silva, merchant capital is a mechanism for unequal exchange: it ensures that commodity production under conditions of non-valorized labour or underemployment can produce an appropriable surplus. For Kay, merchant capital not only makes surplus transfer possible, but also ensures that local development of the productive forces is subverted by the fragmentation of local social formations via environmental destruction and disorganized atomization of production units. What I have tried to outline in the discussion above is that regardless of the degenerative effects of merchant capital's dominance (and for whatever reasons), what must also be considered is the fact that despite the degenerative effects, for some people, however untoward the prospects, merchant capital may be all there is to deal with.

Chapter 8

Maintaining the Image of Sustainable Development

If an Amazonianist anthropologist had happened to fall asleep in, say, 1975, and had awoken in, say, 1991, he or she would have noticed something peculiar: the standard lexicon, one appropriate for discussion of dual organization, couvade, sorcery, the myth of the anteater whose cousin married a dolphin, and patriliny with uxorilocal residence had been overlaid with one loaded with short nutrient cycles, exchangeable bases, *theobroma speciosum*, spontaneously ovulating ungulates, cation exchange capacities, succession management and intellectual property rights.

Said anthropologist, initially perplexed by the list of new keywords, would quickly come to realize that less had changed than was at first sight imagined. Amazonians were still described as 'tribes' if Indian, lumpen 'populations' if not; concepts such as 'adaptation' had been retained; 'nature' was still a steady backdrop.

There are, however, some substantive changes in addition to the change of vocabulary. For some, the definition of 'Amazonian society' has been broadened, if not enough to include all non-Amerindians or the lineaments of a global system, at least far enough to consider the possibilities seriously. Second, much interest is shown in the ways in which Amazonia is an anthropogenic environment not necessarily locked into a Disneyish world of implacable biological stability. Third, it is more widely recognized that change in Amazonia – biological and social – has been prompted by external factors, specifically changing global demand for tropical preciosities and gross basic materials. Fourth, mobilizations by and on behalf of Indian and peasant groups – from the Yanomami to the Rubber Tappers Union – have resulted in some reduction of the effects of the deregulation mania which passes as development policy.

In addition to these changes and continuities, one might also observe that Amazonianist anthropology as a sub-specialty maintains a peculiar relationship with developments in the field as a whole: while many other domains of anthropological inquiry have undergone radical postmodern surgery – most notably with regard to the local savage's having become a generic, international other – in Amazonia, the late modern period has been marked by an upsurge of a vigorously pre-postmodern 'science'. With a few noteworthy exceptions such as Taussig (1987), while non-Amazonianists may, broadly, be pursuing reflexivist strategies, a significant number of Amazonianists have retro-fitted late modern anthropology with all the apparatus of the science now widely condemned as limited, positivistic and parochially Western.

For example, in the pages of *Cultural Anthropology*, to cite one of the more self-consciously vanguardist textualist journals, one finds an article such as Ruth Behar's 'Death and memory: from Santa Maria del Monte to Miami Beach' (1991), opening with quotations from Michel de Certeau ('memory produces in a place that does not belong to it') and Allon White ('Flaccid, diseased cells are swarming and swelling inside my bones'), while in the abstract of a typical, state-of-the-art Amazonianist piece one finds:

> Results are presented for an ethnobotanical study of the Chacobo Indians. ... Information about the history and current status of the tribe is given. This is followed by a description of the study area and the methodology employed. A total of 360 species of vascular plants, in at least 221 genera and 79 families, were encountered' (Boom 1989).

Are these anthropologists talking about the same thing?

Although ostensibly they are not – and the dialogue between the two camps continually draws attention to the gulf between them – in some instances they are probably closer to each other than is immediately apparent. There is, for example, in a companion piece to the last-mentioned article, a study of Bora (Peruvian Amazon) and Huastec (Mexico) resource management in which farmers have 'scripts' which 'regulate synchronous relationships', and in which Conklin's *Hanunoo Agriculture* is trailed in the bibliography by Machery's *A Theory of Literary Production*.

In this chapter attention is focused on one prominent tendency in Amazonian research – the idea of sustainable development – and it is argued that despite its apparent parochialism, the concept of sustainable development is of a piece with the more theoretically vaunted tendencies designated postmodernist. Just as the 'market system has become sheer common sense' (Jameson 1990: 249), within the cultural logic of postmodernism, so is appreciation of the traditional knowledge of Amazonian forest users conceived of not primarily as a matter of anthropological interest in and of itself, but as a possible source of value which can be realized outside of Amazonia.

The relationship between empirical research in Amazonia and the apparatus of postmodernism is not without its ironies, but the fact that some Amazonian ethnography should now appear in highly positivistic dress just at the moment when such garb has been so widely discarded should not obscure the fact both tendencies are pursued by anthropologists, neither botanists on the one hand, nor literary critics and post-metaphysical philosophers on the other. 'Positivism', according to Jameson, 'becomes postmodernism when it has, like philosophy on the older paradigm, fulfilled and thereby abolished itself' (1990: 248).

The major expression of this positivism-born-again-as-postmodernism is found in the economism of arguments which treat Amazonia not as a social space, but as a resource domain to be managed in the name of an abstract market.

Sustainable development is a contradictory notion which combines – as does the postmodern tendency – elements of progressive critique as well as deep conservatism, sharing as well an 'end of history' orientation in which, as Jameson has observed of postmodernism, the past is evoked while history is denied (1991: 19). The concept of sustainable development in Amazonia represents, I think, a special case, not only because of its apparent distance from the discursive preoccupations of much recent anthropological writing, but also because it represents the conjuncture of an overdeveloped ethos of management science – which some take to be a hallmark of postmodernism – and a social object rendered almost invisible by management's commitment to an unreconstructed naturalism. Thus, for example, we have the paradox of the prominence of intellectual property rights on the sustainability agenda, an issue shaped by ultra-modern legal and representational discourses, yet earmarked for application in a setting in which society, if granted much integrity at all, is widely regarded as contingent and not fully formed. That traditional users of the forest should be considered in relation to intellectual property rights when their very existence is threatened by the fact that they are denied access to the property necessary to feed themselves is ironic, to say the least.

The Specificity of Amazonianist Discourse

Amazonian anthropology has always embodied a notion of environmental determinism, expressed in the persistence of adapatationist arguments as well as the intensity of arguments about protein capture and soil fertility. The upshot of this, in the late twentieth century, is that Amazonian anthropology, facing the same global crisis as that presenting reflexive anthropology, does so with a theoretical armoury heavily stocked with naturalism in its various rhetorical and scientific forms. Nature has always been implicated in anthropological explanation in Amazonia, but in the context of rising global eco-consciousness in which Amazonia is seen to have a major role, nature's position is even further enhanced.

Two examples of the overvaluation of natural constraints were noted in earlier chapters, but bear repeating:

1. The priority of natural systems in Amazonia is widely taken as a primordial given. The region is frequently characterized as one in which societies are few and far between, and those which exist are ideal-typically 'primitive', because of the heavy constraints imposed by the humid tropical forest or, in the case of neo-Amazonians, 'flawed' or 'stagnant' by virtue of the peasants' inability to accommodate the demands of the market and nature simultaneously. One of the main reasons why Amazonia appears as a vast natural space unburdened by society is because of the effects of expansionary European systems: most indigenous peoples were exterminated in the first two centuries following

discovery. Amazonia's missing other is not natural in any sense, but a social product.

2. The second example concerns the archaeological record. Archaeology in the neo-tropics has not, for reasons discussed earlier attracted much attention, but the published results of that research which has been done demand major revisions of conventional accounts. At the most general level, the results dispute the view that contemporary Amazonian societies are significantly representative of pre-colonial social formations. The limited evidence demanding a radical rethink is compelling despite the fact, as Roosevelt notes, that 'not one region of Amazonia has been investigated systematically and comprehensively with [modern] methods' (1989: 39)

The point here is three-fold: (1) current ethnographic patterns have been projected back onto pre-history; (2) continue to be so despite evidence that pre-historical (or pre-Conquest) social formations were radically different; and (3) environmental determinism is assumed.

An appreciation of the relationship between pre-colonial and post-colonial social formations in Amazonia is complicated by the fragmentary character of pre-historical reconstruction, and in the absence of knowledge of social systems, the relative significance of the role of natural systems is exaggerated.

Contributing to the perception that Amazonian societies were and are exceptionally subordinated by nature was the way in which the region was incorporated into Empire. The image of the 'noble savage' with which Amazonia is so well associated has an iconic quality which permits it to evade association with the historical world. This is hardly a unique stereotype – one could say the same for 'the African' or the 'Southeast Asian' – and although I would not wish to push the argument too far, I would suggest that the imagery of the Amazonian noble savage has been insulated from the kind of folkloric apparatus which is attached to many other stereotypical primitives. In Euro/New World terms, for example, aside from the single-breasted Amazon herself, and perhaps Chico Mendes, there is no autochthanous folk hero-figure, no Hiawatha, Pocahantas, Sitting Bull or Geromimo. Nor is there anyone who embodies imperial history, no T. E. Lawrence, Custer, Livingstone or Captain Cook (although there is Col. Fawcett). Nor, of course, is there a Gandhi, Toussainte L'Ouverture or Pancho Villa. Nor is there even a neo-tropical literary interloper of Conradian proportions, although some might argue for Euclides da Cunha.

The apparent pristineness of Amazonia *vis-à-vis* a popular or indeed scholarly representational apparatus has to do with the fact that the colony of Brazil not only became the tail that wagged the dog, but indeed a tail that wagged on its own, and from the point of view of developments elsewhere in the colony, Amazonia was, with the exception of the rubber boom era, a remote periphery. The main image of the Amazonian 'noble savage', is thus a generalized feature of Enlightenment Europe more than it is the singular product of a particular imperial history. The image of the generalized Amazonian 'noble savage' has been very durable over time as well as being very accessible. Such contemporary and different chroniclers of the modern condition as Werner Herzog, Sting and John Boorman have been able to tap into Amazonia without difficulty, registering readings of Amazonia which, despite what one might think of the distortions, are easily recognizable and, perhaps more importantly, of a piece: humans whose identity is predicated on the overwhelming 'naturalness' of Amazonia. Put another way, what is noble about the noble savage is not savagery, but the nature of which she/he is an expression.

To recapitulate, the current trajectory of Amazonian research is in part a particular response to the crisis (see Ortner 1984; Roseberry 1989; *Social Analysis* 1986) in anthropology, and what shapes it more than anything else is the special role which the environment is seen to play in accounting for past, present and future forms of Amazonian societies. The fact that the particular form of environmental determinism which prevails does not necessarily accord with the facts, as far as they are known, has not led to a recasting of Amazonian anthropology. In fact, the environment is, if anything, more privileged than it was in the past because it is the perfect idiom for the ideology of management, that in which unreconstructed *homo oeconomicus* reigns supreme.

Sustainability versus Social Reproduction

Scholarly discussions of Amazonia – revitalized especially by new research into biological systems – are now also informed by the effects of two new forces. These are, on one hand, *sindicatos rurais, movimentos populares* and other grassroots and trades union organizations which have emerged in the wake of *abertura*, and on the other hand, by environmentalist lobbies of various types (international agencies, NGOs, rainforest preservationists, 'green' businessmen and women, federal agencies). There is considerable overlap of personnel of these two tendencies as well as with human rights/indigenist rights groups long active in the region.

A theme addressed by all these constituencies is 'sustainable development'. At one extreme, sustainability is short-hand for a panglossian programme consisting of the unlikely combination of capital accumulation and environmental conservation: the assertion is that economic growth can be sustained and untoward environmental impact mitigated. This programme is actively discussed at the 'north/south', international agency level; it is, in many respects, the official view and treats Amazonia as but one piece within a globalist environmental model.

At the other extreme, sustainability is a euphemism for subsistence, as the term used to appear more frequently in anthropological discourse. In the Amazonian context, this reading refers to the fact that historical peasantries have managed to persevere despite their having been cut loose from formal colonial apparatus, after the rubber boom, for example. The object of analysis in this reading is a local society whose viability depends on achieving a balance between social need and the capacity of biological systems to accommodate human intervention.

More or less in the middle there is a usage which draws attention to the possibilities for satisfying the demands of both local communities and the global economy. In this formulation, sustainability refers to a programme of replacing a profitable if environmentally destructive resource use with a more profitable and environmentally non-destructive form. One of the most celebrated formulations is that outlined by Peters, Gentry and Mendelsohn (1989). In this article they argue that two of the major products of gross forest conversion (cattle and timber) are, in the long term, far less profitable than is the environmentally sound extraction of diverse non-timber forest products. This conception combines – in a manner still not realistically assessed

– some of the goals of the other two readings: eco-geopolitical stability and recognition of the rights of direct producers. It is what might be called the realist/utopian position.

What the sustainability arguments have in common is an ostensible concern for environmental conservation and economic viability. What they also share, although infrequently addressed, is an interest in maintaining social systems as they exist, albeit in some formulations in a reformed way (e.g. through the establishment of extractive reserves). All acknowledge that something is terribly wrong, but all seek a solution which involves minimal disruption of the status quo. None, for example, suggests that agrarian change at the national level is a realistic goal however desireable it may be as precondition for implementing policies of sustainable development (Cleary 1991: 42). None, for example, proposes anything as positive as stopping road-building Amazonia, much less closing existing roads. Indeed, despite the recommendations of its own environmentalists (and followed some years later by the public admission of error by Barber Conable), the World Bank has pushed for road improvements (Cleary 1991: 54).

The Tropical Forest Action Plan – which epitomizes the panglossian prescription – argues for a change of management; the 'grassroots' plan argues for the appropriation of direct producers' knowledge; Peters, Gentry and Mendelson (1989) appeal to the taking of a long-term perspective in which short-term gain is sacrificed for long-term growth. What they share, however, despite differences in orientation, is the idea that Amazonia is basically a management problem, a social landscape to which technical expertise can be applied.

Specialist conceptions of Amazonia as a 'problem' requiring top-down solutions are part of a wider discourse on Amazonia and environmentalism. The non-specialist attention now paid Amazonia is, generally speaking, driven by an inchoate environmental concern in which the object of analysis is not so much 'deforestation and its consequences for Amazonians', but the 'globe' (the greenhouse effect, London will flood, etc.). This elevation of the status of Amazonia (lungs of the earth, genetic warehouse etc.) is problematic. There is an unreality about the 'global concern' for Amazonia which is, upon even brief reflection, self-serving of those interests whose activities have generated the global environmental crisis. Amazonia is now important, it seems, not because Amazonians have a basic right to exist, but because without Amazonia, the globe is at risk. This is a *volte-face* of considerable proportions. Most Amazonians were eradicated as a result of the 'discovery' of the New World; most deforestation has taken place as a result of development schemes enthusiastically pursued by the putative saviour interests. The invasion/rediscovery of Amazonia (*c.* 1970) was prompted by the demands of a cynical programme of national integration. In short, the professed sensitivity toward the plight of Amazonia and Amazonians has chequered antecedents.

The condition in which Amazonia currently finds itself is not the result of arbitrary shifts of misguided policy, but rather is the result of policies formulated and acted upon by real human agents in real positions of power. Despite the claims that the condition of Amazonia is the result of bungled development, one might ask why, if Amazonian development is so flawed, investment there is still so enthusiastically pursued? If this is the case – and continued interest in Carajás and *Polonoroeste* would seem to confirm it – it might also be worth considering the provenance of some sustainability prescriptions.

The sustainability thesis in Amazonia represents the convergence of three tendencies: (1) action undertaken by Amazonians, (2) initiatives by multilateral lending agencies and NGOs agencies, and (3) an eco-informed research community.

In bald form, sustainability represents the claim that natural resources can be continuously and profitably appropriated without untoward environmental degradation. In its weakest version, this looks like a greenish analogue of a perpetual motion machine and scepticism, not to mention cynicism, is the appropriate response. In its strong form, however, the notion of sustainable development has a number of appealing features. For one thing, it proposes that issues relating to social reproduction be cast in strongly materialist terms: the viability of social systems depends in great measure on recognizing that social reproduction has preconditions which defy so-called cultural logic. Animists, Pentacostalists and Catholic, are equally bound by the conditions presented by aluminium toxicity and the short nutrient cycle. Beyond that, the sustainability thesis holds up the promise that the historical peasantries of Amazonia will be recognized as integral societies which have not merely adapted to Amazonia.

From the perspective of the North–South debate, sustainability (in what I would call the restricted form) is put forward as central to the future of the planet. In its benign form, this represents a plea to recognize that the global interaction of degraded biological systems separated by transparent political boundaries will have catastrophic global consequences which can only be forestalled if national interests are subsumed under pan-national ones. In its less benign form, it represents a claim that the constituencies on the periphery are incapable of recognizing that their best interests lie with and should be managed by remote green-tinged mandarins.

At the local level, however, sustainability addresses a different constituency, albeit using the same term of reference: an abstract market. For this constituency, as I shall discuss shortly, sustainability does not represent a novel solution to an old problem. Rather it represents an accommodation to a new social reality in which Amazonia-the-resource-domain is recast in newly global terms. For many Amazonian producers, the lexicon of sustainability may be new, but the activities it describes and prescribes are already well established.

The viability of sustained forest management is a main focus of research, much of it now published (see Anderson 1990; Posey and Balée 1989, for good examples), and the studies of indigenous and *caboclo* sustainable systems already in place have debunked many long-held views about the allegedly ad hoc character of Amazonian societies. It is in the relationship between empirical studies and programmatic accounts of sustainable development, however, that certain difficulties arise particularly concerning (1) the discrepancy between globalist goals and local goals; and (2) the relationship between maintenance of biological systems and social systems.

Objections to Sustainability

The research which has contributed to the high profile of the sustainability thesis in Amazonia has mainly been prompted by the construction of *Transamazônica* and falls into two classes: (1) that which debunks the modernizationist project (e.g. Fearnside 1988a); and (2) that which shows that there are alternative forms of resource-use (Amerindian and neo-Amazonian, e.g. Anderson 1990; Posey and Balée 1989). Both classes of research have produced results which have, by most reckonings, significantly altered long-held views about the prospects for Amazonian development, but what may interest future historians is the fact that the same research serves such diverse interests: the results of sustainability research are hailed both by those who view Amazonia as a resource domain whose fate is to serve remote consumers and by those who argue for the self-determination of Amazonians.

This contradiction can be dismantled by examining sustainability not as a new remedy for an Amazonian pathology (although it does represent some novelties), but as a compromise effected in a climate of limited political expectations. The sustainability thesis emerges after a period of severe political represssion, in a region in which the army has historically wielded considerable power (cf. the secrecy surrounding Calhe Norte[1]), and after a period during which multilateral agencies – especially the World Bank – were instrumental in setting the terms of development virtually unopposed, and to the degree that it is a critique, the sustainability thesis is already deeply embedded in the *realpolitik* of Amazonia development. What is strongest about the sustainability thesis already exists in practice (*caboclo* society) and what is weakest about the sustainability thesis is the idea that, as administered by the same interests which have been responsible for late-modern 'Amazonian development' to date, sustainability will succeed in redistributing the wealth of the region. Most cynical of all is the claim that in order to maintain biological systems (about which developmentalists to date have shown little concern) mollification of the manifest injustices of social systems must be deferred.

One of the consequences of the unevenness of capitalist development on the periphery has been the coexistence of capitalist relations of production and ersatz relations of production, petty commodity forms, for example, in their various manifestations. At the national level – in Brazil, for instance – one has an economy which by the usual aggregate measures is the eighth largest in the world while at the same

1. Calhe Norte is a national security-cum-resource zone projected to serve as a buffer on Brazil's northern border. When publicly disclosed, the extent of secret military planning attracted much commentary.

time, upwards of 40 per cent of the urban working population labours outside the formal sector; while Brazil is a major industrial nation, about half of its foreign revenue is still derived from the export of agricultural and other raw materials; agricultural land is highly concentrated, but most of the food for the internal market is produced by smallholders working only a small proportion of land (and then under parlous conditions of tenure). These are not merely dramatically contrasted facts about Brazil: they depict a social reality, the outcome of well-documented historical processes.

In a recent article outlining the prospects for sustainable development in Amazonia, David Pearce and Norman Myers argue that 'sustainable development suggests that certain traditional objectives of economic growth can be served without the capital depletion process' (1990: 383–4). This may be true, but the historical record is not reassuring. In fact one could argue, plausibly, that the current plight of Amazonia (and Brazil) may be attributed precisely to the pursuit of certain traditional objectives of economic growth and that sustainable development is making a tardy appearance. That aside, however, one could also object that as a formula for a green future, sustainable development is not beginning with a blank slate, but rather a complex – if largely obscured – historical object: historical Amazonian peasant societies.

Pearce and Myer's article, which in many respects exemplifies the globalist sustainability perspective, is expansively critical of the way in which Amazonian development has proceeded to date, but it presents primarily a view of Amazonia as a resource domain, a landscape to be managed, for better or worse. While relying on reputable recent research to substantiate its claims, it adheres to a standard rendition of the place of actual Amazonian societies in the debates about sustainability: they exist as analogues of natural species, viz. 'the Gavioes of western Brazil' (p. 393; in fact the only society mentioned by name; otherwise: squatters, e.g. 398).

It could be argued that actual Amazonian societies are irrelevant to the arguments marshalled by Pearce and Myers, that, for example, the formalism of the economic concepts employed does not demand acknowledgement of empirical realities. That is an argument, although not a very good one. More to the point is the fact that what Pearce and Myers refer to as 'the sustainable development paradigm' (1990: 383) is not the only model of sustainable development. If one looks at the record of so-called 'traditional' users of forest and riverine resources one finds numerous historical models of sustainable resource use and much of the more recent Amazonian research has significantly expanded the range of examples.[2]

In this light, the sustainable development paradigm put forward by Pearce and Myers among others is actually a highly specialized model, one addressed to a current global problem – how to maintain global eco-security, the maintenance of so-called natural capital – not Amazonia in particular. Amazonia is a mere sub-set of natural capital, which is the concept that 'future generations should have roughly equal access to that stock [forests, soil, water], serving the basic objectives of intertemporal equity – i.e., fairness between generations' (1990:383). This concern for fairness is laudable, but there is another dimension relevant in considering the maldistribution of the benefits of natural capital and this is that current consumption of user values is hardly equitable, thus before inter-generational fairness can have any content, it is incumbent on proponents of the sustainable development paradigm to say a little about how the preconditions of that future – which are manifestly iniquitous – are going to result in 'optimal use' (1990: 390). Pearce and Myers note that: 'The whole exercise of making optimal use of a natural capital asset is complex. But we can be sure that it is a procedure that is not even approximated in Amazonia' (1990: 390). Nor, one might observe, is such a procedure much in evidence elsewhere. That aside, however, Pearce and Myers say that a first stage 'is to obtain some idea of the values at stake in deforestation' (1990: 390). These are (followed by my glosses):

2. The archaeological record shows that pre-colonial Amazonia sustained very large populations without significant environmental degradation; research among contemporary Indian groups – by Balée and Irvine, for example – shows that far from tolerating narrow environmental limits, such groups consciously manipulate the environment in such a way as to ensure that the management of forests for social ends does not exceed the reproductive capacity of biological systems; third, studies of neo-Amazonian *caboclo* societies show that the tendency has been for such societies to diversify their production forms in order to mollify the effects of environmental degradation (Anderson and Ioris (1989) in a survey of land use in six East Pará *municipios*, show that there is significantly more forest destruction in *newer settlements* and in those *without floodplain*, that is to say in non-*caboclo* settlements.)

1. Biodiversity: 'biodiversity' addresses a key feature of research in the humid tropical forest: many species, low concentration of species, highly interdependence among species. The complex interdependency means, crudely, that relatively, for any to survive, all must survive. Biodiversity argments have been developed in studies of swidden agriculture (Harris 1971) and agroforestry (Ewel 1986) and have been implicit in proposals for both extractive and biological reserves.
2. Agriculture: 'agriculture' is noted as a value because of the increasing recognition that a broad genetic base must be maintained in order that new sources of germplasm be available to counter the effects of depredation of currently preferred cultivable species.
3. Medicinals: medicinals are noted because of the high commercial value of neo-tropical plants. For examples of pharmaceutical companies' interest in 'sustainable development' see Rainforest Alliance (1992).
4. Industrial materials: 'industrial materials' refers to such plants as babassu palm, a cheap and widely available source of oils.
5. Environmental services: 'environmental services' refers to the forest's role as global carbon-sink and regulator of global rainfall and temperature.
6. Humanitarian concerns: 'humanitarian concerns' refers to the knowledge of which 'traditional' Amazonians have yet to be debriefed.

The gloss provided by Pearce and Myers on the last mentioned provides a major insight into the principles underlying this agenda (1990: 393):

> These forest-dwelling tribes represent a fund of traditional knowledge that is critically relevant to pharmacologists, industrial researchers, agronomists and others who seek to identify key raw plant materials for modern economies.

For whom are these values? While it could hardly be denied that these represent values for Amazonians themselves, they are not the target group. Indeed there is no target group *per se*, but humanity at large, the global community, 'the market'. It is perhaps unfortunate that the Pearce and Myers article appears in a volume entitled *The Future of Amazonia* rather than *The Future of the Globe*, for the Amazonia portrayed is one whose sense is primarily defined in terms of its exploitable utility for non-Amazonians. The maintenance of biodiversity will ensure the relative intactness of genetic stock crucial to the maintenance of a productive agriculture while agriculture in Amazonia is profoundly unsupported in terms of credit provision, extension, marketing, co-operatives. Medicinals will help sustain the pharmaceutical industry, but if current GATT talks are anything to go by ('free trade' except in the area of patents and copyrights, intellectual property rights so-called), the direct benefits to the 'fund of traditional knowledge' are hard to foresee. Such products as babassu will provide fats, but the very reason for their desirability (cheapness) leaves direct producers at the wrong end of the commercial chain. The environmental services will militate against the greenhouse effect while it is widely acknowledged the societies responsible for the main contributions to the greenhouse effect strenuously resist self-regulation. Traditional knowledge will provide new commercial products while the bearers of traditional knowledge find themselves more often subject to the predations of mining and timber companies (cf. Greenbaum 1989; Price 1989; Baines 1991) than the inquiries of provisioners of hair conditioners.

The emphasis in this list is on marketable products, 'natural services' and the biological systems required to sustain output, and the perspective is that of the world market. What, one might ask, is the role of Amazonians in all this except as spear-carriers for global eco-management?

Pearce and Myers present one fairly concrete example of how this version of sustainable development enhances the lives of Amazonians. Using data drawn from studies in the Ecuadorian Amazon, they argue that based on the extraction of wild meat, hides and primates for medical research, it is possible to calculate an income of $200/ha compared with $150/ha to be got from commercial logging. The example serves to show how, in narrow price terms, one could begin to mount an argument for the utopian sustainable development paradigm: the forest is preserved and greater profits realized, a pared-down version of the Peters, Gentry and Mendelsohn (1989) blueprint.

It is a very weak argument. For one thing, $200/ha is not very much, even in Amazonia. For another thing, most Amazonians live in cities and towns from which the exotic bounty of nature has long disappeared: primates for medical research are as likely to be prospective organ-donors as they are spider monkeys, and the hides widely available are attached to dogs host to world-class collections of parasites.

While one can only agree with Pearce and Myers that current government policy in Amazonia is counterproductive in the short and long term, it must be objected that the Amazonia they describe is one whose character is derived primarily from external market considerations. For instance, after a cursory review of non-timber forest products they note that:

> The Amazon forests thus offer many outputs apart from the few conventional products, notably hardwood timber, and space for large-scale cattle ranching and small-scale cultivation, that have hitherto been virtually the sole modes of exploitation. (1990: 393)

The version of sustainable development discussed above is by no means the only one, but it is significant that it is one which speaks with the self-claimed authority of the global community and while one could argue, effectively, that this view of the role of the Third World in general and Amazonia in particular reflects entrenched First World interests, there is a more general point of criticism. This is that the concept of sustainable development is taken as seriously as it is. That it is taken so seriously – or at least not subject to more serious critique – is a testimony to the degree to which the market system has become not simply common sense, but the only sense. In the concluding section of their article, Pearce and Myers mull over possible policy outcomes informed by the sustainable development sensibility. They write that:

> The answer is to devise an institutional mechanism that would enable tropical forest countries to receive some sort of 'rental fee'. The same applies in the case of other forest outputs that contribute markedly to human welfare in lands far removed from the source country: notable instances include plant genetic resources that support modern agriculture through regular germ-plasm infusions to upgrade the productivity of crops such as rubber. (We can note too that Brazil benefits significantly from germplasm supplies for its coffee crop, imported from Ethiopia). (1990: 402)[3]

3. It is noteworthy that the example employs two Third World Countries, and no First World one. How might the contribution of the potato – to take one obvious example of First World/Third World germplasm exchange – be evaluated in this scheme?

This proposal of a 'rental-fee' – admitted by the authors to be a 'taxing challenge' – indicates as clearly as anything the major subtext of this version of sustainable development: in order for economic growth to continue in the core, it is no longer enough to rely on the traditional armoury of institutional mechanisms, colonialism, imperialism, unequal exchange, coups. What is required now is the complete economic intervention which will ensure the continued conditions of existence of those peripheral domains such as Amazonia whose paths have taken a perhaps ecologically fatal turn for the worse as a result of 500 years of economic development. By this vision, everything is to be valorized, indeed even the distinction between use value and exchange value is eroded, or as Pearce and Myers put it:

> Perceived within an expanded evaluatory framework, exploitation of Amazon's forests could come to include all manner of activities. Genetic reservoirs should count together with forest; a national park[4] could sometimes prove as valid a use as a paperpulp plantation. Maintenance of climatic stability could be seen as a form of 'use' that ranks alongside timber harvesting. In certain localities, 'use' could even entail outright preservation of forest ecosystems for scientific research, especially applied-biology research as it relates to new modes for man to reap Earth's natural bounty in Amazon forests as the most productive ecosystem anywhere. (1990: 402)

This is postmodernism as morphic resonance: the butterfly flaps its wings in the forest and the Stock Market comes to life.

Combú and Forest Management

The study of traditional forms of resource use in Amazonia has produced a highly fragmented literature. While there are many distinguished monographs of Amerindian societies (see Jackson 1975 for a survey), the resulting overall picture is composite rather than nomothetic. Studies of *caboclo* societies are few, for one of the same reasons that archaeological research has been sparse: the assumption has been that there is nothing worth researching. Following *Transamazônica*, however, and in part motivated by the rising concern for the inclusion of

4. Michael Crichton's *Jurassic Park* (1990) presents one scenario.

environmental impact studies within the programmes of development, *caboclo* society came to be granted – albeit reluctantly – some salience. Parker (1985a) represents post-*Transamazônica* recognition and Posey and Balée (1989) and Anderson (1990) represent the extension of 'traditional forest-users' to include caboclos.[5] The new rendering of the caboclo, however, is strongly shaped by the instrumentalist concerns which dominate discussion of the dilemmas of Amazonian development, indicated, for example, even in the realist/utopian version of sustainable development by the high priority placed on the (real or imagined) profitability of petty production (cf. Peters, Gentry and Mendelsohn 1989). The viability of *caboclo* petty commodity production is not, however, in dispute unless the existence of Amazonia's historical peasantries is totally effaced, but if one looks at the historical development of such a peasantry, the prospects for future development still depend on a number of factors outside the control of direct producers.

Combú is an island within easy reach of Belém, the capital of Pará and the largest city in Amazonia. In the past five years, the fortunes of Combú have improved decisively and in the context of rising interest in the prospects for sustainable peasant production, Combú has achieved a certain celebrity: through the intensive management of riverine forest, previously economically marginal Combuites now earn incomes several times that of the national minimum salary (the standard unit of income measurement in Brazil).

With 600 inhabitants, Combú has a relatively high population density: 43/km^2. Half of the inhabitants belong to land-holding groups (average size 15 ha); 23 per cent have free access to forest products; 24 per cent have restricted access via contractual arrangements; half the population is native (Combú-born), 84 per cent have lived there more than ten years; 16 per cent work in town; 92 per cent make a significant part of their living from extraction. Mean household income (1988) is $2,773/annum (compared with $1,828 in Tomé-Açu) (Anderson and Ioris 1989).

The main source of income are managed forest crops, all heavily manipulated. *Açaí* is the main crop, a native palm, which provides the fruit from which juice is extracted and sold on the local market, and palm heart which is tinned and exported. The

5. See also Padoch et al. (1987) and Hiraoka (1985c).

high level of *açaí* output is a result of conscientious management of riverine forest and profitability is enhanced by the proximity of the market.

Cacau is an introduced species and is treated as an extractive rather than agricultural species. The largest producer on Combú claims to have 10,000 trees under cultivation; other producers also have thousands of trees. *Hevea* is not managed in the same way, but the fact that hevea is denser on sites where *açaí* and *cacau* are managed suggests its having been incorporated within a wider regime of forest management (Anderson and Ioris 1989). *Hevea* and *cacau* differ from *açaí* not only in terms of being less lucrative products and less easily manipulated (longer period for maturation in the case of *hevea*, subject to 'witches broom' in the case of *cacau*), but also in being crops which do not have to be sold immediately upon harvesting. *Açaí* spoils rapidly and should be delivered to market within 48 hours.

As with other examples of historic peasantries, Combúites exploit a wide range of forest and riverine resources as well as pursuing specialist craft vocations (boat-building/carpentry) and day labour on Combú (*açaí* gathering) and in Belém. In addition to the three main three products, other sources of extractive income include hardwoods, shrimp, fish, oils (e.g. *andiroba*), various perennials (*limão*). Populations of skin and meat-bearing animals have declined to the point where hunting is not a significant activity. Agriculture, difficult because of the high water table, is virtually absent, although in leaner times it has been more widely practised.

In the context of recent discussions about sustainable development, Combú represents a strong example of wise forest management: Combúites are able to exploit the forest for marketable produce in a manner which, as far as is known, results in negligible disruption of the environment. If one were looking for examples which matched the prescriptions of Pearce and Myers, Combú would certainly have some relevance.

Upon closer examination, however, some problems arise. In the first instance, the market for Combú produce is local, not global, and the connection between local conservation and global benefit is not obvious. The consumers of Combú produce are Belenenses. Second, Combú is not merely a place where wise extractivists live: extractivists are divided between those who control the forest which they exploit and those who have no control. The major producers of *açaí* (who are also the main producers of *borracha* and *cacau*) are tenants who give half of their proceeds to an absentee landlord. Following them in terms of income are producers who have secure title to land, but only enough land to meet their needs as long as the *açaí* market holds up. Were they forced to revert to a broader-based livelihood they would find themselves in straitened circumstances.

The observation here is that Combú's existence is conditioned by factors largely beyond the control of local economies. Belém's growth, which has presented a substantial market for *açaí*, is the result of a process which has little to do with Combú. Combuites reproduce themselves through the market via *açaí* and in doing so shift away from a complex of activities which in previous years constituted their 'traditional management of the forests'. On a small scale, the situation is not dissimilar to that which prevailed during the rubber era: under the impact of external demand for a particular commodity, independent smallholder production is distorted, albeit in this case to the distinct advantage of smallproducers.

One reading of this state of affairs, and that to which proponents of sustainable development are likely to be drawn, is that Amazonian peasantries are capable of riding out the vicissitudes of haphazard development in Amazonia and emerge as relatively well-remunerated petty producers.

There are other examples, however, which do not fit this reading. Not far away from Combú, on the Tocantins, the small producers around Cametá have been less capable of accommodating externally generated shifts. Those who depend on fish and *cacau*, for example, have found that the consequences of the construction of the Tucuruí dam have presented insuperable obstacles to their wise management of Amazonian resources.

A notion of sustainable development which focuses only or primarily on the management of biological systems runs the danger of mystifying the social and historical contexts in which so-called traditional wisdom is mobilized. For example, Combuites' activities as forest managers are predicated on unambiguous relations between landowners and landusers. Those, for example, who treat the forest as public domain, as a 'natural' resource are not regarded as 'wise extractivists', but rather as thieves. At the moment, the management of the forest for *açaí* – and to a lesser extent seringa and *cacau* – represents an adequate return from the point of view of the landowners and extractivists, and embodies the utopian prescription outlined in Peters, Gentry and Mendelsohn (1989) (and others): the profitable extraction of non-timber products without overt environmental destruction; but this stability is not one over which direct producers have much control. Indeed, the major landowner on Combú has already begun to experiment with other forms of resource use, some of which – like water buffalo ranching – bode ill for extractivists. If one views the current *açaí* period in historical perspective, the wise management of the forest seems less the culmination of traditional extractivist practices than it does a respite from a series of disenfranchisements, and these are necessarily part of the story of sustainability as well. The life histories of Combuites include a long list of petty commodity and marginal activities in Combú, Belém and the estuary, and two of them in particular illustrate the way in which smallholders' livelihoods in Amazonia have been reactions to broad shifts in resource use. The first of these is the collapse of wood-fired steam technology (declining through the 1960s) and the introduction of refrigerated fishing vessels, late in the 1960s. Both subverted major extractive activities of Combuites – collection of firewood and shrimping – with the result that the current focus on *açaí* is not simply a result of the expanded urban market, but also reflects an absolute decline in extractable resources.

From the perspective of the debate on sustainable development, Combú represents a strong example of a peasant community able to exploit biological systems in a manner which does not result in environmental degradation and which results, overall, in a high level of income. From the perspective of the community itself, however, there is clear differentiation: there are landowners (resident and absent), land-controllers (groups with customary ownership of land not necessarily backed up by title and tenant-extractivists), members of land-controlling groups who are unabsorbable within the extractivist economy (and who must work in Belém as a result), and landless extractivists of two sorts, those who are recognized as having kinship links with land-owners/controllers, and those designated as *posseiros*, squatters with no recognized links to established members of Combú communities.

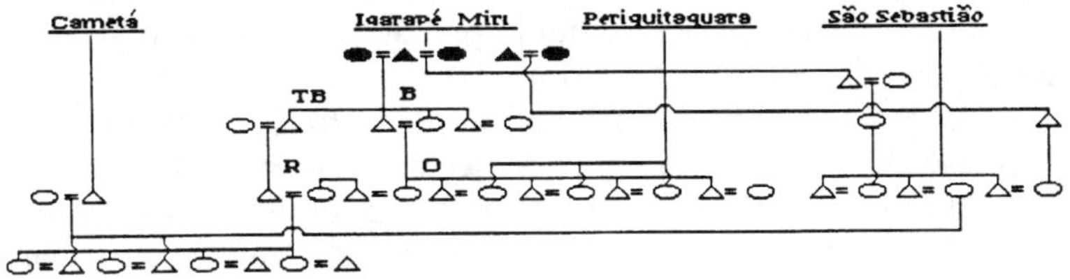

Figure 8.1 Combú kin groups

From a third perspective, Combú is itself merely the most successful segment of a larger community other segments of which are located in adjacent *terra firme* communities and elsewhere in the Guamá estuary. The nearby community of Boa Vista, for example, is the cynosure of a number of *terra firme* households maintaining links with Combú households.

If the most charitable reading of sustainable development, however provisional, is to provide the beginning of a reassessment of the role of historical peasantries, it is necessary to examine the social relations according to which this version of economic rationality has emerged. On Combú, for example, it seems quite clear that kingroup organization – and in particular sibling solidarity – reveals crucial limits on economic activity. In Figure 8.1, for example, marriages between sisters of 'Periquitaquara' and brothers of 'Igarapé-Mirí' represent a significant amalgamation of land-holding groups on Combú groups dominant on their respective *furos* (Combú itself and Periquitaquara). Another group of brothers, Cametá, are represented as spouses of the female cousins of the 'Igarapé-Mirí' brothers. The brothers of São Sebastião, by contrast, are share-tenants (and among the largest producers on the island) whose parents emigrated from a nearby *terra firme* settlement. As a general observation, in the absence of marrying-in prospects, share-tenancy and wage-labour represent alternative strategies, delaying for a generation the possibility of livelihood deriving from kin group membership, and overall, the social universe of Combú is very rigid.

With just these few points in mind, the utopian/realist version of sustainable development quickly becomes more problematic than it first appeared. For one thing, the diverse resource base – widely, and usually justifiably, regarded as a hallmark of *caboclo* livelihood (cf. Padoch 1988) – is illusory: on Combú it exists in principle, but in practice a disproportionately large part of income is derived from a single source. Second, the 'public' character of the resource base is contradicted by private ownership (whether sanctioned by legal title or not) of the most valued resources. Even fishing, by and large undertaken only for immediate domestic consumption, may be regarded as intrusive when nets are set too frequently or too close to someone else's waterfront. Third, the conscientious exploitation of the forest does not take place in an unweighted social environment: on Combú, 'wise forest management' is predicated on clear notions of property, access to which is largely afforded by kinship or clientage, and in the absence of a significant market for extractive products (characteristic until the *açaí* boom of the immediate past), Combuites are propelled into the diversified informal sector.

Fourth, Combuites are fluent in the language of 'sustainability'. The owner-manager of the island's only significant commercial establishment – long married to a daughter of Combú's major resident landowner – represents a most elaborated version of modern *cabocloism*: he produces the main extractive items, cultivates a menagerie of local fauna (particularly useful for amusing his guests), has long experience in various non-local trades (e.g. merchant marine), and, most significantly, runs a bar/restaurant located at the mouth of the *furo* from which it can serve Belenense water-skiers and the researchers and makers of television programmes who, because of Combú's proximity to Belém, take advantage of the easy access to a 'traditional' *caboclo/ribeirinho* community.

A second example is provided by a member of the same kindred (the restaurant owner's WB) who can rattle off an inventory of local tree species providing the necessary detail to satisfy the foreign seeker of local wisdom. In a conversation with a European timber researcher, this *ribeirinho* ran through a list of more than a dozen species (*acaçu, jarandeia, imbauba, uxirana, ingacipo, taperiba, ucuuba, anani, mututi, andiroba, genipapa, sapucaia, geniparana, mauba*) providing details of predators, growth rates, maximum height, girth, uses, etc. (e.g. '*taperiba* produces fruit good for *refresco*, but parrots like it too; the fruit can be sold; lots of fruit in the summer, too much for the market;

it's good if you can find it out of season; grows rapidly; the wood is useless for burning, too much water; but it's good for making bridges in *igapó* because it doesn't rot; rises to 25 m and is about 1 m in circumference; it's well distributed, grows rapidly, and is never planted).

A third example is provided on the occasion of a visit by a European film crew. Well prepared, the director knew that *açaí* and *cacau* were major products, but he didn't know that *cacau* was out of season. Having filmed a Combuite ascending an *açaí* tree and cutting off the fruit-laden branches, the director asked for *cacau*, and an old man led the crew further into the forest and offered to be filmed cutting down the *cacau* pods. Filming complete, the crew packed up to return to the boats. Everyone but the crew knew that the old man had scoured the forest to find out-of-season pods and tie them onto convenient branches.

Ribeirinhos' facility with the language of sustainability is both important and – from the point of view of most sustainability prescriptions – trivial. It is important because it draws attention to *ribeirinhos'* awareness of the constructions placed on them by those who now profess interest in the 'wise management of the forest', and trivial because little of the interest shown in *caboclo* sustainability is concerned in the first instance with what sustainable practices mean to those who practise them. Such practices have salience in resolving 'the dilemmas of development' only in so far as they have relevance for the constructions of those who, at this late date, have discovered yet another Amazonian resource.

The relatively high levels of disposable income derived from expanded *açaí* production have produced undoubted material benefits: motorized boat ownership is high (and those without can rent transport space from neighbours); many houses have refrigerators and television sets (run on butane and car batteries respectively); and collective organizations have been able to construct a community centre and pay for local primary education, but the local community is still significantly disenfranchised. Access to the *açaí* market takes place via personalized relations between producers and merchants; the largest single holding on the island belongs to an absentee landlord whose attempts at diversification (e.g. introduction of water buffalo) have potentially subversive effects *vis-à-vis* the extractive economy; there is no infrastructure for sanitation and public health, and the seat of municipal power is eight hours away (by boat). Recent economic success (although by no means equally distributed) has mitigated some of the effects of this disenfranchisement, and a forest ecology/extension programme directed by foreign researchers has attempted to broaden the base of extractive resources, but what is sustained in the development of Combú is direct producers' dependence on an urban market for a single lucrative crop.

The Future of Sustainabilty in Amazonia

The restricted notion of sustainable development as applied to Amazonia requires recasting. As it stands, it treats issues of Amazonian development as though they are exhausted by consideration of the possibilities of maintaining ecological viability which will in turn ensure the flow of neo-tropical products. The notion of social reproduction, hardly a controversial one, has thus far been kept out of the frame because of the undoubted complications it raises, among which are the following:

1. It entails recognition that there are integral social forms in Amazonia, historic peasantries whose existence challenges the conventional prortrayal of Amazonia as merely a vast resource domain.
2. It draws attention to the fact that in company with the gross environmental degradation which has taken place in Amazonia is a pattern of social injustice which can only begin to be rectified once there is a serious programme of land reform.
3. Such an orientation would draw attention to the fact that the calls for the 'rational management' of Amazonia come from the same quarters that in previous epochs have wreaked havoc in the region.
4. It draws attention to the fact that a model of development is already being implemented in Amazonia, one for which the 'sustainable development' discussion is something of a useful distraction. As Tony Hall has argued, it is basically a '*latifundio*-biased model which is based on strengthening corporate interests at the expense of small farmers who are

being pushed further and further into more distant frontier zones by a combination of market presures and heightened land conflicts' (1989: 39). It is significant, as Hall goes on to note, that: 'in terms of the general expansion of State influence in the region ... Calha Norte and Carajás together embrace fully half of Brazilian Amazonia.'

Without a grounding in actual rather than provisional versions of Amazonian social forms, the restricted sustainable development thesis merely obscures Amazonia as a social domain with a vision of Amazonia as a natural landscape.

The role of recent anthropologically informed research into sustainability in Amazonia has been equivocal. On the one hand it has challenged the received view that traditional Amazonian societies are merely highly adaptive social forms whose configurations are no more than the strained outcomes of coping in an inhospitable environment; but on the other hand, the uncritical promotion of the possibilities of sustained development (a concept for which few are willing put forward any but the most qualified definitions)[6] has meant that the specific contributions of historical peasantries of Amazonia have been casually absorbed by the discourse of the market. In its most pitiless form, the discourse of the market says that Amazonians may have the right to live as long as they can manage to sustain themselves between the dual demands of the market and environmental conservation. That they have done so unrecognized until the current assault on Amazonian resources is a mere historical footnote.

6. See Redclift (1987) for overview.

Bibliography

Agassiz, Louis, *A Journey in Brazil*, Boston: Ticknor and Fields, 1868

Alcarde, Henrique Gastao, *O Caboclo 'Indolente' e as Riquezas de Amazonia*, Belém, 1926

Allegretti, Mary Helena, *'Reservas extrativistas: desfios a sua implantação'*, *Tempo e Presenca*, 244/45, 32–4, 1989

Allen, Elizabeth, 'Brazil: Indians and the new constitution', *Third World Quarterly*, 10(4), 148–65, 1989

'Amazonia 1990: the burning question', *Third World Quarterly*, 12(1), 229–35, 1990

Alves, Maria H.M., *Estado e Oposição no Brasil 1964–1984*, Petropolis: Vozes, 1984

Amnesty International, *Brazil Briefing*, London: Amnesty International Publications, 1988

Anderson, Anthony B. (ed.), *Alternatives to Deforestation*, New York: Columbia University Press, 1990

and Ioris, Edviges, 'The logic of extraction: resource management and income generation by extractive producers in the Amazon estuary', Paper presented at the International Workshop, 'Traditional Resource Use in Neotropical Forests', The Center for Latin American Studies, University of Florida, Gainesville, 1989

and Posey, Darrell A., *'Refloresamento indígena'*, *Ciencia Hoje*, 6(3), 44–50, 1987

Hecht, Suzanna B., and May, Peter, 'The subsidy from nature: shifting cultivation, successional palm forests, and rural development', *Human Organization*, 17(1), 25–35, 1988

Anderson, Robin, 'The *caboclo* as revolutionary: the cabanagem revolt, 1835–36', in Parker (ed.) (1985a), 51–87, 1985

Anonymous, *Grande Enciclopédia Portuguesa e Brasileira*, Lisboa and Rio de Janeiro: Ed. Enciclopédia Ltda, 1945

Anonymous, *Enciclopédia Brasileira Merito*, São Paulo: Ed. Merito Ltda, 1957

Anonymous, Novo *Dicionário Brasileiro* Melhoramentos, 2nd ed, São Paulo: Melhoramentos, 1964

Anonymous, *Dicionário Brasileiro*, São Paulo: Mirador Internacional, 1977a

Anonymous, *Grande Enciclopédia Delta Larousse*, Rio de Janeiro: Ed. Delta S.A., 1977b

Ardener, Edwin, 'Social anthropology and the decline of modernism', in J. Overing (ed.), *Reason and Morality*, London: Tavistock, 1985

Arruda, Marcos et al., *The Multinationals and Brazil: the impact of multinationals in the contemporary Brazilian economy*, Toronto: Brazilian Studies, Latin American Research Unit, 1975

Asad, Talal (ed.), *Anthropology and the Colonial Encounter*, London: Ithaca Press, 1973

Aspelin, Paul L. and dos Santos, Silcio Coelho, *Indian Areas Threatened by Hydroelectric Projects in Brazil*, Copenhagen: IWGIA, 1981

Associação Commercial do Amazonas, Brazil: the land of rubber, New York: Brazilian Commissioner, 1912

Ayres, Deborah de Magalhaes Lima, 'The social caboclo: history, social organization, identity and outsider's social classification of the rural population of an Amazonian region (the middle Solimóes)'. Unpublished PhD thesis, University of Cambridge, 1992

Ayres, Marcio J., 'Some aspects of social problems facing conservation in Brazil', *Trends in Ecology and Evolution*, 1(2), 48–9, 1986

Baines, Stephen, 'The Waimiri–Atroari and the Paranapanema company', *Critique of Anthropology*, 11(2), 143–53.

Bakx, Keith, 'Planning agrarian reform: Amazonian settlement projects, 1970–1986', Ms., n.d

'Peasant formation and capitalist development: the case of Acre, S-W Amazonia', unpublished PhD thesis, University of Liverpool, 1986

'From proletarian to peasant: rural transformation in the state of Acre, 1970–1986', *The Journal of Development Studies*, 12(2),141–60, 1988

Balée, William, 'The ecology of ancient Tupi warfare', in Brian B. Fergis (ed.), *Warfare, Culture and Environment*. New York: Academic Press, 1984

'Cultural forests of the Amazon', *Garden*, Nov./Dec., 12–32, 1987

Banaji, J., 'Modes of production in a materialist conception of history', *Capital and Class*, 3, 1–44, 1977

Barbira-Scazzochio, Françoise (ed.), *Land, People and Planning in Contemporary Amazonia*, Cambridge: Centre for Latin American Studies, 1980

Barnet, R. J. and Muller, R., *Global reach: the power of multinational corporations*, London: Jonathan Cape, 1975

Barrow, Chris, 'Environmentally appropriate, sustainable small-farm strategies for Amazonia', in Goodman and Hall (eds.) (1990), 360–82, 1990

Bates, Henry W., *The Naturalist on the River Amazons*, London: John Murray, 1964

Beckerman, Stephen,'Does the swidden ape the jungle?', *Human Ecology*, 11(1), 1–12, 1983

Behar, Ruth, 'Death and memory: from Santa Maria del Monte to Miami Beach', *Cultural Anthropology*, 6(3), 346–84, 1991

Bernstein, Henry, 'Underdevelopment and the law of value: a critique of Kay', *Review of African Political Economy*, 6, 51–64, 1976

'Notes on capital and peasantry', *Review of African* Political Economy, 10, 60–73, 1977

'African peasantries: a theoretical framework', *Journal of Peasant Studies*, 6(4), 421–43, 1979

Bettelheim, Charles, see Emmanuel, Arrighi, (1972)

Binswanger, Hans P.,1987 'Fiscal and legal incentives with environmental effects on the Brazilian Amazon', Research Unit, Agricultural and Development Department, Operational Policy Staff, World Bank, 1987

Black, Jan K., *United States Penetration of Brazil*, Philadelphia: University of Pennsylvania Press, 1977

Bodard, Lucien, *Massacre on the Amazon*, London: Tom Stacey, 1971

Boom, Brian, 'Use of plant resources by the Chacabo', in Posey and Balée (eds.) (1989), 78–96, 1989

Bourne, Richard, *Assault on the Amazon*, London: Gollancz, 1978

Bradby, Barbara, 'The destruction of the natural economy', *Economy and Society*, 4(2), 127–61, 1975

Branford, Sue and Glock, Oriana, *The Last frontier: fighting for land in the Amazon*, London: Zed, 1985

and Kucinski, Bernardo, *The Debt Squads: the U.S., the banks, and Latin America*, London: Zed, 1988

Brasil, Raimundo Pereira, *O Rio Tapajós na Exposi(No Nacional de Borracha en 1913*, Belém: Municipio do Para, 1913

Browder, John (ed.), *Fragile Lands of Latin America: strategies for sustainable development*, Boulder and London: Westview Press, 1989

Buarque de Hollanda Ferreira, Aurelio, *Pequeno Dicionário Brasileiro da Lingua Portuguesa*, Rio de Janeiro: Ed. Civilizacao Brasileira, 1964

Bunker, Stephen, 'Forces of destruction in the Amazon', *Environment*, 22(7), 14–43, 1980

Underdeveloping the Amazon: extraction, unequal exchange, and the failure of the modern state, Urbana: University of Illinois Press, 1985

Campbell, Alan, *To Square with Genesis: causal statements and shamanic ideas in Wayapi*, Edinburgh: Polygon, 1990

Cardoso, Fernando H. and Muller, Geraldo, *Amazonia: expansão do capitalismo*, São Paulo: Editora Brasilense, 1977

Chomsky, Noam, *Towards a New Cold War: essays on the current crisis and how we got there*, New York: Pantheon, 1979

and Herman, Edward S., *The Political Economy of Human Rights*, Volume I: *the Washington connection and Third World Fascism*, Nottingham: Spokesman, 1979

Crichton, Michael, *Jurassic Park*, New York: Knopf, 1990

Clark, William, 'Managing planet earth', *Scientific American*, 261(3), 18–26, 1989

Clastres, Pierre, *La Société Contre l'état: recherches d'anthropologie politique*, Paris: Editions Minuit, 1974

Clay, Jason, *Indigenous Peoples and Tropical Forests: models of land use and management from Latin America*, Cambridge, Mass.: Cultural Survival, 1988

Cleary, David, *Anatomy of the Amazon Gold Rush*, Basingstoke: Macmillan and St Antony's College, Oxford, 1990

The Brazilian Rainforest: politics, finance, mining and the environment, Economist Special Report No. 2100, London: Economist Intelligence Unit, 1991

Clifford, James, *The Predicament of Culture: twentieth-century ethnography, literature, and art*, Cambridge, Mass.: Harvard University Press, 1988

'Introduction: partial truths', in Clifford and Marcus (eds.) (1986), 1–26

and Marcus, George (eds.), *Writing Culture: the poetics and politics of ethnography*, Berkeley: University of California Press, 1986

Coontz, Sidney, *Productive Labour and Effective Demand*, London: Routledge and Kegan Paul, 1965

Crosby, Alfred W., *Biological and Cultural Consequences of 1492*, Westport: Greenwood Press, 1972

Ecological Imperialism: the biological expansion of Europe 900–1900, Cambridge: Cambridge University Press, 1986

Cummings, Barbara, *Dam the Rivers, Damn the People*, London: Earthscan, 1990

Cunha, Euclides da, '*A margem da historia*', in *Obra Completa*, Coutinho, Afranio (ed.), Vol. I, 223–384, Rio de Janeiro: Jose Aguiar Editora, 1966

Davenport, William, 'Nonunilinear descent and descent groups', *American Anthropologist*, 61, 557–72, 1959

Davis, Shelton, *Victims of the Miracle*, New York and Cambridge: Cambridge University Press, 1977

Dean, Warren, *Brazil and the Struggle for Rubber: a study in environmental history*, Cambridge: Cambridge University Press, 1987

Denevan, William, 'Development and the imminent demise of the Amazon rain forest', *The Professional Geographer*, XXV(2), 130–5, 1973

'The aboriginal populations of America', in W. Denevan (ed.), *The Native Populations of America in 1492*, Madison: University of Wisconsin Press, 1976

'Swiddens and cattle versus forest: the imminent demise of the Amazon rain forest', *Studies in Third World Societies*, 13, 25–44, 1981

Denslow, Julie and Padoch, Christine (eds.), *People of the Rain Forest*, Los Angeles and London: University of California Press, 1988

Di Paolo, Pasquale, *Cabanagem: a revolução popular da Amazonia*, Belém: Conselho Estadual de Cultura, 1985

Dietschy, John M., 'The origins, genetics and diseases of Mexican-Americans', *Medical Grand Rounds*, University of Texas Southwestern Medical Center, 1990

Drennan, Robert D. and Uribe, Carlos A. (eds.), *Chiefdoms in the Americas*, New York and London: University Press of America, 1987

Economist, 'Special supplement: a survey of Brazil', 7 December 1991

Eden, Michael J., 'Ecology and land development: the case of Amazonian rainforest', *Transactions of the Institute of British Geographers*, N.S. 3, 444–63, 1978

Ecology and Land Management in Amazona, New York and London: Belhaven Press, 1990

Edwards, Michael, 'The irrelevance of development studies', *Third World Quarterly*, 11(1), 116–35, 1989

Ellen, Roy, 'Patterns of indigenous timber extraction from Moluccan rain forest fringes', *Journal of Biogeography*, 12, 559–87, 1985

Emmanuel, Arrighi, *Unequal Exchange*, London: New Left Books, 1972

Ennew, Judith, Hirst, Paul and Tribe, Keith, '"Peasantry" as an economic category', *Journal of Peasant Studies*, 4(4), 295–322, 1977

Enzensberger, Hans Magnus, *Dreamers of the Absolute*, London: Radius, 1988

Evans, Peter, *Dependent Development: the alliance of multinational, state, and local capital in Brazil*, Princeton: Princeton University Press, 1979

Ewel, John J., 'Designing agricultural ecosystems for the humid tropics', *Annual Review of Ecology and Systematics*, 17, 245–71, 1986

Fabian, Johannes, *Time and the Other: how anthropology makes its object*, New York: Columbia University Press, 1983

Falesi, I. C., 'Soils of the Brazilian Amazon', in Wagley (ed.) (1974)

Faria e Sousa Calvet de Magalhaes, Manuel de, *Dicionário Trilingue*, Lisboa: Confluencia Ltd, 1960

Fearnside, Philip M., 'Cattle yield prediction for the Transamazon highway', *Interciência*, 4, 220–25, 1979a

'The development of the Amazon rainforest: priority problems for the formulation of guidelines', *Interciência* 4, 338–42, 1979b

'Development alternatives in the Brazilian Amazon: an ecological evaluation', *Interciência*, 8(2), 65–78, 1983

Human Carrying Capacity of the Brazilian Rainforest, New York: Columbia University Press, 1986a

'Spatial concentration of deforestation in the Brazilian Amazon', *Ambio*, 15(2), 74–81, 1986b

'Prospects for sustainable agricultural development in tropical forests', *ISI Atlas of Science*, 251–6, 1988a

'Causa do desmatamento na Amazonia Brasileira', *Pará Desenvolvimento*, 23, 24–33, Jan./June 1988b

'A prescription for slowing deforestation in Amazonia', *Environment*, 32(4), 16–20, 39–40, 1989a

'Extractive reserves in Brazilian Amazonia', *BioScience*, 36(6), 387–93, 1989b

Fernandes, Francisco, *Dicionário Brasileiro Contemporaneo*, Porto Alegre: Ed. Glob, 1974

Fittkau, E.J., 'Introduction', in E. J. Fittkau et al. (eds.), *Biogeography and Ecology in South America*, The Hague: Dr W. Junk, 1969

'Crocodiles and the nutrient metabolism of the Amazon', *Amazoniana: limnologiea et oecologia regionalis systemae fluminin Amazonas*, IV, 103–33, 1973

Forman, S., *The Brazilian Peasantry*, New York and London: Columbia University Press, 1975

Foster-Carter, Aidan, 'The mode of production controversy', *New Left Review*, 107, 47–78, 1978

Foweraker, Joe, *The Struggle for Land: a political economy of the pioneer frontier in Brazil, 1930 to the present*, London: Cambridge University Press, 1981

Freeman, J., 'On the concept of kindred', *Journal of the Royal Anthropological Institute*, 91, 192–220, 1961

Friedman, Jonathan, 'The further adventures of phallus in blunderland', in L. Nencel and P. Pels (eds.), *Constructing Knowledge*, London: Sage, 1990

Friedmann, Harriet, 'Household production and the national economy: concepts for the analysis of agrarian formations', *Journal of Peasant Studies*, 7(2), 154–84, 1990

'Postscript: small commodity production', *Labour, Capital and Society*, 19(1), 117–26, 1986

Friends of the Earth, Briefing paper: 'Hydroelectric dams and rainforest destruction in the Amazon basin: Kayapo Indians' appeal to Europe and North American', Nov., 1988

Furtado, Lourdes, *'Pesca artesenal: um delineamento de sua historia no Para', Boletim Antropologia do Museu Paraense Emilio Goeldi*, 79, 1981

Galvao, Eduardo, *Santos e Visagens – um Estudo da Vida Religiosa de Itá, Amazonas*, Brasiliana, Vol. 284, São Paulo: Companhia Editora Nacional, 1955

Garrido Filha, Irene, *O Projeto Jarí e os Capitais Estrangeiro na Amazonia*, Petropolis: Ed. Vozes, 1980

Gates, R. Ruggles, *A Botanist in the Amazon Valley*, London: H.F.& G. Witherby, 1927

Genovese, Eugene and Elizabeth Fox-Genovese, *Fruits of Merchant Capital*, Oxford, New York, Toronto, Melbourne: Oxford University Press, 1983

Gentil, Janete, *'A juta na agricultura de várzea na area de Santarém – medio Amazonas', Boletim do Museu Paraense Emilio Goeldi – Antropologia*, 4(2), 118–99, 1988

Gjertsen, Derek, *Science and Philosophy: past and present*,

Harmondsworth: Penguin, 1989
Goodenough, Ward, 'Kindred and hamlet in Lakalai, New Britain', *Ethnology*, 1, 5–12, 1962
Descripton and Comparison in Cultural Anthropology, Chicago: Aldine, 1970
Goodland, Robert J. and Irwin, Howard S., *Amazon Jungle? Green hell to red desert?*, New York: Elsevier, 1975
Goodman, David and Hall, Anthony (eds), *The Future of Amazonia: deforestation or sustainable development?*, London: Macmillan, 1990
and Redclift, Michael, *From Peasant to Proletarian: capitalist development and agrarian transitions*, Oxford: Basil Blackwell, 1981
and Redclift, Michael (eds.), *Environment and Development in Latin America: the politics of sustainability*, Manchester and New York: Manchester University Press, 1991
Gordon, Lincoln, *A New Deal for Latin America: the Alliance for Progress*, Cambridge, Mass.: Harvard University Press, 1963
Review of R. Leacock, *Requiem for Revolution: the United States and Brazil, 1961–1969, Journal of Interamerican Studies and World Affairs*, 1990
Gough, Kathleen, 'Anthropology: child of imperialism', *Monthly Review*, 19(11), 12–27, 1968a
'New proposals for anthropologists', *Current Anthropology*, 9, 403–7, 1968b
Gradwhohl, Judith and Greenberg, Russell, *Saving the Tropical Forests*, London: Earthscan, 1988
Greenbaum, Linda, 'Plundering the timber on Brazilian Indian reservations', *Cultural Survival Quarterly*, 13(1), 1989
Gross, Daniel, 'Protein capture and cultural development in the Amazon basin', *American Anthropologist*, 77(3), 526–49, 1975
Hall, Anthony, *Developing Amazonia: deforestation and social conflict in Brazil's Carajás programme*, Manchester and New York: Manchester University Press, 1989
Harris, David, 'The ecology of swidden cultivation in the Upper Orinoco rain forest, Venezuela', *Geographical Review*, 61(4), 475–95, 1971
Harriss, John, *Capitalism and Peasant Farming: agrarian structure and ideology in Northern Tamil Nadu*, Bombay: Oxford University Press, 1982
Hayter, Teresa, *Exploited Earth: Britain's aid and the environment*, London: Earthscan, 1989
Watson, Catherine, *Aid: rhetoric and reality*, London: Pluto Press, 1985
Hayward, Tim, 'Ecosocialism – utopian and scientific', *Radical Philosophy*, 56, 2–14 (Autumn), 1990
Hebette, Jean and Marin, Rosa, '*Colonização espontanea, politica agária e*

grupos sociais', in J. M. da Costa (ed.), *Amazonia: desenvolvimento e ocupação*, Rio de Janeiro: IPEA/INBPES, 1979

Dall 'Agrol, Roberto and Souza, Andre Luiz, *Pan Amazonia: processo de ocupação, uso de recursos naturais e suas consequencias*, Belém: UFPa/NAEA, 1989

Hecht, Susanna B., 'The evolution of agroecological thought', Ms., n.d.

'Agroforestry in the Amazon basin: practice, theory and limits of a promising land use', in S. B. Hecht (ed.), *Amazonia: agriculture and land use research*, 331–71, Cali: Centro Internacional de Agricultura Tropical (CIAT), 1982

'Environment, development and politics: capital accumulation and the livestock sector in E. Amazonia', *World Development*, 13(6), 663–84, 1985

'Chico Mendes: chronicle of a death foretold', *New Left Review*, 173, 47–55, 1989

and Cockburn, Alexander, 'Land, trees and justice: defenders of the Amazon', *The Nation*, 22 May, 695–702, 1989

and Cockburn, Alexander, 'Rain forest politics', *The Nation*, 18 September, 2, 1989

and Cockburn, Alexander, *The Fate of the Forest: developers, destroyers and defenders of the Amazon*, London and New York: Verso, 1989

Hemming, John, *Red Gold: the conquest of the Brazilian Indians*, London: Macmillan, 1978

Amazon Frontier: the defeat of the Brazilian Indians, London: Macmillan, 1987

Heriarte, Mauricia de, *Descripção de Estado do Maranhão, Pará, Corupa de Rios das Amazonas*, Vienna: Imprensa do Filho de C. Gerold, 1974

Herman, Edward S., *The Real Terror Network*, Boston: South End Press, 1982

Hewlett, Sylvia, 'Dynamics of economic imperialism: the role of foreign direct investment in Brazil', *Latin American Perspectives*, 11(1), 136–48, 1975

The Cruel Dilemmas of Development, New York: Basic Books, 1980

Hine, James, '*Peasants, Politics and Agrarian Structure in Eastern Amazonia*', PhD thesis, University of Liverpool, 1991

Hiraroka, Mario, 'Floodplain farming in the Peruvian Amazon', *Geographical Review of Japan*, 58, 1–23, 1985a

'Changing livelihood patterns in the Peruvian Amazon', *Institute of Geoscience, The University of Tsukuba, Tsukuba Studies in Human Geography*, IX, 243–75, 1985b

'Cash cropping, wage labor and urbanward migrations: changing floodplain subsistence in the Peruvian Amazon', in Parker (ed.), (1985), 199–242, 1985c

'Mestizo subsistence in riparian Amazonia', *National Geographic*

Research, 1(2), 236–46, 1985d. Also (1986) 2(3), 54–71

Hoben, A., 'Anthropologists and development', *Annual Review of Anthropology*, 11, 349–75, 1981

Hoogvelt, Ankie, *The Third World in Global Perspective*, London: Macmillan, 1982

Hopper, Janice (ed.), *Indians of Brazil in the 20th Century*, Washington D.C.: Institute of Cross-Cultural Research, 1967

Huguet, Louis, 'The future of the world's tropical forests', *Commonwealth Forestry Review*, 62(3), 195–200, 1983

Huyssen, Andreas, *After the Great Divide: modernism, mass culture, postmodernism*, Bloomington: Indiana University Press, 1986

Hymes, Dell (ed.), *Rethinking Anthropology*, New York: Vintage, 1974

Ianni, Otavio, *Colonização e Contra-reforma Agrária na Amazonia*, Petropolis: Vozes, 1979

Projeto Jarí – a Invasão Americana, São Paulo: Brasil Debates, 1980

IBGE (Instituto Brasileiro de Geografia e Estastica), *Anáurio estatístico do Brasil*, 1950

Enciclopédia dos municípios Brasileiros, Vol. XIV, Pará, Amazonas, territórios, 1957

Santarém – censo industrial, censo demográfico, censo agro-pecurário, 1960

Plano de ação imédiata, 1969

Sinopse preliminar do censo demográfico, censo agro-pecuário, censo indústrial, Santarém, 1970

Sinopse prelíminar do censo agro-pecurio, Santarém, 1971/2

Sinopse prelíminar do censo demográfico, censo agro-pecuário, censo indústrial, Santarém, 1973

Sinopse prelimínar do censo agro-pecuário, Santarém, 1974a

Importações, exportações, sinopse, Santarém, 1974b

Sinopse prelíminar do censo indústrial, Santarém, 1975

IDESP (Instituto do Desenvolvimento Económico-Social do Pará) *Seminário Sobre a Pesca Artésenal*, 1984

Estudos e Problemas Amazonicos: História Social e Económica e Temas Espéciais, 1989

Irvine, Dominique, 'Succession management and rainforest distribution in an Amazonian rainforest', in Posey and Balée (eds.) (1989), 1989

Jackson, Jean, 'Recent ethnography of indigenous northern lowland South America', *Annual Review of Anthropology*, 4, 1975

Jameson, Frederic, *Late Marxism: Adorno, or, the persistence of the dialectic*, London and New York: Verso, 1990

The Cultural Logic of Late Capitalism, London and New York, Verso, 1991

Jordan, C. F. (ed.), *An Amazonian Rain Forest: the structure and function of a nutrient stressed ecosystem and the impact of slash-and-burn agriculture*, Man and the Biosphere Series, Carnforth, UK and Park Ridge, New

Jersey: UNESCO and Parthenon Publishing Group, 1989
Kahn, Joel, *Minangkabau Social Formations: Indonesian peasants and the world-economy*, Cambridge: Cambridge University Press, 1980
'Peasant ideologies in the third world', *Annual Review of Anthropology*, 14, 49–75, 1985
and Llobera, Josep (eds.), *The Anthropology of Pre-capitalist Societies*, London: Macmillan, 1981
Kaplan, Joanna Overing, 'Endogamy and marriage alliance: a note on continuity in kindred-based groups', *Man*, 8(4), 555–70, 1973
Katzman, Martin, 'Paradoxes of Amzonian development in a "resource-starved" world', *Journal of Developing Areas*, 10, 445–60, 1976
Cities and Frontiers in Brazil: regional dimensions of economic development, Cambridge, Mass. and London: Harvard University Press, 1977
Kay, Cristobal, *Latin American Theories of Development and Underdevelopment*, London: Routledge, 1989
Kay, Geoffrey, *Development and Underdevelopment: a Marxist perspective*, London: Macmillan, 1975
King, C. and Chandler, M. T., *The Wasted Lands*, Nairobi: ICRAF, 1978a
'Editorial: what is agroforestry?', *Agroforestry Systems*, 1(1), 7–11, 1978b
Kleinpenning, J. M. G., *The Integration and Colonisation of the Brazilian Portion of the Amazon Basin*, Nijmegen: Institute of Geography and Planning, Catholic University, 1975
Kolko, Gabriel, *The Roots of American Foreign Policy: an analysis of power and purpose*, Boston: Beacon, 1969
and Kolko, Joyce, *The Limits of Power*, New York: Harper & Row, 1972
Labour, Capital and Society, Special Issue on the informal sector, 19(1), 1986
Laclau, Ernesto, *Politics and Ideology in Marxist Theory*, London: New Left Books, 1976
Langguth, A. J., *Hidden Terrors*, New York: Pantheon, 1978
Lappé, Francis Moore, Schurman, Rachel and Donaher, Kevin, *Betraying the National Interest*, New York: Grove Press, 1987
Lathrap, Donald, 'The "hunting" economies of the tropical forest zone of South America: an attempt at historical perspective', in R. B. Lee and I. Devore (eds.), *Man the Hunter*, Chicago: Aldine, 1968
The Upper Amazon, London: Thames & Hudson, 1970
Leal, Aluízio Lins, '*Amazonia: o aspecto político da questão mineral*', Belém: mimeo, 1988
Leacock, Seth, 'Economic life of the Maué indians', *Boletim do Museu Paraense Emilio Goeldi*, N.S. 19, 1964
Leacock, Ruth, *Requiem for Revolution: the United States and Brazil, 1961–69*, Kent, Ohio: Kent State University Press, 1990

and Leacock, Seth, *Spirits of the Deep: a study of an Afro-brazilian cult*, Garden City, NY: Anchor/Doubleday, 1972

LeRoy, J. P., '*O bote contra a geleira, os pescadores de Santarém em busca de sua afirmaçãofase*, in *Pescadores artesenais, entre o passado e o futuro*, Rio: FASE, Proposta (*Experiencias em Educação Popular*), No. 38, 1988

Lévi-Strauss, Claude, *Structural Anthropology I*, Garden City, NY: Anchor/Doubleday, 1967

The Elementary Structures of Kinship, Boston: Beacon Press, 1969

Loureiro, Violeta Refkalefsky, '*Modernização e conflito numa população de pescadores do Pará*', in IDESP (1984), 37–46

Os Parceiros do Mar, Belém: CNPq/MPEG, 1985

A Miseria da Ascensão Social: capitalismo e pequena produção na Amazonia, São Paulo: Ed. Marco Zero, 1987

MacLachlan, Colin, 'The indian directorate, forced acculturation in Portuguese America', *The Americas*, April, 357–87, 1972

'The Indian labor structure in the Portuguese Amazon, 1700–1800', in D. Alden (ed.), *Colonial Roots of Modern Brazil*, 199–230, Berkeley, Los Angeles and London: University of California Press, 1973

'Africa slave trade and economic development in Amazonia 1700–1800', in R. B. Toplin (ed.), *Slavery and Race Relations in Latin America*, London: Greenwood Press, 1974

Mahar, Dennis, *Government Development Policies and Deforestation in Brazil's Amazon Region*, Washington D.C.: World Bank Publications, 1989

Mangin, William, *Peasants in Cities*, Boston: Houghton Mifflin, 1970

Marcus, George and Fischer, Michael, *Anthropology as Cultural Critique*, Chicago and London: University of Chicago Press, 1986

Martine, George, 'Recent colonization experiences in Brazil: expectations versus reality', in Barbira-Scazzocchio (ed.) (1980), 80–94

Marx, Karl, *Capital* Vol. I, London: Lawrence & Wishart, 1954

Capital, Vol.III London: Lawrence & Wishart, 1959

Maxwell, Kenneth, 'The tragedy of the Amazon', *The New York Review of Books*, 7 March, 24–9, 1991

Maybury-Lewis, David (ed.), *Dialectical Societies*, Cambridge, Mass.: Harvard University Press, 1979

Meggers, Betty, *Amazonia: Man and Culture in a Counterfeit Paradise*, Chicago: Aldine, 1971

'Aboriginal adaptation to Amazonia', in G. T. Prance and T. E. Lovejoy (eds.), *Amazonia*, Oxford: Pergamon Press, 1985

Meillassoux, Claude, *Femmes, Greniers et Capitaux*, Paris: Maspéro, 1975

Mendes, Chico, *Fight for the Forest: Chico Mendes in his own words*, London: Latin American Bureau, 1989

Mintz, Sidney, *Caribbean Transformations*, Chicago: Aldine, 1974

Mitchell, W. E., 'Theoretical problems in the concept of kindred', *American Anthropolgist*, 65, 34–54, 1963

Monbiot, George, *Amazon Watershed: the new environmental investigation*, London: Abacus, 1992

Moran, Emilio, 'The adaptive system of the Amazonian caboclo', in Wagley (ed.) (1974), 136–59

Developing the Amazon, Bloomington: University of Indiana Press, 1981

(ed.), *The Dilemmas of Amazonian Development*, Boulder: Westview Press, 1983

'An assessment of a decade of colonisation in the Amazon Basin', in J. Hemming (ed.), *Change in the Amazon Basin*, Vol. II, Manchester: Manchester University Press, 1985

Motta Maués, Maria Angelica, '*A literatura oficial sobre a pesca na amazonia: uma tentativa de revisão critica*', in IDESP (1984), 103–29

'*A questão etnica: indios, brancos, negros e caboclos*', in IDESP (1989), 195–204

and Maués, Raymundo Heraldo, *O Folclore da Alimentação: tabus alimentares da Amazonia*, Belém: Falangola, 1980

Moulder, Frances, *Japan, China and the Modern World Economy: toward a reinterpretation of East Asian development*, Cambridge: Cambridge University Press, 1977

Murphy, Robert, *Headhunter's Heritage: social and economic change among the Munduruсu*, Berkeley and Los Angeles: University of California Press, 1960

and Steward, Julian, 'Tappers and trappers: parallel process in acculturation', *Economic Development and Culture Change*, 4(4), 335–55 ,1956

Murphy, Yolanda and Murphy, Robert, *Women of the Forest*, New York: Columbia University Press, 1974

Myers, Norman, *The Sinking Ark*, Oxford: Pergamon, 1979

Conversion of Tropical Moist Forest: a report prepared by Norman Myers for the Committee on Research Priorities in Tropical Biology of the National Resources Council, Washington D.C.: National Academy of Sciences, 1980

Nimuendaju, Curt, 'The Tapajo', *Kroeber Anthropological Society Papers*, 6, 1–12, 1952

Nugent, Stephen, 'Amazonia: ecosystem and social system', *Man*, N.S. 16, 62–74, 1981

Big Mouth: the Amazon speaks, London: Fourth Estate, 1990

'The limitations of "environmental" management: forest utilisation in the lower Amazon', in Goodman and Redclift (eds.) (1991), 141–54

Observer, 'Underwater chainsaw', 19 November 1989

Odum, H. T., Brown, M. T. and Christianson, R. A., *Energy Systems*

Overview of the Amazon Basin, Gainesville: Center for Wetlands, University of Florida, 1986

Ortner, Sherry, 'Anthropological theory since the sixties', *Comparative Studies in Society and History*, 26(1), 126–66, 1984

Padoch, Christine, 'People of the floodplain and forest', in Denslow and Padoch (eds.) (1988), 127–40

et al., 'Market-oriented agroforestry at Tamshiyacu', in W. Denevan and C. Padoch (eds.), *Swidden-Fallow Agroforestry in the Peruvian Amazon*, 90–6, New York: New York Botanical Garden, 1987

Palmatary, Helen, 'The pottery of Marajó Island, Brazil', *Transactions of the American Philosophical Society*, (n.s.), 39(3), 1950

'The archaeology of the lower Tapajós valley', *Transactions of the American Philosophical Society*, (n.s.), 50(3), 1960

Parker, Eugene P. (ed.), *The Amazon Caboclo: historical and contemporary perspectives*. Studies in Third World Societies 32, Williamsburg: College of William and Mary, 1985a

'The Amazon *caboclo*: an introduction and overview', in Parker (ed.) (1985a), xvii–li, 1985b

'Caboclization: the transformation of Amerindian in Amazonia, 1615–1800', in Parker (ed.) (1985a), 1–49, 1985c

'A neglected human resource in Amazonia: the Amazon *caboclo*', in Posey and Balée (eds.) (1989), 249–59, 1989

Parker, Phyllis, *Brazil and the Quiet Intervention*, Austin: University of Texas Press, 1979

Payer, Cheryl, *The World Bank: a critical analysis*, New York: Monthly Review Press, 1982

Pearce, David and Myers, Norman, 'Economic values and the environment of Amazonia', in Goodman and Hall (eds.), 1990

Pearce, Fred, 'Kill or cure? remedies for the rainforest', *New Scientist*, 16 September 1989a

'Felled trees deal double blow to global warming', *New Scientist*, 16 September 1989b

Pearse, Andrew, *The Latin American Peasant*, London: Frank Cass, 1975

Pehrson, R.N., 'Bilateral kin groupings' in J. Goody (ed.), *Kinship*, Harmondsworth: Penguin, 1964

Perlman, Janice, *The Myth of Marginality*, Berkeley and Los Angeles: University of California Press, 1976

Peters, Charles, Gentry, Alwyn and Mendelsohn, Robert, 'Valuation of an Amazonian forest', *Nature*, 339, 655–6, 1989

Pfeil, Fred, 'Makin' flippy-floppy: postmodernism and the baby-boom PMC', in M. Davis, F. Pfeil and M. Sprinker (eds.), *The Year Left: an American socialist yearbook*, London: Verso, 1985

Phelps, Gilbert, *Green Horizons: travels in Brazil*, New York: Simon and Schuster, 1964

Piazza, Paulo Della, *Santarém*, São Paulo: SPLAN (Sociedade de Pesquisas e Planejamento), 1963

Polier, Nicole and Roseberry, William, 'Tristes tropes: post-modern anthropologists encounter the other and discover themselves', *Economy and Society*, 18(2), 245–64, 1989

Pompermeyer, Malori Jose, '*Estrategias do grande capital na fronteira Amazonica Brazileira*', mimeo, Minas Gerais: UFM, 1982

Posey, Darrell and Balée, William (eds.), *Resource Management in Amazonia: indigenous and folk strategies (Advances in Economic Botany*, Vol. 7), New York: New York Botanical Society, 1989

Prance, Ghillean T., 'Notes on the vegetation of Amazonia III: the terminology of Amazon forest types subject to inundation', *Brittonia*, 31, 26–38, 1977

Pratt, Mary Louise, 'Fieldwork in common places',in Clifford and Marcus (eds.) (1986), 27–50.

Price, David, *After the Bulldozers*, Cabin John, MD and Washington D.C.: Seven Locks Press, 1989

Rainforest Alliance, *Tropical Forest Medical Resources and the Conservation of Biodiversity*, Symposium presented in conjunction with the New York Botanical Garden's Institute of Economic Botany, 24 May 1992

Ramirez-Faria, C., *The Origins of Economic Inequality Between Nations: a critique of Western theories on development and underdevelopment*, London: Unwin Hyman, 1991

Ramos, Alcida Rita, 'Ethnology Brazilian style', *Serie Antropologia*, No. 89, Brasilia: University of Brasilia, 1990a

'An economy of waste: Amazonian frontier development and the livelihoods of Brazilian indians', *Série Antropologia*, No. 90, Brasilia: University of Brasilia, 1990b

'Hall of mirrors', *Critique of Anthropology*, 11,2, 1991

Rangel, Alberto, *Inferno Verde*, Tonis: Typografia Arrauetllia, 1972

Redclift, Michael, *Sustainable Development: exploring the contradictions*, London: Macmillan, 1987

Redclift, Nanneke, 'The contested domain: gender, accumulation and the labour process', in N. Redclift and E. Mingione (eds.), *Beyond Employment: household, gender and subsistence*, Oxford: Blackwell, 1985

Reinhardt, Nola, *Our Daily Bread: the peasant question and family farming in the Colombian Andes*, Berkeley, Los Angeles and London: University of California Press, 1988

Renner, M., 'A critical review of *Tropical Forests: a call for action*', *The Ecologist*, 18(1), 35–40, 1988

Rey, Pierre-Philpppe, *Les Alliances de Classe*, Paris: Maspéro, 1973

Ribeiro, Darcy, 'Indigenous cultures and languages of Brazil', in Hopper (ed.) (1967)

Rich, Bruce, 'The challenge of sustainable development', The *Global Reporter*, 1(3), 9–12, 1983

Richards, Paul, *Indigenous Agricultural Revolutions*, London: Hutchinson, 1984

Richards, P. W., *The Tropical Forest: an ecological study*. Cambridge: Cambridge University Press, 1952

'The tropical rain forest', *Scientific American*, 229(6), 58–67, 1973

Riviere, Peter, *The Forgotten Frontier: ranchers of northern Brazil*, New York: Holt, Rinehart & Winston, 1972

Roberts, Bryan, *Cities of Peasants*, London: Edward Arnold, 1978

Rocque, Carlos, *Grande Enciclopédia da Amazonia*, Belém: Amazonia Ed. Ltda, 1968

Rocque, Carlos, *'Historia dos municípios de estado do Pará'*, Edição especial 6, *A Província do Pará* (Belém), 1982

Roosevelt, Anna, *Parmana: prehistoric maize and manioc subsistence along the Amazon and Orinoco*, New York and London: Academic Press, 1980

'Chiefdoms in the Amazon and Orinoco', in R. D. Drennan and C. A. Uribe (eds.), *Chiefdoms in the Americas*, New York and London: University Press of America, 1987

'Resource management in Amazonia before conquest: beyond ethnographic projection', in Posey and Balée (eds.) (1989), 30–62

Moundbuilders of the Amazon: geophysical archaeology on Marajó island, Brazil, New York and London: Academic Press, 1991

Roseberry, William, 'Peasants as proletarians', *Critique of Anthropology*, 3(11), 3–18, 1978

Coffee and Capitalism in the Venezuelan Andes, Austin: University of Texas Press, 1983

Anthropologies and Histories: essays in culture, history and political economy, New Brunswick and London: Rutgers University Press, 1989

Ross, Eric B., 'The evolution of the Amazonian peasantry', *Journal of Latin American Studies*, 10(1), 193–218, November 1978

Rostow, Walter W., *The Stages of Economic Growth: a non-communist manifesto*, Cambridge: Cambridge University Press, 1960

Roxborough, Ian, *Theories of Underdevelopment*, London: Macmillan, 1979

Ruckelshaus, William, 'Toward a sustainable world', *Scientific American*, 261(3), 114–20, 1989

Sahlins, Marshall, *Moala: culture and nature on a Fijian island*, Ann Arbor: University of Michigan Press, 1962

Said, Edward, *Orientalism*, New York: Pantheon, 1978

'Opponents, audiences, constituencies and community', in H. Foster (ed.) *Postmodern Culture*, London: Pluto Press, 1983

Santos, Roberto, *História Econômica da Amazonia, 1800–1920*, São Paulo: Queiroz, 1980

Sass, Louis, 'Anthropology's native problems: revisionism in the field', *Harpers*, 49–57,May, 1986

Schmink, Marianne, 'Land conflicts in Amazonia', *American Ethnologist*, 9(2), 341–57, 1982

'São Felix do Xingu: a caboclo community in transition', in Parker (ed.) (1985a), 143–66

'Big business in the Amazon', in Denslow and Padoch (eds.) (1988).

and Wood, Charles (eds.), *Frontier Expansion in Amazonia*, Gainesville, Florida: University of Florida Press, 1984

Schwabe, G.H., 'Towards an ecological characterization of the South American continent', in Fittkau et al. (eds.) (1968), 113–36

Shane, Douglas, *Hoofprints on the Forest: cattle ranching and the destruction of Latin America's tropical forests*, Philadelphia: Institute for the Study of Human Issues, 1986

Shanin, Teodor, *Russia as a Developing Society. The roots of otherness: Russia's turn of the century*, Vol. I, London: Macmillan, 1985

Shiva, V., 'Forestry myths and the World Bank: a critical review of *Tropical Forests: a call for action*', *The Ecologist* 17(4/5), 142–9, 1987

Shoumatoff, Alex, *Murder in the Forest: the Chico Mendes story*, London: Fourth Estate, 1991

Shweder, Richard, 'Storytelling among the anthropologists', New York *Times Book Review*, 21 September, 1, 38–9, 1986

Silva, Roberto da, *The Political Economy of Underdevelopment*, London: Routledgeand Kegan Paul, 1982

Sioli, Harold, *Amazonia: fundamentos da ecologia da maior região florestas tropicaís*, Petropolis: Vozes, 1985

The Amazon: limnology and landscape ecology, Dordrecht: Dr W. Junk, 1984

Skidmore, Thomas, *Prêto no Branco: raça e nacionalidade brasileiro*, Rio de Janeiro: Paz e Terra, 1976

Skillings, Robert F., 'Economic development of the Brazilian Amazon: opportunities and constraints', *The Geographical Journal*, 150(1), 48–54, 1984

Smith, Carol, Review of William Roseberry, *Coffee and Capitalism in the Venezuelan Andes*, *Critique of Anthropology* , 5(2), 87–94, 1985

Smith, Nigel J.H., *Rainforest Corridors: the Transamazon colonization scheme*, Berkeley, Los Angeles and London: University of California Press, 1982

Social Analysis, Special Issue on the Peripheral Situation, No. 19, 1986.

Sousa Santos, Antonio Maria, *'Aritapera: uma comunidade de pequenos produtores na várzea Amazonica', Boletim do Museu Paraense Emilio Goeldi*, No. 83, 1982

Spruce, Richard, *Notes of a Botanist on the Amazon and Andes*, New York and London: Johnson Reprint Co, 1970

Staniford, Philip, *Pioneers in the Tropics: the political organization of Japanese in an immigrant community in Brazil*, London: Athlone Press, 1973

Stepan, A. (ed.), *Authoritarian Brazil: origins, policies and future*, New Haven and London: Yale University Press, 1973

Sternberg, Hilgard O'Reilly, *The Amazon River of Brazil*, Wiesbaden: Franz Steiner Verlag, 1975

Steward, Julian, 'Introduction', in J. Steward (ed.), *Handbook of South American Indians.* Vol. I: *The Marginal Tribes.* Washington D.C.: Smithsonian Institute, 1946

'Culture areas of the tropical forests', in J. Steward (ed.), *Handbook of South American Indians.* Vol. III: *The Tropical Forest Tribes*, Washington D.C.: Smithsonian Institute, 1948

Stoler, Ann, 'Sumatran transitions: colonial capitalism and theories of subsumption', *International Social Sciences Journal*, 114, 543–62, 1986

Stone, Roger, *Dreams of Amazonia*, Harmondsworth: Penguin, 1986

'The politics of deforestation', *Issues in Science and Technology*, Spring 1990

Subler, Scott and Uhl, Christopher, 'Japanese agroforestry in Amazonia: a case study in Tomé-Açu, Brazil', in Anderson (ed.) (1990) 153–66

Taussig, Michael, *Shamanism, Colonialism and the Wildman: a study in terror and healing*, Chicago: University of Chicago Press, 1987

Taylor, Kenneth, 'Indian rights in Amazonia', in Denslow and Padoch (eds.) 1988

Tigar, Michael and Levy, Madeleine, *Law and the Rise of Capitalism*, New York: Monthly Review Press, 1977

Treece, David, *Bound in Misery and Iron*, London: Survival International, 1987

Trimberger, Ellen K., 'State power and modes of production: implications of the Japanese transition to capitalism', *Insurgent Sociologist*, VII(2), 85–98, 1977

Turner, Terence, 'Production, exploitation and social consciousness', *Social Analysis* 19, 91–115, 1986

Tyler, Stephen, 'Still RAYTING', *Critique of Anthropology*, 7(1), 49–51, 1987

Uhl, Christopher, *'Extração seletiva de madeiras: impactos ecológicos em Paragominas', Pará Desenvolvimento*, 23, 46–52, 1988

'Comer um hamburger pode ser um reforço para devastação', O Liberal, 16 July 1989

and Jordan, C. F., 'Succession and nutrient dynamics following forest cutting and burning in Amazonia', *Ecology*, 63, 1476–90, 1984

and Buschbacher, R., 'A disturbing synergism between cattle ranching burning practices and selective tree harvesting in the Eastern Amazon', *Biotropica*, 17(4), 265–8, 1985

Velho, Otavio, *Frentes de Expansão*, Rio de Janeiro: Zahar, 1972

Verissimo, Jose, *Estudos Amazonicos*, Coleção Amazonica, Serie Jose Verissimo, Belém: Universidade Federal do Pará, 1970

Wagley, Charles, *Amazon Town: a study of man in the tropics*, New York: Macmillan, 1953

(ed.), *Man in the Amazon*, Gainesville: University of Florida Press, 1974

Preface to revised version of Wagley (1953), New York: Oxford University Press, 1976

Welcome of Tears: the Tapirape indians of central Brazil, New York: Oxford University Press, 1977

'The Amazon caboclo', in Parker (ed.) (1985a), vii–xvi, 1985

Wallace, Alfred J. R., *A Narrative of Travels on the Amazon and Rio Negro*, London: Ward, Lock and Co., 1889

Wallerstein, Immanuel, *The Modern World System: capitalist agriculture and the origins of the European-world economy in the sixteenth century*, New York and London: Academic Press, 1974

Warren, Bill, *Imperialism: pioneer of capitalism*, London: Verso, 1980

Weinstein, Barbara, *The Amazon Rubber Boom, 1850–1920*, Stanford: Stanford University Press, 1983

'Persistence of *caboclo* culture in the Amazon: the impact of the rubber trade', in Parker (ed.) (1985a), 89–113, 1985

Wesche, Rolf, 'The transformation of rural caboclo society upon integration in Brazil's Amazon frontier: a study of Itacoatiara', in Parker (ed.) (1985a), 115–42, 1985

and Bruneau, Thomas, *Integration and Change in Brazil's Middle Amazon*, Ottawa, London and Paris: University of Ottawa Press/Institute for International Development, 1990

Wolf, Eric, *Peasant Wars of the Twentieth Century*, New York: Harper and Row, 1969

Europe and the People Without History, Berkeley, Los Angeles and London: University of California Press, 1982

and Hansen, E.C., *The Human Condition in Latin America*, New York, Toronto and London: Oxford University Press, 1972

Wolpe, Harold, 'Capitalism and cheap labour-power in South Africa: from segregation to apartheid', *Economy and Society*, 1(4), 1972

Wood, Charles and Carvalho, Jose Alberto Magno de Carvalho, *The Demography of Inequality in Brazil*, Cambridge: CUP, 1988

Woodroffe, J. F. and Smith, H. H., *The Rubber Industry of the Amazon*, London: T. Fisher Unwin, 1916

Worsley, Peter, 'The end of anthropology?', *Transactions of the Sixth World Congress of Sociology*, 3, 121–9, 1970

Wright, Robin, 'The great Carajás: Brazil's mega-programme for the '80s', *Global Reporter*, 1(1), 3–6, 1983

Wyer, June, *'Ideology and economic organisation of urban migrants in an Amazonian City'*, Unpublibhed PhD thesis, University of London, 1983

Index